The Youth Culture
and the Universities

other works by the same author

THE YOUTH CULTURE
AND THE UNIVERSITIES

by

Bryan Wilson

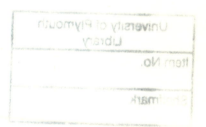
FABER AND FABER
London

First published in 1970
by Faber and Faber Limited
24 Russell Square London WC1
Printed in Great Britain by
Latimer Trend & Co Ltd Plymouth

SBN 571 09233 0

© Bryan Wilson 1970
Alienated Intellectuals and
The Writing on the Redbrick Wall
© Malcolm Bradbury and Bryan Wilson

For Nancy and Harry Higginson
who in their gentle and sensitive way
taught me so many valuable things

Contents

Acknowledgements   *page* 9

Introduction   13

1. The Trouble with Teenagers (1959)   21

2. Alienated Intellectuals (1961)[1]   33

3. Mass-Media and the Public Attitude to Crime (1961)   41

4. The Teacher's Rôle (1962)   51

5. The Writing on the Redbrick Wall (1962)[1]   73

6. The War of the Generations (1964)   86

7. The Changing Universities (1964)   101

8. The Needs of Students (1965)   106

9. The Social Context of the Youth Problem (1965)   150

10. An Approach to Delinquency (1966)   173

11. In Defence of Oxbridge (1966)   185

12. The Age of Majority (1966)   190

13. The Hippies: A Sociological Analysis (1967)   195

14. Technology and the Socialization of the Young (1968)   204

15. The Youth Culture, the Universities and Student
    Unrest (1968)   218

16. Social Values and Higher Education (1968)   234

Index   267

[1] With Malcolm Bradbury

7

Acknowledgements

'The Trouble with Teenagers' first appeared, under a slightly different title and in slightly amended form in *Twentieth Century* in August 1959; 'Alienated Intellectuals' is an amended version of an article, written with Malcolm Bradbury for *The Yorkshire Post*, in October 1961. 'Mass-Media and the Public Attitude to Crime' was specially written, at the editor's request for the *Criminal Law Review*, and appeared in June 1961. 'The Teacher's Rôle' was a paper given to a conference on education, and subsequently appeared, in a form only slightly different from that in which it appears here, in the *British Journal of Sociology*, March 1962. Collaboration with Malcolm Bradbury led to the production of the article, 'The Writing on the Redbrick Wall', which was published in *The Sunday Times* in March 1962.

A version of the essay, 'The War of the Generations' appeared in the *Daily Telegraph* in August 1964 as two articles: it is extended and amended in the form in which it appears now. The article, 'The Changing Universities', was written as one of a series specially commissioned by *The Guardian*, in the columns of which it appeared, in somewhat amended form, in November 1964. 'The Needs of Students' is an expanded version of a paper given to an education conference, and appeared in its present form among the conference papers under the title of *Eighteen Plus*, edited by Marjorie Reeves, and published by Faber and Faber, 1965.

The Trustees of the Charles Russell Memorial Lecture invited me to give their 1965 lecture, for which I chose to talk on 'The Social Context of the Youth Problem'. The chapter in this volume is a slightly amended version of the lecture as published by the Trustees. 'An Approach to Delinquency' is an abridgement of an article written for *New Society*, and which appeared in February 1966. The two short papers, 'In Defence of Ox-

Acknowledgements

bridge' and 'The Age of Majority', were written for the *Spectator*, and were published in April and September 1966, respectively.

Whilst I was staying in Berkeley, California in 1966–7, the *Observer* requested me to write something about the Hippies, who were then a thriving mode of youth cultural expression in Berkeley and San Francisco: the essay in this volume includes some of the points made in the article that appeared in the *Observer* in March 1967, but is in itself an extended discussion not previously published. Similarly, the essay, 'Technology and the Socialization of the Young' is a very much extended version of a Foreword that I was invited to write by Mr. H. A. Rhee for his book, *Office Automation in Social Perspective* (Oxford: Blackwell, 1968): in this version issues of more relevance to the theme of this book have been considerably developed. Dr. Peter Mann, the editor of *British Universities Yearbook*, invited me to contribute a paper on contemporary student troubles to the edition appearing for the session 1968–9. The result of that invitation was the paper, 'The Youth Culture, the Universities and Student Unrest', in very much the same form as it appears in these pages. The paper, 'Social Values in Higher Education', has not previously appeared in print. It is a very much amended version of a study paper written for the University Teachers Group of the Christian Frontier Council and the S.C.M. at their request: (perhaps I should make it clear that I am not a member of the Group nor of either of the sponsoring organizations).

Conversation and day-to-day association with a number of people have been of particular importance in my acquaintance with student affairs, and it would be impossible to mention all the graduates and undergraduates who have kept me informed, by how they behaved as well as by what they said, of their responses to university life and to life in a hall of residence. In particular I should like to express my gratitude for a great deal of thoughtful conversation and sometimes, also, written comment from Robin Biswas, now a lecturer at York University, Toronto; Brian Barton; Manuel Carballo, now teaching at Loyola University, New Orleans; David Eastwood, now a master at Fettes; Paul Harris, now teaching at Reading University; Trevor Matthews; K. H. Nield, now at the University of Birmingham; Frank Riley, once again at the University of Leeds, though now in a senior capacity; and R. E. G. Tyler.

Not all that there is to know about students is known to them, however, and I gained a great deal from sharing responsibility for the running of Sadler Hall, Leeds, with Dr. J. A. Hiddleston, now at Exeter College, Oxford, with whom I am happy to say, my discussions still continue. Dr. J. V. Loach, Registrar at the University of Leeds, as an administrator of rare sensitivity and immense goodwill towards students, taught me a great deal for which I have remained most grateful.

In a very different context, I have considerable debts to several Americans who discussed with me at different times, or who introduced me to, the youth culture in America in its various forms, and I should like to record my thanks to Philip Baity, Jon and Judy Clark, Albert Johnson, Tony Krupa and Rafa Varga.

One or two essays in this volume has been very much improved by the helpful criticism of friends, and I should like in particular to thank John Sparrow, Warden of All Souls, for his comments on the essay on student unrest, and Dr. Marjorie Reeves, of St. Anne's College, Oxford, for improvements to the essay, 'The Needs of Students'. At a much later date in the making of this book I was fortunate to have the care and attention of Mr. T. P. Bull when the proofs were being read, and I am pleased to acknowledge all his help. Two of the earlier essays that are included in this volume were written in collaboration with Malcolm Bradbury, but that reveals only a part of the sustained conversation that has gone on between us over the years on a range of topics that are covered in all the essays in this book. To my association with him I owe not only the benefit of things that he has said, but also the stimulation to think about and say things myself. My gratitude to him naturally extends to Elizabeth, his wife, who, on so many occasions and with so little fuss, made the most congenial arrangements for two men who wanted to talk and to write. All that I learned from Dr. J. H. Higginson when he was Warden of Sadler Hall in the University of Leeds, and from Nancy, his wife, receives its far too modest acknowledgement in the dedication of this book.

Introduction

The 1960s have been a decade of violence and disturbance, beginning among the young people milling about the streets of big cities, and passing finally to the universities. What has occurred has not *merely* been a diffusion of styles of deviance from the least educated to those enjoying expensive education —although it has certainly been that. It has been a development in which the dissidence of the mass youth culture has become a generational response to the point where it has absorbed even elements of the *élite* of the younger generation. From being a mood of disaffection bursting out into civic disturbance under the influence of the mass-media of the pop culture, it has been transformed, with the help of an ideology evolved largely by refugee sociologists, into a movement that justifies itself in grandiose and idealistic terms. Even this development is by no means self-explanatory, however, and it is the sustained emphasis of the essays collected in this volume that to understand the spread of youthful unrest in our times, and what I frankly call the war of the generations, it is necessary to examine some of the processes of social change that are found in the basic areas of social structure, in the work order, the family and in the response of these institutions to changing technological development.

There are, of course, other, perhaps autonomous, factors influencing the course of this development, in particular the changing ways in which children are brought up (in these pages only the secondary socialization—the way in which the individual is taught in school and university, and is prepared for his job—are examined, not the primary process of socialization of the baby). And there are unintended consequences that have followed from deliberate innovation in economic policy and social legislation, particularly from the redistribution of income.

In the background of all these developments there is national demoralization (and this may be more generally the demoralization of western society). A nation experiencing acute decline in power, and aware, as a public matter, for the first time of the fragility of its economic resources in a world which competes in terms increasingly unfavourable to a country that industrialized early and that lacks modern sources of power, might expect to experience demoralization. This is, put in another way, related as a sickness of the soul to the economic problems that constitute a sickness of the body. Paradoxically, there was far more social resilience, fuller expressions of loyalty, patriotism and commitment, and greater willingness to work, in tougher conditions, in the days when many lived lives of great hardship and insecurity between 1880 and 1940, than has been evident in the last decade or two. Despite affluence, the conquest of unemployment, elaborate and comprehensive social welfare, the public are more aware of national economic uncertainties than ever they were before. They experience higher taxes, rising prices and perennial crises of confidence in money. In a world in which extravagant promises have become political stock-in-trade, even comfortable reality has been worse than disappointing. The inflation which in its early phases was an enjoyable ailment for all but fixed income receivers has now become a more malignant disease the long-term consequences of which have become steadily more apparent. The sense of general misfortune persists. Counting blessings is not an exercise to which modern men have been much exhorted, since democratic politics, unlike transcendental religions, has few compensatory devices for disappointed hopes. The threshold of aspirations has been raised far beyond the national capacity for their realization. The changes in society that arise from these conditions are less tangible than are the hard facts of economic change or power politics: they have to do with a mood which is in many respects collective, a shared apprehension of disappointment and relative deprivation. As phenomena these moods are elusive, yielding neither to measurement nor to conceptual rigour, and yet can we doubt their importance?

Demoralization of this kind is something known in other nations of the world, and in part it may stem from the fact that whilst we have learned to recognize problems (for example in economics) much more effectively, we are also aware that their detailed comprehension surpasses the capacities of any one man or group of men. Because we recognize the problems we cannot even take refuge in convenient fictions that lay responsibility in the hands of Providence, as less knowledgeable men did in the past. There may be a special significance in the loss of earlier confidence by a nation like Britain, which was not merely another empire, but an empire founded in the last days of the discovery of the ends of the earth, and an empire built, much more than any forerunner, on certain avowed principles of a civilizing kind. The Victorian conscience was in many ways a remarkable phenomenon, and the standards of public service and disinterested commitment that were evoked in response to that national ethic and ideology were perhaps of an order unlike those known in earlier epochs. They depended in large part on a strongly internalized sense of morality, on principles of public decency and on a growing sense of social justice. Fashionable as it is to poke holes through the elborate façade of Victorian hypocrisy, it can scarcely be gainsaid that that was an era of public confidence in the maintenance of disinterested goodwill, and the moral education of the emotions for the attainment of socially prescribed ends. Whatever the deficiencies of the system of economic reward and social status—and they are evident—this aspect of what Victorian Britain enjoyed may be a *sine qua non* of stable society, whether capitalist or socialist. No western nation of today has this confidence or this widely diffused moral commitment of individuals to the public good. No nation now appears to have the combination of resources—economic, political, social, moral and civic—for effective leadership or even for internal cohesion. Civil strife in America; economic weakness, perversity and isolationism in France; political uncertainty and self-conscious fear of her own economic strength in Germany—disqualify them, as the deterioration of cultural and social life and of civic conscience in Britain disqualify her, for such a rôle. But this is far from the burden of this book or its introduction.

If the changes of mood in nations are largely induced, tertiary responses (although no less significant for that) to deeper-laid real causes, how much more so are the changes that we have admitted into our way of life under the influence of the mass-media, and the manufacture of pop-culture. [The hedonism of contemporary society, the expectation that organized mass entertainment will be available throughout all our leisure hours, indeed all of the time, is part, perhaps, of a compensatory response to a society in which we are less confident, as well as an indication of the abandonment of the work ethic.] As work grew more boring the idea of being entertained whilst at work developed: *Music While You Work* was the war-time spearhead of the assault on a work ethic that had become increasingly difficult to sustain (even in war-time) as work tasks lost their direct human involvements and acquired only the imposed rhythms of the machines. Enough is said of the mass-media of communication, and more especially of the mass-media of entertainment, in the following pages to make unnecessary any further discussion here. [Mass-media are seen as a crucial element in the moulding of contemporary modes of social disenchantment and social unrest, as providing their own contribution to the growing shapelessness of social life.] Their importance is symbolic as well as intrinsic, of course, since they epitomize more than anything else the making of Britain as a mass society, a society that has lost much of its traditional resilience, its traditional ethical and cultural resources, and its citizens their sense of distinctive identity. The new agents of acculturation have ceased to be those who imitated—if they did not belong to—more educated and more leisured social classes. They have become a much more professional body of communicators, whose interests are to titillate the emotions rather than to inform the mind or mould the manners of men.

The essays collected in this volume span the decade from 1959 to 1969, and they may be taken as 'progress' reports of a cultural process that I should not care to call 'progress'. Although I have deleted some repetition, there remain inevitable notes of repeated emphasis as new phases of the youth problem have demanded attention to persisting structural elements of explanation, and these it has seemed as well to leave in order not to vitiate the argument of any one particular chapter. In a collection of pieces on associated themes, such echoes of earlier thoughts seem as natural and as forgivable as they would in any other genre of a creative kind.

Introduction

In abridging some of these essays, and expanding the analysis in others, I have been forcibly struck by points made years ago that have subsequently appeared to have particular cogency and which in some of the later works I had taken up again in more extensive discussion. Thus, in the first essay, 'The Trouble with Teenagers' (1959), there was an allusion to the 'routinization of work tasks and the rationalization of the industrial process' that is a much more central focus of attention in the piece, 'Technology and the Socialization of the Young' (1968); and to 'the breakdown of trust between generations' which, five years later, seemed a much more conspicuous phenomenon. Writing on CND in 1961, Malcolm Bradbury and I, in what is the second chapter of this volume—more presciently than we knew in the light of the student uprisings that occurred six or seven years later—referred to that movement as 'the first mass protest movement of modern times', that, 'has begun a whole new era of public protest'. Early in 1969, following riots in St. Paul's Cathedral on the occasion of a unity address there by the Roman Catholic Cardinal Heenan, Lord Coleraine, in a letter to *The Times*, reminded Canon Collins, the leader of CND, that the type of demonstration that suddenly seemed so wanton to the Church of England had been begun by the movement he had led.

In 'The Writing on the Redbrick Wall' (1962) my co-author and I pointed to the growing malaise in the universities at a time when the Robbins Report dealt in terms of glowing confidence with the prospects of university expansion. As Chairman of the Governors of the London School of Economics, at the time of the closure of the School in 1969, Lord Robbins was himself brought face to face with the message that we had deciphered seven years before. It must be said, now that the chalked obscenities are written not only on the walls of Redbrick, but also on the walls of Balliol College, Oxford, that the writing we saw in 1962 did not tell us so very clearly of the extent of the discredit into which a minority of students would bring the universities in less than seven years. Some sort of breakdown, particularly of quality, we fully expected, but the political exploitation of university vulnerability as a conscious act of a minority of students is a phenomenon we did not foresee.

B

When the disadvantages of large universities of the American type were discussed in 'The Needs of Students', I suggested that undergraduates did not need specialist courses taught by experts such as American state universities have typically provided. What I suggested was needed was the sustained involvement of committed teachers of basic, not specialist, subjects. Just as this book is going to press there comes an account from Berkeley of discontent with specialist course-work for undergraduates at the University of California, and of an experiment with an undergraduate educational programme designed almost completely in accord with (but, need it be said, entirely independently of) what is advocated in the essay in this volume.[1]

In discussing the 'Social Context of the Youth Problem' in the Russell Memorial Lecture (1965), I emphasized that the Mods and Rockers who were merely the passing temporary style of the persisting youth culture, were not able to explain their own riotous behaviour, and the analysis pursued there offers some explanation of the shift from 'rational' (economic) rioting to 'irrational' affrays for which the explanation lay in unexamined social causes of which the rioters themselves were unaware. But by the time youthful unrest had reached the universities a couple of years later, it had acquired—as would be expected of the more educated population now affected—a distinctive ideology. What emerges is that whereas the social disturbances of the less educated proceed spontaneously from disgruntlements the social causes of which are unknown to the people concerned, disturbances in the universities arise from widely canvassed beliefs and propaganda that are patently false causes. Such is the power of rationalization and the demand for at least the appearance of intellectual justification for behaviour that is prompted by much less rational factors.

Such are some of the conclusions that seem to emerge from re-reading these various pieces. I have included two or three rather shorter items which pick up particular issues of topical significance, and which serve as afterthoughts to some of the longer articles, and at some points I have permitted myself the liberty of a number of prescriptive comments. They serve now to show how far my thinking was from the social legislation that

[1] See Joseph Tussman, *Experiment at Berkeley*, Berkeley: University of California Press, 1969.

was subsequently enacted—most particularly, and I would consider disastrously, that arising from the Latey Report on the Age of Majority. In general, however, my concern has not been prescriptive but diagnostic. The concern has not been to attribute blame, but to chart the course of moral change and institutional change in a particular and important field. At one point, in 'Social Context of the Youth Problem', I have set out the assumptions in the background of my discussion, and this might serve for all the essays in the volume. I make plain there that I take as the base line for a discussion of change the moral intimations in the received ideas of our society: these are the point of departure for an assessment of social developments in Britain in the last two decades.

The essays in this volume are written from a sociological perspective, but they do not stem from the conventional exercises of sociological research. They are not the result of administering a large research grant (or even a small one) on secretaries and research assistants. They do not rest on the supposed 'hard data' of responses to questionnaires, attitude tests and scientifically constructed rating scales. Neither do they proceed from abstract theoretical formulations or deductive models. I have relieved myself of the task of setting forth a conceptual framework. These essays, then, claim no more than to issue from reading and thinking, and from living in particular contexts relevant to the subject, as a teacher at Leeds in the earlier part of the decade, and then at Oxford, and as Warden of a hall of residence in the University of Leeds. They are the product of reflection in a genre that might at its best be regarded as analytical sociological commentary. This I hope sets modest bounds to their claim as a contribution—and may offset my earlier immodesty in this introduction in recalling the accuracy of some prophetic points in the earlier essays. For the benefit of my colleagues in sociology, I might add that these points were prophetic and *not* predictive. But prophecy is perhaps the most that we can expect of the discipline at the present time, since, whatever claims may be made for it to the contrary, sociology cannot be said as yet to have a reliable record of prediction.

I

The Trouble with Teenagers
(1959)

Teenage frustration and aggression are part of the common context of our everyday lives, even if we realize it only by the daily reports in the provincial evening press. Adolescent crime and violence increases, and there is much which occurs which never reaches the newspaper: garden fences are destroyed; park benches up-ended; flower beds trampled; cinema seats ripped open (some cinemas in working-class districts have whole rows of seats out of commission because teenagers have cut open the upholstery). Weapons are used in gang fights, and such affrays are commonplace in some working-class districts. So far Britain has escaped the more dramatic evidence of teenage disturbance such as has occurred on the Continent—riots, car-burning, unruly spontaneous eruptions of teenagers for no known reason—but the frustration and need for self-expression in young people, evident in socially deviant attitudes, behaviour and dress, is common to the Teddy boy, the Austrian *Schlurf,* the German *Halbstarken* and the Russian *Stilyagi.* And the Teddy boy, of course, is only one of a series of adolescent deviants, of whom the spiv, the yob and the cosh-boy were earlier variations.

In any age adolescents are necessarily one of the most vigorous elements of society. Young people are usually in the van of assertive action; they have the physical vigour, the impulsive disposition, lack of the inhibitions of wider experience and the commitments which give older people a stake in respectability. But initiative for purposive social action is less likely to spring from the young, and contemporary teenage activity is largely unpurposive, a release of inner tensions rather than a pursuit of articulate social ends. It is more than a vague uncertainty

21

attendant upon biopsychological changes associated with puberty, and part of its explanation is in the changing social situation in which modern youth finds itself. In a period of accelerating social change there are always certain social costs of social progress—costs unseen in the calculated systems of rational accounting which dominate the political thinking of our society. Such change has a differential impact on different segments of society, and youth is inevitably a most vulnerable section. Young people who have acquired no stable life-orientation in a changing society are rendered insecure by the changes which occur. The values of the society, the texture of social relationships, the rôle of authority, are least understood by the young: they can accept changing values most readily, accept them as an ally in their own rebellion, but lose their social balance in the process.

Various aspects of social change have relevance for the problem of teenage frustration and aggression.

(i) New production methods and changing techniques in industry set long experience at a discount and latest training at a premium. This situation clearly favours the young worker. The position and prestige of older workers, once derived from their practical knowledge gained in years at the job, is undermined: they become 'has-beens' who lack the know-how of modern methods. Yet these workers are the fathers of the youngsters who now, in the work sphere, no longer accord prestige to the older hands. As older workers lose importance as economic providers (since high wages accompany modern 'know-how') so too they are likely to suffer loss of respect in other rôles, in the social, political, moral and spiritual spheres. This occurs because of the dominance of the work-rôle in contemporary society, even though there are no short-cut modern techniques to social and moral wisdom, where experience and length of years are alone adequate teachers. Hence both the example of the older generation and the transmission of its values and norms, are disrupted by the changing technological context of our lives.

(ii) Full employment and inflation have had a differential impact on the economy, and unskilled and semi-skilled workers have enjoyed most of the benefit. Income differentials have declined, been eliminated or have even been reversed, and these differentials provided, in earlier periods, the objective basis for the differing life-styles of, for example, the skilled and clerical class as against the manual and unskilled groups. Inflation has meant continually rising money incomes, but has undermined, especially for young workers, any stable conception of the value of money or the things which money buys. Inflation has had significant effects on young people, in providing high money incomes for a group without serious social responsibilities, stable commitments, knowledge of educational, cultural and creative outlets. The connection of high wages and contemporary anti-social behaviour, frustration and criminality is a subject of frequent magisterial comment. Money becomes the standard in terms of which young people think— a key to the socially significant ends which are presented to them, and yet high wages do not bring them effectively nearer to permanent satisfaction, in that they lack a sense of values which enables them effectively to cultivate inner resources. Inflation has given consumption power to groups which have never had the opportunity to cultivate sustained standards of taste, and such groups become the most important market for the capitalist precisely because they are on the one hand wealthy and on the other manipulable and under-educated.

(iii) With new industrial techniques and an increasingly equal distribution of increasing income, mass produced consumer goods have become more and more profitable. The individual, subtle, well-wrought and well-designed, which once epitomized cultivated standards of taste is less readily available, and the groups which had leisure to establish such values have disappeared. Today's high income receivers are without background, education and information necessary to the cultivation of stable tastes. They are exposed in innumerable ways to commercial exploitation, and induced to pay high prices for the merely novel and ephemeral. Mass-production establishes a certain egalitarianism of taste—things sold at equal prices are somehow to be regarded as equally tasteful. Expense becomes the criterion of aesthetic quality, and the basis of social prestige. Advertising emphasizes prestige rather than established reputation, and prestige becomes a commercialized, saleable commodity, all the more eagerly sought because the rewards system offers high but near-equal incomes to large masses of people.

In competitive society the decline of objective class divisions engenders deeper status anxieties, and hence the value of prestige as a selling-point. Advertising is, however, only a method for the manipulation of consumers, it does not express a stable value system: its techniques and gimmicks are employed indiscriminately, with wide disjunction between advertised claims and real quality. Consequently, people, and especially young people, become confused about their norms, values, tastes and standards. High-pressure sales techniques induce the development of powerful cynicism which men need in order to resist commercial enticements. But cynicism does not render men immune from the competitive struggle in which prestige must be constantly renewed by reinvestments in the latest prestige-conferring products.

(iv) With the rationalization of industrial processes specialization of the work-task has increased, and with it the impersonality of work relations, and a lack of comprehension of work activity. Alienation from the means of production, which Marx recognized as a crucial social factor in industrialization, has been followed by alienation from work itself. In the old-time structure of industry there were real relationships of masters and men, even if they were sometimes relationships of tension. Today the bigness of the concern, the routinization of tasks, and the development of bureaucracy create a sense of personal insignificance for the individual worker, and particularly for the young worker who knows less of the folk-lore, tradition and history of the industry, or of workers' movements, in which his interest is often limited to his desire to minimize rewards. Increasingly the worker is the adjunct of the machine which dictates his work patterns and rhythms. Personal investment in the job is diminished, and the cash nexus becomes crucial. Work becomes the irksome routinized activity to provide money for leisure—the 'real' part of life. The taxes and stoppages which reduce income are often only vaguely understood, they are an unfair levy which 'they' impose for no reason except 'their' general hostility to 'us'.

(v) Spatial separation of home and work has been more or less consciously promoted by local authorities who build housing estates well away from factories and from city centres. This vicinal separation enhances the social distance between the two most vital social institutions—the work organization and the family. The rôles of the individual become increasingly disparate, and a socially induced 'rôle-schizophrenia' occurs. One of these institutions must suffer from the division: by and large it is the family. For most of his waking hours the individual is effectively removed from the cohesive, affective functioning of the family, whose members come together less than ever before, and whose control of its younger members is diminished as the work organization becomes more dominant. School meals, youth organizations, mothers going out to work, all promote this attenuation of relationships. The agency for transmission of social values, experiences and aspirations is hopelessly impaired. Honest work attitudes, receptivity, allegiance to family, good name, are all vitiated by the breakdown of association between generations, and as a consequence public promotion of education, literacy and culture fail to have their full cumulative effect. Teachers and club-leaders lose contact by this breakdown of trust between generations and cannot tap the same affective responses as parents, even assuming ideal levels of enlightenment in these specialists themselves. Increasingly the young person gathers his social clues from workmates and peer-group members. Parents, recognizing the different interests and outlook of the younger generation, have experienced a serious failure of nerve: they have surrendered oversight in a changed social situation which they feel themselves not fully to understand.

The entertainment industry diversifies its products along generational lines, and re-emphasizes the separation of work from home by catering for different age groups. Its main concern is to exploit the undiscriminating taste of the big money teenage market: as the rock 'n' roll singer Marty Wilde has said, '. . . the whole country's ruled by what the teenagers like.' Creative use of leisure is not inculcated, and the cumulative effects of educational advance is undermined. The new uses of leisure involve high expenditure and low personal effort, except for the direct release of tensions in an extreme way as in rock 'n' roll dancing. The management of personal tensions and frustrations is unlearned, and outlets of a neurotic type come into their own. Sustaining relationships and cultivated interests are replaced by merely novel and ephemeral satisfactions which eventually serve only to perpetuate the cycle of boredom and release as a self-sustaining pattern. Some young people have the crudest notions of social values and social organization. The establishment—police, law and church—are simply nuisances who stand in the path of gratifications: they are actively despised as being totally irrelevant to the real business of life as these youngsters know it.

(vi) Most young people today are not expected to internalize the 'work ethic' of the last century and the religious values with which it was associated. The remnant of the work ethic in contemporary society has become subsumed into a success ethic, which stresses work, not as a positive good in itself, as a fulfilment of the self, or as a character-building process, but only as a means to the attainment of status. The work-ethic emphasized creativity, integrity, the sense of calling: the success ethic emphasizes prestige, involves competitiveness, a struggle for pre-eminence, and the pleasures of consumption. Success is partly recognized by the use of leisure, and this ethic espouses hedonism. Alienation from work means that the individual's interests focus on leisure pursuits, which have become divorced from the activities of work, as from the texture of family life. The use of leisure becomes an escape from the real world, rather than the refreshment, revitalization and re-creation of it. Vicarious release of frustrated energies, the display of crude aggression, the flight into fantasy, characterize increasingly the leisure activities of the young. Self-improvement, the cultivation of the mind (the very terms sound curiously archaic and moralizing in our own age), even *Erholung*, are alien ends. Leisure tends to be passive without being restful, titillating without being educative: it has ceased to be 'of a piece' with the world of serious and necessary labour and stable sustaining affections.

(vii) Today's young people are exposed by the various mass-media to a wide and motley range of influences. With such abundant diversity little is permanently absorbed in a way which is meaningful: real educational media are highly selective, repetitive, intense, integrated, coherent, sustained—qualities totally alien to the presentations of our mass-media, which are concerned with the novel, bizarre, sensational and fantastic. Media seeking to stimulate their own sales operate on the principle of providing easy, escapist gratifications for a bored public, and ultimately perpetuate the vicious circle of limited interest and heightened sensationalist appetites. They help to establish unreasoning and emotional attitudes of mind: they play on crude sentiments and mobilize emotional responses rather than stimulating intelligent appreciation and understanding. They thus negatively condition young people for more serious appreciation of literary and artistic expression. The presentation of the sensational becomes a competitive race, feeding upon social tensions and stimulating them further, driving down the standards of all media which compete for a mass audience. Feeding on fantasy increases the ennui and nausea of everyday circumstances which, as we have seen, overwhelm the individual in their impersonality. The process makes it more improbable that at any future time the individual's inner resources will be cultivated in ways that will enrich his life. The stimulation of taste for the crass and vulgar destroys both fine feeling and the appreciation of objects of subtle beauty made with care, and the integrity of craftsmanship.

The values expressed in the mass-media are rarely those of the dominant social tradition. Frequently they are the values of aimless rebellion, deviance and criminality. Youth's mistrust and frustration are made the subject of dramatic musicals, or written presentation, and thus, in some sense, are vindicated. The censorial demand for 'a moral' with the triumph of virtue, has no significance for a teenage audience, which watches only the episodes of violence and tension. Dialogue is often unheard, and there is impatience for the depiction of action. There is widespread identification with young violators. The old 'baddies and goodies' have disappeared, and there is only 'us', the youngsters, and 'them'. The American films *High School Confidential, Teenage Rebel, Rebel without a Cause, Blackboard Jungle, The Bad Seed*, and the British film *Violent Playground*, are examples, and so is *West Side Story*. A new type of *cultural hero* emerges, an exaggerated and glamorized representation of a teenager at odds with the world, capable of extreme deviation: he is presented to a largely teenage audience, whose attitudes and orientations are sustained, titillated and emboldened by the process. The old-type hero, a romantic rough diamond, is replaced by the violent disturbed teenager who defies law and causes the pompous and established to suffer dreadful indignities. In some measure the new model hero reflects the contemporary problems of society, but the very presentation provides a tacit vindication for the behaviour it depicts. The issues of right and wrong are surrendered, replaced by crude allegiance to one side, and for the teenage audience there can be no doubt about the direction of their enmity.

There is also the hero who dramatizes sudden 'something-for-nothing' success to be got by virtue of purely natural talents and good looks, without hard work or intelligent effort. This desire is almost hysterically demonstrated in the enthusiasm for the entertainer who emerges from the obscurity of 'an ordinary background', who has not advanced by normal educational channels, who typifies, personally and in the screen rôles he performs, the limitations and frustrations of the ordinary teenager, who displays the currently accepted talents (usually musical, occasionally athletic) which provide vicarious gratifications for his public. The success of Elvis Presley, Terry Dene, Marty Wilde and Tommy Steele is the dream of many a youngster whose only prospect of 'success' in a status-dominated, entertainment-oriented society is a suddenly discovered talent for some 'socially deviant' type of entertainment. Success is closed to most teenagers once they are committed to the secondary modern school, except by a win on the pools or by sudden 'stardom'. Modern youth identifies itself with the ordinary boys 'who make good', whose success is objectified by the disproportionate money rewards which entertainers obtain: the cumulative cultured tradition, the fruits of education, artistic endeavour and intellectual rigour, are all rejected.

Because material of very diverse quality, depicting very divergent social values, are given screen time, they all acquire a superficial equality, which suggests that all tastes are equally valid. Mass-media make no effort to discriminate, or to guide taste. The demand for a mass market is rationalized into a phoney democratic ideology of taste, which denies the positive value of education. Consumer-demand implies that jazz, bebop, rock 'n' roll are as worthy and legitimate as those things that demand educated and cultivated taste. Mass agencies, even the B.B.C. have surrendered their educational mission. But worse, they have also made the effort of more committed educators more difficult, in that the attempt to transmit a sense of values, serious critical standards and informed taste are threatened by the indiscriminate presentations of screen, stage and press.

(viii) Contemporary society is highly status conscious, and promotes the search for social mobility and the desire to 'get on'. For large sections of modern youth who have fallen out of the normal system of advancement via the education system, this cultural goal of success can have only an ironic quality. They must, perforce, acquire prestige, but increasingly for teenagers, this is not by getting a good job, acquiring security, a respectable home, a happy family, a good reputation as a man of character. These things are undervalued in favour of ability to consume, high wages and expenditures, luxury and fun. These new ends may be sought by new means, if need be by delinquency. Advertising holds out the new ends, and the mass-media at least half condone the delinquent means. The reference group in whose eyes status is sought has changed. Failure in the educational system in particular propels the young individual to seek prestige elsewhere, from those with other values. For the highly frustrated a certain prestige can be won by spiting society and its norms by aggressive behaviour. A type of adjustment is made between internal tensions and external approval, the inner need of aggression now acquires social support in these deviant groups. Like neurotic behaviour, the adjustment is a way of managing tensions, but it does this at a false level, perpetuating the problem, rather than solving it. The wider the social group in support the more deviant may the behaviour be; when other sections of society are also suffering frustrations, they too may gain vicarious satisfaction, and provide a context of approval for violence—the case in the Notting Hill race riots.

(ix) Allusion to the youth culture has already been made. Modern youth is fashion-conscious and spending-prone: it can be induced to take up novelties, and to cast them off once their prestige value of being 'in fashion' has become outworn. Youth has surplus income for prestige items, particularly for drink and dress. Careful choice, durability, inherent subtleties of design, care and attention which clothes require if they are to continue to please, are alien pre-occupations to modern young people. Smartness is a concept divorced from economy, affection for clothes, pleasure in keeping things in good condition; instead, smartness depends upon newness, upon external and extrinsic factors, not on the associated suitability of the wearer and his clothes; ultimately it depends on crude money criteria and the fact that certain young entertainers are wearing the same style.

The redistribution of wealth, which has occurred between age classes as well as between social classes, has altered the fashion market. New fashions, once for higher strata, now pass quickly to the highly-paid youngsters, who use fashion to flout convention and to signalize the gap between themselves and 'squares'. Since commerce directs itself to this market catering for these demands becomes a priority. Anticipation of teenage demand becomes vital to big business. Youth becomes a clientele which is taste-determining, and yet objectively its taste is so uneducated. Particularly in entertainment its own condition of lostness, disorder, cultural neurosis is reflected; if youth is 'crazy, mixed up', 'shook up', 'beat' so too must be its entertainment. There is an erosion of established values, of real self-expression, the cultivation of inner resources and articulated understanding of themselves. The youth culture also means the disappearance of commodities and shops which catered for a more discerning trade. Mass production, the 'dear and nasty', the novel, the garish and bizarre, displace the items of quality and the retail units which were devoted to their sale. The tradition even of sales people passes, and there is a new generation of sales people which knows only how to push a sale, and does not know the intrinsic qualities and character of the goods it sells. Yet although youth has acquired this new commercial significance it is manipulated rather than participant in social arrangements; it is first exposed to alien values and then blamed for accepting them.

British youth culture imitates the American: for some time we have been a major 'cultural importer' from the United States, although American ideals act erosively on our traditional values, which, to the young, appear 'out-moded'. Rapid social change in the advancing capitalist economy places a great emphasis on youth, but in Britain this developing emphasis has been accelerated by the importation of ideas from a country more advanced in technical and material standards. Instead of

the classic 'cultural lag' of social institutions and attitudes behind economic and technical changes, we have, because of
this process of cultural borrowing, something of the reverse
process in operation—a 'cultural drag'. In the cultural drag
certain cultural goals, attitudes and ideals are imported and
developed. These social ends, which through media such as
screen, television and cheap literature, are disseminated as
prestigious goals, draw commerce and industry to import and
produce commodities along the lines suggested by the prestige
system of another culture. Standards are affected, and the local
and national character of produce fades before the imitation of
commodities current in the United States. The very word
'American', as a tag for adolescent clothing and other goods, is
a prestige-selling device. Yet the disparity between the material
standards of America and Britain cannot but create further
frustrations for those exposed to all this propaganda for the
American way of life, in a society which cannot yet—and may
never—be able to support a similar standard, even if that were
genuinely and widely desired.

(x) Since the war geographic mobility has increased—mainly
on the assumption that labour should be ready to move to areas
where new opportunities exist. It is easy to assume that new
towns can be populated with rootless families, drawn away
from older environments, but there is an immense social strain
involved. The loss of roots, of stable community sentiments,
isolate the family, which has already lost much of its own inner
resilience. Just as the new form of work organization has
jeopardized family life, so the new geographic mobility has
destroyed community life. The strong family exists only in the
strong community. Social control, stable tradition, cumulative
experience, the deeper process of social education, the strength
of local character, the distinctiveness of local vigour, allegiance
to local government, are all lost as this process develops. Young
people in particular suffer in the disruption. The crude attraction of money is the incentive whereby people are manipulated
into mobility, and this pursuit of gain comes to justify all sacri-
fices in the minds of young people exposed to the system. One
consequence is the boredom of youth with its surroundings, and
its inability to obtain local satisfaction and stimulation; just as
so many young people have no knowledge of ways in which to

cultivate inner resources, so, too, they have no inducement to draw enrichment from their surroundings. Instead, places featured on the screen are thought to be the only places where life is really worth living. For most people the genuine richness of life must rest on the vigour, stability and strength of local tradition, which in its best form does not exclude the infusion of culture and knowledge from without. These values fade not only because people are on the move, but also because local contexts are being standardized and made uniform. Young people suffer most in that mobility becomes normal to them. The local context offers less, and they remain less long to discover such richness as it has; social relationships become superficial, and deep-laid isolation, with its many attendant social and psychic strains, becomes a basis for further anti-social behaviour.

2

Alienated Intellectuals
(1961)

The Campaign for Nuclear Disarmament is a movement that dramatically focuses attention on the discontents of our time. Unlike so many popular causes of the past, it is not a mere rabble of the economically underpriviliged seeking redress for personally felt grievances and the means of subsistence. It has within its ranks a significant minority of the more intelligent and more articulate members of society, and there can be no doubt that their discontents are deeply felt. C.N.D. is not only important as a focus of opinion, however: it has social significance in successfully presenting an image as the movement to which enlightened, forward-looking young people should obviously belong. 'Anti-bomb, of course', is the self-recommendation of *New Statesman* advertisers seeking friends, lodgers or even baby-sitters. Its demonstrations are as much publicity as protest, and do more, in fact, to recruit followers than to influence governments. Its ostensible aim is one to which, all else being equal, few could take exception: it appears to offer a simple but high-minded goal against which there are no respectable intellectual arguments, but only blind subservience to governments that lack objective reasons for nuclear armament, but which indulge themselves in power fantasies. Many of those who support C.N.D. are writers, churchmen, university dons and students—'good', 'intelligent' people. The movement concentrates the fears and insecurities of our age. But to many of these fears the bomb is itself only incidental.

C.N.D. is the first *mass* protest movement of modern times that has not been either a political party or a messianic movement: it has begun a whole new era of public protest, and has recruited and mobilized against the government sections of society whose political interests would otherwise have remained passive. Persons who would normally favour the maintenance of public order have been aroused into demonstrations under the influence of C.N.D. As with motoring offences, many basically law-abiding people have found themselves aligned unexpectedly against the police.

The issue with which C.N.D. is concerned is potentially apocalyptic, and the movement itself acquires something of an apocalyptic urgency, since it is dealing with nothing less than the prospect of the end of the world. Certainly, the movement is differently related to the apocalyptic idea than are, say, Jehovah's Witnesses, who engage in special pleading for their own salvation when Armageddon comes. The Campaigners are more rational: they know that mankind's fate will be their own. But they are like the Witnesses in pressing their solution on others. They share a similar urgency and communicate similar fervour, albeit among a very different section of the population. They differ in being fired not by a saviour, a god-man, but by a simple idea for government action—a stroke of policy. The explanation of the emergence of apocalyptic movements is usually sought somewhere other than in their own self-acclaimed goals, and it may be not out of order to ask whether such explanations might not be at least partly relevant to C.N.D., despites its intellectual constituency.

Ostensibly C.N.D. has a one-article creed—to abandon the nuclear bomb in the interests of the survival of mankind. The simplicity and the attractiveness of this idea explains the movement's hold over its adherents: it needs no platform, and experiences no arguments about positive prescriptions. It has no strategy for survival, only a single-minded demand. It can thus avoid internal sectarian schism on ideological issues. Its only programme is a programme for protest action, and because it has devised a pattern of action, and can communicate a sense, however illusory, of instant achievement, the movement succeeds. The achievement, however, is not towards its declared ends, and yet it undoubtedly meets the needs of C.N.D. adherents.

What C.N.D. stands for is a new style in living. Its badge is the symbol of that style, and a way of communicating to others the values one lives by. Since Suez there has been a growing

34

section of the public, particularly among the young, that has become ashamed of, and self-conscious about, the nation's image and history; they feel only guilt about our colonial past, and, by extension, about our whole cultural heritage. Although often professing a type of idealism themselves, they are completely cynical about the motives of men in the past, and, indeed, about those who do not espouse the same causes as they do themselves. For these young people, living in a declining nation is obviously a difficult experience. Much of the past must obviously be abandoned—the imagery of imperialism, and the self-confidence that the British used to know as the world's dominant nation. But many young people cannot relinquish all that without debunking everything identified with the past, and this includes its culture and its morality as well as national loyalties and social obligations. Many of the younger generation are only lightly tied to their cultural past, and only mildly committed to the kind of society in which they live. In particular, they find the very notion of society as an authority and as an order both constraining and damaging—and this even though they are often self-styled socialists.

Their cast of mind is cynical about the real world and utopian about the alternatives. Their demand for emotional liberty finds expression in jazz, plays about working-class life and defiant young men, and in C.N.D. Their strong moralistic attitude about the nation's past and their feelings of moral concern about the nation's activities are often combined with a moral unconcern about their own. This displacement of moral responsibility, from the individual to 'the establishment' is a way in which C.N.D. manages to combine the appeal of being a moral arbiter whilst, simultaneously, providing a morally permissive context for its own adherents. Blame is attached to authorities and freedom is demanded for the faithful: it has been a common feature of apoclyptic movements of the past. Because they define the political situation in stark terms, and because they reject the idea of diminishing the threat of nuclear war by diplomacy or strategy (the bankrupt methods of the past world which they condemn) they can permit themselves considerable license in the conduct of their campaign and the life-style it fosters. They demand an outright solution, whatever the consequences for the survival of their own national culture or of social democracy and the procedures that it has developed over the centuries. Because they are not, finally, negotiators, but believers in an urgent creed, their opinion justifies any form of expression even if it is little more than high-minded delinquency.

Breaking conventions without losing the respect of those one accepts as the most important reference group, has its own special satisfactions, and violating normal codes of behaviour has become very much the public style of C.N.D. in its passive resistance, and no less informs the private life-style of many of those who identify themselves with the movement. Again, this dual assertion of freedom from normal social constraints, which also reveals the breakdown of social control in modern society, reflects the pattern established by religious apocalyptic movements. The urgency of the message, and the special position of the truly enlightened, sanction deviance from the existing moral order, and this deviance is justified as a necessary part of the challenge to authority and apathy.

The challenge to established mores has another function— it provides the basis by which adherents can see themselves as a new, separated, community of friends, linked in the cause of salvation. The badge, the jargon, the revivalist appeal of the march and the pilgrimage, and the common assumptions about what is justified public behaviour and what is appropriate private behaviour, are all readily paralleled in other millennial movements.

Although the bomb itself is undoubtedly a focus of concern for campaigners, the other functions that the movement fulfils suggests that in many ways the bomb serves as a scapegoat for a range of frustrations that intellectuals encounter in contemporary society. As a scapegoat the bomb has special attraction—it appears as an objective issue over which individuals are rightly concerned; the call for nuclear disarmament appears to imply no vested interests—only a disinterested humanitarianism that rises above the sectional interests of other social groups. The call for action that transcends parties and denominations has been common among new religious movements impressed by the drama of their own times (which, of course, is often a drama of their own making). The disinterested humanitarianism is underlined by the sacrificial aspect of C.N.D. activities—by marching in foul weather, sitting on wet pavements, and the general sanctifying air of undertaking personally uncomfortable and publicly discomforting acts for the sake of the universal good. From their involvement, the campaigners acquire a faint air of saintliness, and even their violence, whatever its social consequences, assumes the quality of virtue.

Objectivity and disinterested virtue combine with the widespread disenchantment with traditional democratic political processes. Since there appears to be little opportunity for significant action within party politics, and since, for the young, all parties appear hopelessly 'established', their procedures highly routinized and their authority-structures bureaucratic, C.N.D. is a vehicle for those who want to be in something that is very much alive, and where at least the illusion of purposive politics is maintained. The increasing passivity of modern leisure time pursuits enhances the attraction of a movement that marches under one simple, clear-cut slogan. That intellectuals should be attracted to C.N.D. is itself an indication of their increasing feeling of helplessness, and an expression of the extent to which they feel their sense of separation from the centre of power. It is a confession that they are no longer convinced that they can influence people by what they write, what they say from the pulpit, or even by the special techniques that they have gone to university to acquire. This comes out sharply when one recalls that scarcely any of the writers associated with the movement have written novels and plays about the movement: they have chosen the curiously unskilled activities of marching and sitting it out. As in a millennial movement, men divest themselves of their social status and cultural skills in order to express the commonality of their condition, in a symbolic gesture of willingness to abandon what is inherited from the old world for the sake of the promise of the new. Of course, C.N.D. promises far less, and its ideological position differs greatly from those of millennial movements, but the style that they have adopted bears striking resemblance.

For intellectuals in Britain to be so heavily represented in a mass movement given to socially disruptive demonstrations is a new phenomenon. In the nineteenth century there was no such disobedience among the equivalent class, because they would have been nearer the centres of power, and would have had much more influence and a stronger sense of social responsibility. The intellectual's situation in contemporary society, however, is one in which he is easily disillusioned with democracy: in its nature democratic processes reflect only very partially and only very laggardly the issues that intellectuals take to be important. In the less perfect democracy of the nineteenth century those intellectuals who wanted to be involved in politics had much more of a chance of being so. The expansion of the intellectually educated class, its recruitment from very different sections of society, and the increasingly specialist and technical nature of politics, economics, society and work-patterns all militate against any individual intellectual's having much sense of influence or power. In their greater numbers they become an alienated section of society, often experiencing their sharpest tension with the mass of the unintellectual population, although they prefer to represent this conflict as a confrontation with what they call the upper-class establishment.

Perhaps because they are more acutely aware of themselves as a class, they readily interpret the social situation in class terms, and this at a time when social mobility, social legislation and the changing structure of industry is significantly blurring all the old class lines of traditional Marxist analysis. The conflict that they experience in their relation to the rest of society, permits them to espouse conflict analysis of social systems generally. They have less hope of democratic processes, and in consequence are disposed to seize simple-minded slogans that establish for a group that behaves in defiance of the nation the sense that it really is, in a superior way, the conscience of the nation. Because the struggle that they see between classes is beyond solution by democratic means, they move the arena of politics out of its traditional institutions and into the streets under the banner of C.N.D.

In its beginnings, when the movement's character was not fully articulated, C.N.D. was not at once an expression of disillusionment with modern democracy. Then it had no necessity to promote protest demonstrations. As long as it regarded itself as primarily an expression of moral feeling, calling governments generally to their responsibilities, and insisting on the supremacy of humane action over any other, it had a place in a democratic system. But as the movement developed, so its hard-core supporters intensified its activity, and inevitably it became a magnet for many who were socially discontented. For some it was a valuable front-organization: these were the Communist sympathizers who, though proclaiming that it was better to be red than dead, were inclined to believe that it would be better to be red anyway. For others it was a focus of anti-German feeling which, under the guise of being anti-Fascist, at times became almost racist in character. The recruitment of such elements probably enhanced the disenchantment of the movement with its prospects as a democratic pressure-group, and stimulated its tendency to become a movement of mass protest taking increasingly extreme measures. C.N.D. promotes a policy that no government can espouse—no government can voluntarily reduce its power to negotiate or revoke its protective alliances. The zenith of that phase of the campaign's activity in which its leaders still hoped to influence normal political processes was reached at the Scarborough Conference of the Labour Party. Its failure to influence the Labour Party policy, freed the campaign from normal democratic responsibilities, and the movement has now passed into a more extremist phase. Its political aims grow less certain, and it now seeks principally to embarrass the government, the Labour Party and the public authorities generally.

The movement has thus entered a phase of deliberate alienation. The pattern of its response now enacts a self-fulfilling prophecy: because it finds difficulty in pressing its policy on to democratic parties, the more it is likely to engage in action that convicts its members that they have no prospects in democratic systems, and the more they are encouraged to engage in acts subversive of democracy, because the system is not worth preserving anyway. Yet all this is done to achieve one particular goal, and the dependence of individuals on democratic institutions in other respects is easily ignored. The urgency with which their view on war is felt presses the movement into modes of action that are surprising and socially significant. At a time when teenage groups of a semi-delinquent kind frequently create disturbances, C.N.D. organizes such occasions for the intellectually-better-to-do. Its disturbances are messages, primarily assertions of faith, demands for immediate access to public debate of particularly strident and ultimately irresponsible kind. But the disturbances and the way of life that goes with them is more than merely political protest. Unlike old riots, the movement *co-ordinates* disruption, and permits its own spearhead of activists to make propaganda for the cause that the moderates nominally disavow. But in all this the movement inevitably attracts to it, and increasingly tolerates, not only those who are only marginally committed to our form of society, but also those who are actively enlisted against it. The Committee of 100 makes no secret of the nihilists and anarchists that it attracts: its supporters are increasingly drawn from the alienated, socially-hostile persons who care neither for the lives they lead nor the society in which they live. The mass of the movement recruits young people who are little informed—and whom the movement steadily misinforms—about democratic political processes, but who doubtlessly enjoy the sideshows of moral abandonment that have always accompanied marching movements.

3

Mass-Media and the Public Attitude to Crime
(1961)

In the 1930s it was a fairly common thing for the mass-media
—in particular the cinema—to receive rather intemperate
blame for the extent of crime and juvenile delinquency then
prevailing. Much of the criticism was superficial and ill-
informed, and in these circumstances it was not difficult for the
cinema industry to rebutt these attacks as unfounded and
alarmist. But, even at that time, the thesis was taken more
seriously by some investigators, and, even in early studies, evidence was accumulated to show that the cinema had some
significant effect—albeit as one of a number of influences,
among which others were perhaps more profound—on children's social behaviour.[1] Because the cinema was presenting
almost entirely fictional material it tended to draw more
criticism than did the newspaper press which was, at least
theoretically, presenting largely factual material. The advent
of television has, in some ways, made more apparent the similarity of the types of influence which all the media of mass communication may exert, and has made the previous distinction
of fictional and factual material seem rather less relevant.

No serious writer on the subject would, today, suggest that
the mass-media were the principal causes of crime and delinquency. What might more reasonably be suggested is that these
media have played a considerable part in altering our attitude

[1] See for example Herbert Blumer and Philip M. Hauser, *Movies, Delinquency and Crime*, New York, 1933, and M. I. Preston, 'Children's Reaction
to Movie Horrors and Radio Crime', *Journal of Pediatrics* (19), 1941, pp.
147–68.

to crime, in providing our society with a new structure of values, and in disseminating information, and providing models for social deviance. A thorough-going analysis of crime in contemporary Britain would necessarily take into account the changing structure of our society; the strains of increased social and geographic mobility; the breakdown of patterns of stable community life; the consequent loss of agencies of social control, and the wider experience of social disorder. In the anonymous context of urban living the strength of received custom and stable convention is diminished, and social control operates directly and abrasively at its lowest level—that which the law enforces, without the lubricating effect of a climate of moderating social practice and opinion. The mass-media are an increasingly important part of changing social conditions: the transmission of information and the business of communication has come to occupy a central place in modern society, and so they exert increasing influence in the moulding of social behaviour. Even if the mass-media were concerned only with the transmission of ideas, it would be reasonable to postulate that they must thereby influence the attitude and behaviour of the public. In fact they do more than this: they set out to appeal much more to the emotions than to reason, more to the deeper-laid sources of motivation than to the intellect. Similarly, we know that they exert a selective influence—greater on those groups from among whom delinquents are principally drawn: just as the cinema has tended to attract as most frequent attenders those of low intelligence, and those in need of escapist activities, so too television is viewed less by intelligent children who are more easily bored by what it presents.[1]

Discovering by direct inquiry the exact effect of mass-media on the attitudes and behaviour of the public is difficult, and some would say impossible. Attitude-testing is one of the least satisfactory areas of social inquiry. This is so because the situation in which tests are undertaken is arranged so as to eliminate the influence of extraneous factors; but, in consequence, ques-

[1] UNESCO, Reports & Papers on Mass Communication, No. 31. *The influence of the cinema on children and adolescents*, Introduction. See also, H. Himmelweit, 'Television & Radio' in *Popular Culture & Personal Responsibility*, Verbatim Report of a Conference, October 1960, N.U.T., London, p. 157.

tionnaire procedure is so artificial that the information obtained must always be of doubtful value and validity. The effects of exposing people to a particular programme or news-story must necessarily be slight and of short duration. The really significant influence of the mass-media is necessarily more subtle and cumulative. There are, however, other methods of analysis which, if not conclusive, are at least suggestive. One approach is to examine those who are most addicted to mass-media, and to discover their particular social circumstances and psychological dispositions. From such research it is possible to say that maladjusted children show a marked preference for violent and traumatic material.[1] (Most of this research has been undertaken with children because children are more susceptible to direct influence; the public is generally more concerned about what influences them; and they lend themselves to easy testing in standard circumstances in school.) A perhaps more relevant approach is the content-analysis of the material presented by the mass-media themselves, and the examination of the possible functions of this type of material in contemporary society.

Even those who have been most reserved in their opinion on the effects of mass-media on crime and delinquency have not doubted that much of the material presented by these media is in itself nauseous and tasteless.[2] Certain more specific points may also be made, to some of which I shall return below:

(i) Mass-media have given a great deal of attention to criminal activity as such: they have exaggerated its extent and frequency, and provided the purely factual with a context of drama. They have been particularly attentive to violence, both criminal violence and violence which, in the context of the programme, is not specifically criminal.

(ii) From various studies we know that mass-media have provided those with anti-social dispositions with vivid

[1] Mark Abrams, in *Popular Culture & Personal Responsibility*, *op. cit.*, p. 62.
[2] Report of the Departmental Committee on *Children and the Cinema*. Home Office, London, 1950; Barbara Gray, 'The Social Effects of the Film', *Sociological Review*, XLII, 1950, p. 12; also Mark Abrams, *op. cit.*, p. 61.

fantasies, and there is some evidence that they have also provided the criminal disposed with ideas and technical knowledge for criminal activity.

(iii) They have served as agencies of cultural diffusion, transmitting criminal ideas from one society to another, and thus providing new forms of expression for social deviance: this is particularly the case with the film, television and comic-books, which readily pass over national frontiers.

(iv) They have created a new value for what they determine is 'news' the content of which, as we have seen, is largely socially deviant activity.

(v) They have thereby helped to create a climate of greater tolerance for deviant behaviour and for their own presentation of salacious materials which can serve as stimulants to social action for those so disposed.

(vi) In fictional presentations they have frequently and increasingly built stories around the 'delinquent-hero' as a cultural type of our society.

(vii) They have presented deviant behaviour as a part of the youth culture, and as a legitimate challenge to the existing social order, so that in some measure it has gained a favourable connotation as something associated with progress. This is particularly true of media directed towards teenagers.

(viii) They have provided the glamour of publicity for criminals, thus adding the appetite for fame (which in our society means 'newsworthiness') to the other motivations for crime.

To suggest that these are functions which mass-media have fulfilled in our society is not to suggest that these influences are unmitigated by other factors. The influence of the media is probably rarely direct, and rarely in evidence in the perpetration of particular crimes except in unusual circumstances. We have already suggested that there are immense and perhaps insuperable difficulties in response-analysis, and yet it is reasonable to suggest, from content-analysis and by inference, that the mass-media are not without effect in our society, although we would expect that effect to be cumulative, widely diffused and gradual in its operation, and not immediate, specific and sudden.

We have to remember that the media are often proud to present themselves as agencies of persuasion. In fixing their advertising rates they have no hesitancy in claiming for themselves a most extensive influence over the general public. Both ITV and Radio Luxemburg, as well as newspapers and magazines, work on the assumption that they do influence people, and that they do it significantly: indeed it is the fact that advertisers believe this claim which alone keeps many media of mass-communication in business. The advertisers themselves are concerned only with the profitability of persuasion, and they have undoubtedly satisfied themselves with the efficacy of these agencies in moulding tastes and preferences, in the short run, and, perhaps, more profound values, in the long run. Advertisers have sometimes set out on quite long-term projects to alter the public's values in particular ways, and from the big business which advertising has become it must be presumed that they have frequently succeeded. The well-known case of the American beer manufacturers who steadily and systematically introduced women into their picture advertisements—at first depicting a benign matron in the background watching men drink, and eventually daring to represent an attractive young woman, glass in hand, drinking with the men—was a delicate campaign to alter women's values in order to increase sales. The vigour of the demand for another commercial television channel illustrates the strength of conviction about the efficacy of mass-media as agencies of persuasion. There is also some evidence to suggest that young people in particular have acquired various sorts of knowledge from the cinema—deportment, courtship responses, manners, the use of cosmetics and —who will doubt?—an extended, if sometimes tasteless, vocabulary.[1] They have learned, undoubtedly, what sort of behaviour is currently fashionable among their peer-groups, what the prestige gimmicks are, and how to 'cut a figure' with the opposite sex. No doubt the public has also learned to resist the persuasiveness of mass-media: a type of cynicism alternates with

[1] See, e.g. William Wall and W. A. Simson, 'The Effects of Cinema Attendance on the Behaviour of Adolescents as seen by their Contemporaries,' *British Journal of Educational Psychology*, February 1949, pp. 53–61.

extreme credulity in public discussion of screened or printed material. There is frequently a deference-acceptance of what the media present, because the media have the prestige of highly technical authority. But even if the public's attitude to these media is ambivalent, there can be no doubt of the immense potential of the mass-media to influence men and to change their values. Predominantly that influence is exerted to undermine received custom and codes of behaviour.

There can be no doubt that the general public has an avid appetite for the criminal, the violent, the salacious and the sensational. But in just what measure it may indulge these appetites depends to a very considerable extent on the values of our mass-media, for it is the mass-media which themselves establish the degree of 'permissiveness'. There has been competitive catering to these appetites and the deliberate stimulation of public interest by creating 'sensations'. The appetite is no doubt there in the public, but it is the media which have stimulated it, as they have vied with each other in the presentation of material to satisfy it. Employing the specious rationalization that the 'public has a right to know', they have extended the range of subjects which can be freely discussed, so that issues that thirty years ago were more or less unmentionable are, today, almost casually discussed in the press. They have built up, around the sensational, a cult of spurious sentiment by interviewing the relatives of victims and seeking statements from anyone connected with the central characters of a crime. Even the B.B.C. has resorted to this type of trading on sentiment and sensation —no doubt aware of its need to compete in these directions in order to hold an audience. Frequently, this approach is accompanied by expressions of moral concern: sometimes, indeed, 'exposures' are justified by the expression of moral indignation on the part of the reporters. For some newspapers, and some television programmes, this is an almost stock pattern for the presentation of material which might otherwise be 'too hot to handle'. The device is not very subtle, but it allows the audience to indulge its appetite for the salacious and sensational and, in the expression of moral concern, to assuage any guilt they might feel at such indulgence. Perhaps the most serious consequence for public attitudes to crime, however, is the fact that repeated presentation of this type of material makes morbid appetites appear to be quite acceptable and normal—sanctioned by the values and standards of the media themselves.

The average individual in Britain, today, gives more time to mass-media—in particular to television—than he gives to general reading or to part-time education; children spend almost as much time with mass-media as they do in school. The media increasingly provide the material which people talk about, the stuff of their conversation. Personal interests and relationships are thus fed by what the media provide, and it is altogether expectable that the attitudes of the mass-media should be taken in with the material. Studies in America have shown us that the public there is extremely uncritical of what is presented to them by television—and there is no evidence to suggest that the contrary is true in Britain.[1] Commentators and writers frequently and glibly assert what people are thinking; they talk and write as if they had hidden and immediate insight into everybody's thoughts. But in doing this they probably help to mould and structure attitudes. More important is the long-term consequence by which these commentators influence popular values. Both commentators and the writers of fiction frequently present crime as a type of cleverness—particularly is this the case with dramatic armed robbery. The skill, imagination and the adventure are emphasized, and the fact that the robbery is a competition of brains between crooks and policemen. There is even the suggestion, sometimes, that if criminals are clever enough, then they deserve to win.[2] In a society where success is held up as the goal for everyone, and where something-for-nothing is a widely sought objective, this type of crime may not appear as too radical a departure from the various other avenues to quick achievement. Physical violence is often presented—particularly in fiction—as the means whereby wrongs are righted, problems solved and disputes settled. Revenge is sometimes depicted as a

[1] Rolf B. Meyersohn, 'Social Research in Television' in *Mass Culture: The Popular Arts in America*, edited by Bernard Rosenberg and David Manning White, Glencoe, Ill., 1958, p. 347. See also, Paul F. Lazarsfeld and Robert K. Merton, 'Mass Communication, Popular Taste and Organized Social Action' in Lyman Bryson (edited by) *The Communication of Ideas*, New York, 1948.

[2] After this article had been published, press treatment of the train robbers produced a new high-water mark of this particular trend.

laudable motivation in social action. Parasytic activities, luxury and 'easy' living are presented as attractive and desirable. All of these values stand in stark contrast to the values entrenched in our existing social institutions—the family, the work-place, the school, the law-courts, the church, and in our social relationships. It is difficult, faced with these facts, to absolve mass-media from the charge of promoting the erosion of traditional social values, and of creating confusion, particularly among young people, about standards of behaviour. The media must bear some responsibility for the climate of indifference towards, and tolerance of, social deviance in contemporary society.

As long as mass-media were rooted in local communities—as newspapers used to be—they tended to reflect the value-consensus of these communities; they had concern for, and felt responsible towards, their public, particularly since this public was identifiable. The growth, technical development and centralization of mass-media, and the declining significance of local agencies in the face of national media, has meant a gradual loss of moral concern. It has meant that the media increasingly reflect London attitudes and values—the morality of the big city which, as sociologists have shown, is a different morality from that of smaller communities. The anonymity; impersonality; the spirit of calculating the consequences of action; the acceptance of money values as the final criterion of achievement; the emphasis on rôle rather than on personality; and ultimately the manipulation of personal sentiments and the 'prostitution' of attitudes of genuine human concern—are well documented phenomena of metropolitan life. In the mass-media, therefore, we see the reflection of these values, together with false sentiment for 'human stories'; the manipulation of sympathy for the relatives of murder victims often accompanied with acts of utter callousness by the reporters who get the interviews; the slick and smooth exploitation of human situations of enduring concern for the purely ephemeral interest in 'a story'. The dissemination of these values, and the corrosive influence which they exert on local communities, has been one of the most spectacular consequences of the great growth of mass-media in the past two decades. Since the media compete with one another they stimulate a common climate, grow curiously more alike and more imitative of each other, and help to drive down each other's standards further.

The way in which mass-media have disseminated criminal ideas can be easily illustrated with a few pertinent examples. Even before the war there was an interesting case in Yorkshire. A girl reported to the police that she had been attacked by an unknown assailant. The story received dramatic publicity in the northern editions of the national press and within a few weeks a large number of cases were reported—the press talked about 'the ripper'. In fact all the cases (except perhaps the first) were discovered by the police to be cases of self-inflicted injury. In one sense, the press had created 'the ripper'—such was the desire for publicity and sensationalism. The rash of swastika-painting last year[1] illustrates even better this process. Anti-semitic activity in Germany received widespread attention in this country, and there followed a series of incidents in which swastikas were daubed by young people in Britain and else-where in Europe. These acts had no political significance in fact—they were simply socially hostile acts which were stimu-lated by the dramatic publicity which the first incidents had received. In this case the rôle of mass-media is indisputable because of the distinctive nature of the deviant activity: in other cases it is probably no less influential, but its influence is more difficult to identify and isolate. The recent outbreak of railway hooliganism might have occurred without the attention of mass-media, but it seems much more likely that publicity plays a significant part in disseminating information and in-influencing people in the pattern of their deviant activities. Railway coaches—now much more frequented by young people than formerly—are public places of sanctioned confinement. There is little likelihood—between stations—of interruption. Their position is exactly similar to the sanctioned darkness of the cinema. Both places are difficult areas for the operation of ordinary social control—for either the expression of common public decency, or the operation of the police. These two places, then, are propitious places in which to commit socially hostile acts—places in which to release the tension of frustration in aggression. Some, no doubt, would act in this way without any incitement—but these hostile acts gain attractiveness because

[1] 1960.

D

they come to the attention of the public—and do so without much risk for the perpetrator. News-stories, television commentaries, photographs in the press become an added source of satisfaction to the miscreant—an occasion for boasting within his peer-group, of having done something which is significant. The publicity, then, becomes an added incentive to misbehave in this particular fashion. Many social deviants are publicity conscious; the tendency for criminals to keep diaries, to collect news cuttings of their crimes, and to be proud of their infamy, is a matter of common knowledge to the police. It is from the mass-media that these extra gratifications are sought—and not sought in vain.

The root causes of crime are not to be found in the mass-media, but the public attitude to criminal and deviant activity is undoubtedly affected by them in various ways. They are increasingly influential in moulding the climate of opinion, and do so, perhaps even more effectively than the educational and religious agencies of our society. The full significance of the influence of television, radio, cinema and press will perhaps never be adequately measured, partly because their influence cannot be isolated, and partly because it is an influence which is gradual and cumulative. There will, no doubt, always be those who present a simple picture of the 'public service' image of these agencies, and who will offer plausible but essentially superficial arguments about 'giving the public what the public wants'. But from an analysis of the content of the materials these media present, and their method of handling them, and from some investigation of the motives of those who produce them, and the dispositions of the general public to which they appeal, it seems quite clear that the mass-media have an important rôle in structuring the public's attitude to crime.

4

The Teacher's Rôle
(1962)

In the true sense of the word, teachers exist as a specialist profession only in advanced societies. In static societies values, techniques, skills and what are taken to be 'facts' are transmitted from father to son. If specialist activities are developed at all, their skills and the mystique which accompanies them is learned from practitioners not from teachers, and the learners are apprentices rather than pupils. Teachers exist as specialists in their own right only where the diffusion of knowledge is an accepted social goal—hence only in dynamic societies.

Certainly in traditional societies there is often a distinctive intellectual *élite*, but they are not so much teachers as guardians of knowledge, and knowledge is esoteric, sacred, aristocratic. It is frequently the knowledge of the gods, revealed to inspired seers; its guardians are priests or literati. In such a society knowledge advances—if it advances at all—by the elaboration of its own internal coherence. It is challenged only when a charismatic figure emerges who propounds new knowledge and new moral precepts. Knowledge in such a society tends to be recondite, literal, sacred—a knowledge of holy texts, of the ancient. The literati do not transmit new ideas, but rather keep pure old dogmas: they are not teachers and disseminators, but custodians of the sacred. Their intellectual institutions are closed—segregated seminaries set in remote places, preserving a shrine-like quality of apart-ness. They function according to a holier dispensation than that which prevails in the wider society. They are not centres from which knowledge is disseminated, but places where it is preserved and stored to be only slowly and carefully transmitted, and then only to the initiated. The approved recipient is marked by the tonsure and the sacred vestment, not by the examination certificate; his knowledge is not to be acquired through routinized courses. The literati discipline new knowledge, which means that they suppress it if it stems from outside sources, since knowledge is exclusive, treasured because of the sacred source from which it stems, not for its practical utility.

Such a system is appropriate to a traditional and static society where the natural and social orders are accepted rather than understood, and where because these orders of things are sacred, nothing is challenged or challengeable.

Teachers, as distinct from literati, really emerge as specialists only in societies where knowledge is secularized. This type of knowledge develops at certain places—particularly at points where there is interchange of produce and ideas. Cultural diffusion is the process whereby new ideas are evolved, and the agency by which secularization begins.[1] When knowledge is to be transmitted and used it ceases to be the exclusive monopoly of the intelligentsia. Much of such knowledge is initially practical, and consequently it tends to be fostered and transmitted in classes different from, and sometimes hostile towards, the literati. This type of knowledge is diffused, and its bearers are characterized by their inquisitiveness rather than by their passive receptivity of ideas from established authorities. Whereas the wisdom of the literati is arcane, vast and unassailable, embracing all that is to be known, the new knowledge is practical, piecemeal, and there is an admission of what men do not know. Knowledge ceases to be a secret hoard which a few men store up and invest with sacred quality—it becomes a circulating specie, the influence of which grows as it is circulated. There is an awareness of the enormity of human ignorance as well as of the profundity of human knowledge. Knowledge becomes commonplace, available to increasing numbers until the right of men to knowledge is gradually accepted as self-evident. Its character also changes and it becomes more changeable—it is imported, exported, borrowed, transmitted and adapted.

[1] See on this subject, the penetrating article by Robert Redfield and Milton Singer, 'The Cultural Rôle of Cities', *Economic Development and Cultural Change*, III, October 1954, pp. 54–73.

The social changes which lie behind this change in knowledge do not concern us here: what matters is the growth of new attitudes towards knowledge and its rôle in society. The new attitudes are attitudes of inquiry, of willingness to interchange ideas, the acceptance of critical standards and desirability of challenging discussion. Doubt replaces faith as the test of knowledge, and the learner's task is made more difficult because, whilst he must learn facts and values, he also has to learn to acquire an open and challenging mind and a critical faculty rather than to learn blind trust, simple faith and good memory. The educational task is thus transformed, and it is made in many ways more delicate because, whilst data has to be transmitted, so has the liveliness of mind which challenges every interpretation of data. Whereas the literati could invoke authority and exert authority, and could ultimately discipline to the point of death those who failed to accept their wisdom, the teacher must cultivate within certain bounds some spirit of heresy in those to whom some more-or-less established information must none the less be transmitted. Their own authority must always be tempered and restricted if the right critical spirit is to be drawn forth in their pupils. And yet there is still something in the teacher's rôle which demands that certain social values be preserved and inculcated. In seeking to cultivate attitudes of mind, the teacher is necessarily involved in propounding certain values, setting standards for personal behaviour and decorum, in eliciting respect for established ideals of personal discipline as behaviour patterns approved of in society. At the lowest level, these standards are necessary as the determinants of the climate within which teaching can occur.

In Britain this development of the teacher's rôle has been radically affected by a set of unique historical circumstances. Before the extension of secondary education in the early years of the present century the upper classes already had a system of education for their children. These schools sought especially to inculcate the particular virtues prized among the aristocracy and the gentry. Their emphasis was less with learning and more with leadership. This was an entirely appropriate schooling for those destined to undertake leadership rôles in a society where military and gentlemanly behaviour was explicitly demanded

in the ruling groups. The formation of a certain type of character, rather than the cultivation of rarified intellect was the educational aim. The schools reflected the values of the social
strata from which their clientele was predominantly drawn. The
absence of social revolution in England allowed this model to
persist unchallenged as the entrenched ideal of education, in
both the public schools and the universities. When secondary
education was extended for a wider population, it was this
model which influenced the character of the new and revived
grammar schools. Some of those who were concerned with these
schools—national and local politicians as well as headmasters
—had themselves received the gentlemanly education of public
school and ancient university: for them it was self-evident that
the educational aim was exactly what their own schooling had
been designed to achieve—these were the best models. Social
emulation is a powerful force, and particularly so in a society
where there is a strong traditionalist ethic, a well-entrenched
upper class, and a growing middle class seeking social acceptance for their expanding pretensions.

Thus it was that the shibboleths of education for gentlemen
were transferred to the sons of traders, shopkeepers and artisans
—the clientele of the expanded system of secondary education.
Character-building on the aristocratic model became a pre-
dominant motive of the schools, and ideals of social honour,
team-spirit and inner discipline were very much their concern,
fostered as they were by team games, house loyalty and house
rivalry and regulated competition. The ideal diverges conspicuously from that of the continent, where social revolution
had eliminated the aristocratic ideal; where, as in Germany,
scholarship and culture was predominantly middle class values;
and where intellect had become the well-entrenched major
concern of the schools,[1] and from that of the American educational system where the necessity of forging an ethnically
diversified clientele into one nation imposed on the educational
system a concern for 'adjustment', which is evident to this day.

As society grows more complex and comes to rely on more
elaborated technical means of production, it is necessary for

---

[1] See *Special Reports on Educational Subjects*, VIII, 1902, cd. 835, Paper 13
(pp. 481 ff.) on Hungarian Education by Catherine Dodd, and the illu-
minating appendix to this report by Dr. Emil Reich, pp. 531-2.

certain basic skills—numeracy and literacy—to be diffused throughout the society, and some more specialist skills to be cultivated in smaller sections of the society. The teacher's rôle grows more significant as this process occurs, and teaching becomes a process to which all must be exposed as a social necessity, rather than a process extended by the whim of charity to only a proportion. The teacher learns increasingly in order to teach, but he becomes more than a mere transmitter of knowledge, and must increasingly cultivate a spirit of inquiry: the educational trend has been from 'telling them' to 'encouraging them to find out'. Whereas the literati transmitted exact knowledge and relied on the closed character of the institution to socialize the acolyte into the scholar, the teacher helps the child to discover knowledge. Because he has lost the support of the closed institution with its rigorous routines, a greater onus is thrown upon the teacher to stimulate the child to respond to, and accept, certain social values. As the educational process extends, society becomes increasingly more aware of the need for children to acquire certain value-orientations from their school experience. A salient shift is that whereas the literati rely on the social control established in the seminary, the teacher, without such institutional support, must do more to socialize the child—to build-in these controls as part of the child's developing personality structure. A further problem arising in the creation of this value-context is the fact that the kind of knowledge which society increasingly demands, tends to be in itself intrinsically further removed from concern with values. Whereas the knowledge of the literati was suffused with social values—a knowledge of religious texts and moral precepts—modern knowledge is increasingly of a more objective and scientific character. Thus the values which the teacher must transmit become in some sense extrinsic to the knowledge which he is assisting young people to acquire. As long as education rested in an essentially sacred matrix, this divorce could not occur: the secularization of knowledge implies the loss, or at least the reduction of specific intrinsic value-commitment. Even those subjects which stem more directly from the concerns of the literati—the literary and humanistic subjects—become more scientifically handled, and subject to more precise critical appraisal. And yet, paradoxically, as this acceptance of the relativity of knowledge grows, as doubt is enhanced, so the awareness grows that society needs for its continuance, and individuals need for their own careers, a certain value-commitment. Increasingly schools and teachers are expected to inculcate social values in young people and to socialize them. Men become aware that scientific knowledge outstrips moral, spiritual and political wisdom and there are periodic demands for more concentration on these aspects of education. And to this may be added the significance of the concern for character which modern education has inherited from upper-class models. It becomes the case that the school is expected to provide for all children what the family used to provide for the more favoured strata. The content of aristocratic education was largely the humanities, which lend themselves much more readily to the transmission of values than do the sciences: character could be formed in the appreciation of the heroes of literature and history. One consequence of acceptance of these models was the in-building of disdain for the practical and useful arts. The humanities were preserved in the top strata of society—the sciences necessarily had their fullest development in the new classes which challenged the older order. Here lies the historical and sociological root of the 'two cultures'. Aristocratic education could afford, from its position of superiority, and in training the 'natural' leaders of society, to disdain the sciences and technology: it did not need the work of Daniel Defoe or Samuel Smiles—which was written for different social groups. But in the long run these disciplines were to be of more account to industrial society than the training for leadership and character of the older system. It was precisely the entrenchment of these newer educational ideals which produced the phenomenal technical developments in Germany, and subsequently in Russia and America. In England the neglect of technical education for so long was the consequence of accepting the public school model. The other consequence has been the growth of technology—when it did occur—without humanistic commitment. A type of reciprocal contempt is evident whereby the technologies today disdain the arts. This is readily evident in the universities and probably builds back to the schools. The vast majority of the most intelligent children are channelled into the sciences, which, in a highly specialized educational system, means that they lose almost all contact with the humanities. The sciences and technologies are moving into the position of dominance in the educational field as an increasing proportion of money is available for their extension. It is in part a consequence of this process that we find the recurrent demand for teachers to transmit social values to young people— a more imperative demand now that the specific content of education has so largely passed from the arts to the sciences.

II. SOCIAL SELECTION AND SOCIALIZATION

In a complex industrial society with a wide diversity of social rôles, where basic education is obligatory for everyone, social selection—the allocation of individuals to particular occupations within society—occurs within the educational system rather than, as in the case of traditional societies, before education is embarked upon. This means that the teacher becomes also a social selector, preparing people in the capacities in terms of which selection will occur. Increasingly selection is made in objective terms of intellect and knowledge, rather than in terms of character and life-style. It is this occupational mobility —imperative in advanced society—which makes the teacher's rôle indispensable. In traditional societies, in which occupational succession prevails, fathers teach sons and mothers teach daughters: but in our society son's occupation will not usually be father's, and we do not even consider that home-making and motherhood are the primary tasks for which girls should be trained. Thus, if the child is to be prepared for some social rôle other than that of its father or mother (and indeed, in our sort of society, even if for that same type of rôle), it is the teacher who is largely responsible for the preparation. Clearly the child brings with it, to the teaching situation, certain equipment derived from home, and this equipment will positively or negatively influence its further development. But the specific terms in which selection must occur and the process of selection itself, are the concerns of the teacher's rôle.

We have already seen that, perhaps because of this dominant intellectual stress, the teacher has taken over from the parent some of the activities of socializing the child. The teacher becomes a social weaning agent—helping the child to acquire new attitudes of mind, new values, new knowledge and new motivations, which are not forthcoming in the home context for most children. Social selection—the knowledge of opportunities, which may be the first necessity for inducing adequate motivation, and the knowledge of how to take advantage of opportunities—has itself become a specialist task, and it is the task of the teacher and not of the parent. The teacher, then, has to help the child towards social mobility. He has to transmit personal standards, orientations, ideals of attainment, which diverge from those which are learned in the home. If he is to help the child to 'get on', he must also help the child to 'move on'—which means to move away from the values and assumptions of parents. The teacher must extend the horizons of the child, diversify its knowledge of opportunity, raise its threshold of aspiration, and induce it to exercise its talents so that it may find a place in the social structure which is different from—and not contingent upon—the rôles of its parents.[1]

Since our society demands continual re-allocation of intellectual resources whilst people are young enough to be trained, it is essential that bright young people be adequately motivated —and it is in this task of inducing motivation that the teacher's rôle becomes crucial. Thus a considerable part of the socializing task—performed by parents in earlier times—has now passed to the teacher. Teachers already supervise meals; supervise play; give religious instruction; give training in hygiene; inculcate ideals of fair play; give instruction about sex ethics, public safety, moral obligation: they transmit values appropriate to the stratum in society to which the brighter child will move. Educating for these ends is not done by rote learning: the process demands an emphatic commitment on the part of the teacher—a basic sympathy with children which is not dissimilar from that of parents. Increasingly the child depends on the teacher—particularly at that stage at which it needs new models for behaviour, some new type of ego-ideal hero. Parents come to appear inadequate, and the teacher is frequently held up to parents as a model of higher standards. The mirror of the teacher can supply a new self-image and self-interpretation for

[1] The importance of the differential threshold of aspiration is brought out in J. E. Floud, A. H. Halsey and F. M. Martin, *Social Class and Educational Opportunity*, Heinemann, London, 1956.

the child. Inevitably this process is not accomplished without strains: two different people with rather different stakes in the socialization of the child may readily experience rivalries. Certainly at a rather earlier perid—in the 1930s—there appear to have been many tensions between teachers with lower-middle or middle-class ideals and the working-class parents of their pupils. Today, increased acceptance of social mobility has done much to reconcile parents to the teacher's influence on the child.[1] The relation of parents and teachers is necessarily muted, but the condition of symbiosis which prevails in contemporary England is not the only way in which this relationship has been regulated. As parents recognize the growing importance of the teacher's rôle for the child, so they may increasingly demand to control teachers and their activities. Thus, in the United States, where the ideal of social mobility is more or less universally accepted, there has developed a strong movement by parents towards control of the teachers through the Parent-Teachers Association. Alternatively in the U.S.S.R., where teachers are seen as the agents of the state, and as the loyal inculcators of the state's official ideology, teachers are accorded a higher degree of autonomy, and greater freedom from parental interference: the teachers are seen as vital socializing agents, and the school is held as a counter influence to the family.

If the teacher is to act as a socializing agent, and to remedy the omissions of the home, he must be in a position to foster a sustained relationship with the child. He must occupy a place in the child's scheme of things which makes the transmission of values, standards and attitudes of mind one which can occur easily and naturally. Such relationships cannot be prescribed by any blue-print of institutional organization: they cannot be written into a contract. They must occur in a favourable climate where the teacher can cultivate children in this way. This particular facet of the teacher's rôle is frequently neglected, although its consequences—the sensitive imagination, the appreciation of scholarly values, and the well-rounded, sensible good citizen—are demanded perhaps more vociferously than

---

[1] On the extent to which social mobility is accepted as an ideal see the interesting discussion in S. M. Lipset and R. Bendix, *Social Mobility in Industrial Society*, Heinemann, 1959, pp. 76 ff.

ever before. Whilst this is the case, it is also true that in an age of specialization the teacher's rôle, like other social rôles, has become more routinized, more impersonalized, more exposed to the time-calculation and the achievement-orientation of our society. The wider social climate would appear to have increased the difficulty of drawing forth any high personal commitment of the kind which appears indispensable to the teaching rôle.

III. DIFFUSENESS AND DIVERSITY

Rôles which involve the provision of personal services are difficult to define briefly: the very debate about what teaching is, or should be, illustrates this difficulty. When we say that a rôle is specific we mean that

 (i) there are set tasks which can be defined in terms of the exact manipulations involved; a set time which these operations take; there is a precise content change in the material handled which results from the rôle performance;

 (ii) the rôle-player has a specialized and easily defined expertise;

 (iii) there is a formal limitation to the competences which the rôle-player exercises in his rôle (any other competences and capabilities and character-values being incidental and gratuitous);

 (iv) the rôle-player's commitment is delimited.

But the business of socializing children—of motivating, inspiring and encouraging them, of transmitting values to them, awakening in them a respect for facts and a sense of critical appreciation —all of this is unspecific. It implies 'what a man is' as much as 'what a man does'. The rôle obligation is diffuse, difficult to delimit, and the activities of the rôle are highly diverse.

If we compare other professional rôles—those of the doctor and the lawyer, for example—we find that their rôles are easier to define. But they, too, must be certain sorts of people. Their relationship with their client must also be one of confidence, since their services cannot be examined beforehand. The professional man is trusted to give a quality of service which cannot be quantified and which therefore cannot be specifically stated or contracted for. He gives his personality.[1] His commitment is moral. This moral commitment to the professional rôle is less evident in other types of work. Because the tasks and the means of performing them cannot be precisely specified, there is discretion and autonomy for the rôle-player. Consequently there have to be some safeguards for the clientele. This safeguard is found in the professional ethic, which is voluntarily accepted and internalized by the members of the profession. The ethic defines what type of man the professional is— and the ethic is regulated by and within the profession, with expulsion for the breaches.[2]

In the case of the doctor and the lawyer there is, however, a definable expertise: the objective body of medical knowledge, or the objective body of law (though both are, inevitably, subject to controversy at the margins). There is for the teacher what appears initially as a parallel—the objective body of mathematical, historical, musical or some other knowledge. But the symmetry of the analogy is not exact. The doctor and the lawyer are applying the rules of their expertise: they are not attempting to inculcate it: they are not socializing by building up attitudes of mind. Doctors and lawyers make *patients* out of persons, and *cases* out of clients. Whereas for the teacher the child must, of necessity, remain a whole person. For the doctor and lawyer there is an end of their concern with the 'cure effected', 'the operation performed', the 'case won'. The 'examination passed' is again not a symmetrical analogy. When the pupil does not get through the *good* teacher's concern does not end—nor does that of the educational system end. Failure cannot be counted in terms of examinations alone, otherwise the system would cease to be interested in 75 per cent of children at the age of eleven. Educating is implicitly recognized throughout all educational institutions as something immensely bigger than the passing of examinations.

To refer to the *good* teacher begs questions. But the fact that

---

[1] For a discussion of the professions and the nature of the fiduciary relationship, see T. H. Marshall, 'The Recent History of Professionalization in relation to Social Structure and Social Policy', *Canadian Journal of Economics and Political Science*, V, 13th August 1939, pp. 325–40.

[2] See Everett C. Hughes, 'The Sociological Study of Work', *American Journal of Sociology*, LVII, 5, 1952, pp. 423–7.

one can refer to a *good* teacher when one does not qualify 'doctor' or 'lawyer' in this way implies the moral commitment of the teacher's rôle—a moral commitment which passes beyond the formulation of a professional ethic. In itself, this usage illustrates the difficulty of defining the teacher's rôle—and the further difficulty of doing so without making value-judgments. This is so because we are ultimately concerned with the quality of the values which the teacher transmits. There are—of necessity—value-judgments implicit in the doctor's rôle and the lawyer's rôle, but they are much less exposed value-judgments, and they are allowed to go more or less unchallenged. Who doubts that sick people *ought* to be made better, and that the accused should have proper defence and the guilty be detected?

The teacher's rôle is more diffuse than the doctor's or lawyer's because their concern is limited to areas of deviation or abnormality within the system—sickness, injury, crime or dispute. These items are not part of our usual experience—they are contrary to our widely accepted normative expectations in society. They are items which we accept should be put right—items needing adjustment, regulation or restoration. Because they are departures from the accepted norms, there is much less dispute about what should be done, and doctors and lawyers have built up a professional expertise which gives them the exclusive knowledge of just how it shall be done. But since the teacher is a socializer, concerned with the whole child and its normal self as a social entity, his involvement is necessarily more enduring, slower, steadier. He is not concerned with the pathological aspects of the person. His rôle appears, in consequence, to be less urgent, less dramatic, even though in fact it is no less vital. Because it is less urgent and less dramatic it receives less social respect, and carries less salary. We confer gratitude and rewards on those who put things right when they go wrong, rather than on those who quietly keep things right. The element of the supererogatory is much more evident in the dramatic situation of the doctor's client, or the lawyer's client than in the teacher's client, in relation to whom supererogatory acts must be more sustained if they are to achieve their end.

Because teaching is a stable, normal need of society it requires more agents than do the law and medicine, which is, of course, another factor influencing social prestige and the conferment of rewards. There is no objective reason to believe that the special skills of the lawyer and of the doctor are particularly scarce in society. The abilities employed are probably potentially more abundant than those of a teacher. But these professions maintain a monopoly of training, and keep lawfully recognized practitioners deliberately scarce. Of course, society needs fewer doctors and lawyers than teachers. The expansion of education has meant that whether people have high abilities for teaching or not they have to be accepted, because large numbers of teachers are needed. As a profession it has never been in a position to choose whom it will have. Teacher training colleges rarely fail people; and graduates, merely by being graduates, are thought to be equipped to teach. There is no explicit professional ethic, no professional control of members and no expulsions—because there have never been conditions in which adequate selectivity has been possible. Thus society accepts as glamorous those professional rôles which 'put things right', and accepts the myth that these abilities are scarce because the need for them is limited. It tends to disparage diffuse rôles which are constantly and universally in demand, because a standard of performance is difficult to establish. This is so because the task is defined in terms of the general ends desired, rather than in terms of the precise activities involved.

Because a teacher is concerned with a whole person over a prolonged period of time—and not merely with his delictual acts or his disturbed health—so *he* tends to become involved as a whole person. Since his rôle is difficult to define by reference to its action-content, so it is difficult to delimit the extent to which the teacher's purely personal virtues are involved in it. The fact that the teacher employs his whole person in his rôle, gives rise to unparalleled satisfactions, but equally to intense frustrations. A total commitment necessarily imposes strains—it means 'living the job'. And this is increasingly uncommon and uncalled for in our type of society, in which specificity, time-calculation and contractual obligations are the rule. The diffuse rôle means diffuse involvement. The teacher carries his work around with him—because he has to 're-create' his rôle continually, to re-interpret, re-enact, re-structure relationships and behaviour patterns. He is the model for the child at a formative period and we know, and most teachers know in their work situation, that a child can be seriously disturbed if he discovers shortcomings in his model. The teacher has to be virtually beyond reproach. It is only because demand is great, and possibilities of selection limited, that society has to put up with the uncommitted teacher. Thus there is no way of delimiting the rôle, either in respect of the person dealt with or in the activity of the rôle-performer himself.

Because our society is a society in which specialization continually increases, prestige increasingly attaches to the specialist. But there are distinct limits to the extent of specialization in teaching because the rôle is diffuse. Again, because our society relies increasingly on technical development, it is instrumental rôles which win social approval—in which clearly defined operations are undertaken and means are manipulated to achieve proximate ends, which in turn become means to further ends. In some measure, increasingly higher rewards are given to those whose rôles involve them in the use of elaborate equipment—both technical and organizational. But the teacher's rôle is not directly instrumental—it is concerned with ends, with values. It is, of its nature, personal and direct. The results of effort are not dramatic achievements issuing from complex manipulation of elaborate mechanical or human machinery. They are imperceptibly gradual—and even when they are recognized the teacher's part in their achievement may not be credited—the boy was a bright boy, anyway! Resu lts are always more manifest in instrumental rôles, and the process—the equipment, jargon, tools, formulae, mystique—is impressive; but teaching has little of all this. Thus, diffuse rôles tend to lack the prestige of specific, instrumental rôles. The process by which instrumental and technical rôles have come so much to the fore has diminished the social prestige of the religious functionary much as it limits the status of the teacher. The process does not occur, of course, where the teacher is regarded as a vital agent of consciously-sought social change in accordance with an entrenched ideology—as is the case in the Soviet Union.

IV. THE AFFECTIVITY OF THE RÔLE

Since the teacher is totally involved, warmth of personality, and affective concern for children, are implicit in the rôle. Rôle-performance is a living process, in which the establishment of rapport, the impact of personality, are necessary to stir the imagination, and awaken that enthusiasm necessary for the learning process. Affection is the first language which man understands, and it becomes the lever by which all other languages can be initially learned. The teacher must engage the sympathy of his class; he must attain a certain contentment in order to teach and to create the atmosphere of learning. And yet this process has to occur in a society in which a limited investment of the self is all that is expected in most rôles—an investment of skills, know-how, time and energy, but not of affection, which is a private affair. The strictly professional attitude—to remember that one's clients are just cases—so much stressed in medicine, law and social work is simply not possible in teaching.

Paradoxically, in a world in which most rôles are affectively neutral the positive affectivity of the teacher's rôle increases in importance. The teacher has to prise the child loose, in some respects, from the values of its family, and the teacher must employ the same agency of socialization as does the kinship group. In our society, the individual's relationships tend to be impersonal, anonymous, dominated by rôle obligations and status expectations. Only kinship, friendship, courtship and marriage stand out as the obvious exceptions to the affective neutrality of most of our daily relationships, and even these relationships are attentuated in significance, and comprise a smaller part of our total relational activity. But individuals still need an affective context in which to gain assurance, support and a sense of identity. And since the family in contemporary society is structurally smaller, functionally more restricted to basic essentials, associationally in decline, and afflicted by the divergent values and ideals that social and occupational mobility imposes, and the growing separation of the generations, it is other socializers who must satisfy these needs. The teacher becomes willy-nilly a type of parent—a person whom the child, however much he may deviate from the teacher's ideals, can none the less trust. And because the rest of society is so dominated by contractual and rôle relationships so there is necessarily greater reliance on this relationship of trust. To take the paradox a stage further, it might be said, that the family itself has become a highly specialized agency for affection.[1] It has lost the other types of social activity which were once so much of its activities—the workplace, the dance hall, the youth club and other institutions have taken over its economic and recreational functions, and its political and religious functions were lost long ago. Even the service-agency aspects of the family have declined, now that more meals are consumed in schools and canteens, and new materials have all-but eliminated stitching and darning. What remains to the family, is the mutuality of affection. And yet, if the family has lost so many of its shared activities on what can these emotional orientations rest besides the biological base? Affection needs activities and commitments on which to grow. The family has become an over-specialized agency in affection and has lost the sustaining concerns in which affection develops. In the educative task affection has a real context—a context of common interest, activity and the cultivation of shared attitudes of mind. But the family is less and less supported as a social entity—as children grow it is increasingly exposed to cross-cutting pressures. It has lost its mystery, its permanence, its persisting meaning and its appropriateness as a context in which the individual is identifiable. The generations are pulled apart in a mobile, rapidly changing society, so that the young quickly grow apart from their families, and, especially in adolescence, reject identification with them and their values. But the school has on-going concerns for young people, and these are concerns in which affectivity has a context and a necessary function.

V. RÔLE-CONFLICTS AND INSECURITIES

All rôles in which there is a high commitment to other people are subject to considerable internal conflicts and insecurities. The most obvious ones—with which we are not concerned here —are the conflicts arising from one person's performance of several rôles some of which may be, at some times, contradictory of each other. But the conflicts which concern us are those intrinsic to the teacher's rôle and the circumstances in which it is performed. These conflicts and insecurities might be grouped in six broad categories:

[1] For this point I am indebted to Norbert Elias.

(i) those inherent in the rôle because of its diverse obligations;
(ii) those which derive from the diverse expectations of those whose activities impinge on the rôle—now referred to as 'the rôle-set';
(iii) those arising from circumstances in which the rôle is marginal;
(iv) those arising from the circumstances in which the rôle is inadequately supported by the institutional framework in which it is performed;
(v) those arising from conflict between commitments to the rôle and commitments to the career-line;
(vi) those arising from the divergence of value-commitments that are appropriate to the rôle and those that dominate the wider society. We shall now turn to each of these categories.[1]

(i) Diffuse rôles are likely to embody internal rôle-conflicts because of the absence of clear lines of demarcation whereby the rôle-player knows when he has 'done his job'. Because the teacher's work—like all socializing tasks—is unending, he must continually ask himself whether he has fully discharged his obligations. There is a tendency for the teacher to over-extend himself in his rôle—even though he also knows that an adequate rôle-performance by which the young will be edified and civilized, really requires constant refreshing with outside interests and activities. In few rôles is the need for creative and alternative activity so necessary. When the teacher is given a heavy teaching load, and receives little inducement to keep alive his own mind, the quality of teaching deteriorates.

A second conflict which inheres in the rôle is the problem of authority in the teaching rôle. The teacher is both the affective agent and the disciplinary agent; he is the advocate of a pupil, but also in considerable measure the objective assessor. He must win approval and respect, but he must also maintain standards. The conflict has been noticed by teachers in respect to headteachers where the rôle becomes somewhat modified. Headteachers have higher authority and less opportunity for affectivity, a more prestigeous but perhaps less directly satisfying rôle. As teacher is to parent, headmaster is to grandparent—

---

[1] For a rather different analysis of rôle conflicts, see Jackson Toby, 'Some Variables in Rôle Conflict Analysis', *Social Forces*, XXX, 3rd March 1952, pp. 323–7.

the 'soft disciplinarian' who seeks the affective contact from which his rôle removes him.[1]

(ii) The conflicts which are associated with the rôle-set have been set forth by the originator of the term, Robert K. Merton.[2] These conflicts are essentially the diverse expectations of a given rôle which are made manifest by all those affected by the rôle-performance—headmasters, the governors, and local education authority; colleague groups; the clientele—both parents and children; and manifold external agencies which put pressures on teachers and criticize teaching. Again, the rôle-set of the teacher is especially formidable because the rôle is diffuse, and because everyone in contemporary society has ready opinions about what the teacher does and should do.

(iii) This particular type of rôle-conflict arises for certain teachers but it is a type of conflict which is probably growing: it arises for the teacher whose rôle is marginal—the humanist in the technical college is a case in point. To a lesser extent the whole arrangement of day-continuation teaching may impose somewhat similar insecurities. The humanist in the technical college is the vendor of precarious values: the material in which he deals has little or no prestige within the context in which he performs his rôle. His values are imposed by the Ministry on reluctant hosts. His subject is thought of—by colleagues and clientele alike—as a trimming, a piece of ministerial whitewash with no significance for the real business of the institution. Even in the universities this type of marginality is not unknown. Clearly the teaching rôle can be adequately performed only if insecurity is reduced by the provision of adequate institutional support.[3]

(iv) Rôle-conflicts and insecurities arise from the vulnerability of the institutions in which the teacher's rôle is performed. The school is subject to political pressure: ultimately it

[1] This suggestive analogy is employed by Margaret Phillips in an unpublished manuscript which she has kindly permitted me to see.

[2] Robert K. Merton, 'The Rôle Set: Problems in Sociological Theory', *British Journal of Sociology*, VIII, 2nd June 1957, pp. 106–20.

[3] This type of analysis is developed by Philip Selznik: see, for example, 'Institutional Vulnerability in Mass Society', *American Journal of Sociology*, LVI, January 1951, pp. 320–32. See also Burton Clark, 'Organizational Adaptation and Precarious Values', *American Sociological Review*, XXI, June 1956, pp. 327–36.

is laymen who determine the character of the school. Of all professions, teachers have least control of the institution in which their rôle is performed. Because the rôle is diffuse the institutional arrangements supporting the rôle influence its performance. Lawyers determine very much more completely the character of the courts in which, or in relation to which, they perform their rôle. Doctors do not run hospitals but have an exalted position within them. In universities it is the professors who—at least theoretically—make the decisions about the institution itself. But schools are much more exposed to public pressure than any of these institutions. This is because the process that is occurring is socialization, which in its own nature, is not an esoteric process. Teachers perform in public—their rôle is unprotected from observation. Indeed it is deliberately exposed to inspection. They cannot protect their rôle by jargon, or by the use of dead languages, as doctors and lawyers do. The children whom they serve are a public who have less automatic trust than the clients of lawyers and doctors; their dependence is less dramatic and less urgent, and the processes less special and less apparently essential. The clientele too, is a clientele in only a partial sense: behind it stand the parents as interested parties in the rôle-performance of teachers, and they may readily be mobilized for the expression of criticism. The institution itself is hierarchic, and ultimately, beyond the school, the highest echelon is laic. The teacher is exposed to much more authority than are other professional rôle-players, and yet he too must wield authority. There is continual dispute about his authority—as for instance in the matter of corporal punishment—which is an indication of the diversity of opinion which exists about just what is necessary for adequate rôle-performance.

An associated type of conflict arises from the growth of size of schools which makes more difficult the affective elements of the teacher's rôle. Economic argument suggests that the provision of new equipment for schools—laboratories, mechanical visual aids, facilities of all kinds—can be supported only when the clientele are concentrated in large numbers. But if increase of school size implies a more impersonal atmosphere, a diminished opportunity for sustained personal contacts, a growth of rational specialism in the staff, then it reduces the affective commitment of the teacher. This may make the formal process of *lecturing* easier, but it may make the business of *teaching* much harder. Much of the satisfaction of the rôle is lost for the teacher when the circumstance in which he can actively stimulate and encourage individuals is lost. If schools are to be very large there is the likelihood of producing the mass atmosphere in which the *quality* of teaching is sacrificed for the *quantity* of instruction. It may mean, too, that instead of teachers socializing children we shall see children socializing children.

(v) Because of the diffuse, affective character of the teaching rôle there is, in contemporary society, a most significant rôle-conflict arising from the divergence of rôle-commitment and career-orientation.[1] The teacher is—like everyone in contemporary society—exposed to the pressure to 'get on'. Achievement and social mobility are the accepted cultured goals for all individuals in our society, and there are well-structured systems of inducement to motivate men to these ends. Yet the teaching rôle demands the cultivation of sustained relationships with particular children, and this necessarily means a continued commitment to a particular situation. But the teacher, and particularly the young teacher, *ought* to want to 'move on to a better job', according to our widely accepted social values. If this is not a possibility, he should want to improve himself in other ways—to move to more congenial schools. There is a considerable horizontal mobility as well as vertical mobility in the teaching profession.[2] Teachers prefer better surroundings, more teachable and brighter children, fewer problems of discipline, and yet the need for committed people as teachers, and as models, is evident. If teachers are 'on the move', the affective aspects of their rôle are less well performed. They become impersonal transmitters of skills, who do not know their children and whose children do not know them—sometimes not even by name! The damage done by high teacher turn-over has not been assessed, and yet a frequent excuse by children and head-teachers for poor performance is the fact that there has been a

---

[1] This type of rôle-conflict is examined in a different context of analysis in Melvin Seeman, 'Rôle Conflict and Ambivalence in Leadership', *American Sociological Review*, XVIII, August 1953, pp. 373–80.

[2] A study of horizontal mobility in America is made by Howard S. Becker, 'The career of the Chicago Public Schoolteacher', *American Journal of Sociology*, LVII, 5th March 1952, pp. 470–7.

change of teachers. Often, the least attractive schools, with the need for the highest commitment, suffer most. Thus it is that the career-line that the young teacher is expected to desire, is a career-line that cuts across his commitment to his rôle. It means reduced loyalty to the institution of which he is a part, to the clientele whom he serves—especially so since his service is of its very nature particularistic. But it is evident, that colleagues and the world at large judge the individual in terms of his career-line rather than in terms of the care, concern and commitment that are involved in rôle-performance. These are largely unseen, and in a highly mobile society are likely to be seen less and less. There is an inducement in this situation to make right impressions on the significant people, rather than significant impressions on the right people—the children. Financial security, social prestige, one's own self-esteem, once these values have been completely internalized, are reflected more and more in the capacity to 'get on', rather than to do the job well. Indeed, inability to do well in the rôle may itself be an inducement to further mobility: the less rôle-committed can become the more career-oriented, and the less adequate teachers can accept the incentive to get ahead more easily than the intensely rôle-committed. In an inner-directed society, the satisfactions of good performance of the rôle would be sufficient; once men are 'other-directed' they become more concerned with success, as acknowledged by others, rather than with their own knowledge of their good performance. Thus it is that there is structurally in-built tension in the teacher's rôle in a society which places a high premium on social mobility.

There is a further implication of a paradoxical kind associated with this particular conflict. The dedication to achievement and the striving for social mobility has its impact on the school at the eleven-plus examination—the first step in the allocation of intellectual resources to suitable training. But intellectual ability is not manifested without motivation, and the teacher's task is thus to motivate his pupils to high achievement. Yet he himself is torn between achievement-orientation and rôle-commitment! His means for inspiring children is essentially affective. The pupils must be won over to accept the inducements of the system, and the teacher's part in this is to use a positive affective approach to strengthen the structure of values which prevail in our society—values which are themselves affectively-neutral, impersonal and achievement-oriented—the pursuit of a career. So the teacher must represent to the child values which, in the nature of his own rôle, he must in some measure eschew, and some of the consequences of which he must also, in his moral capacity, more or less condemn.[1]

(vi) Finally, there is the conflict of a rôle that implies specific value-commitments performed in a society where these values are, at best, only partially supported. It might be asserted that the wider society manifests a considerable confusion in the realm of values, and that different sections of society show a highly differential acceptance of the values that are implicit in the teacher's rôle. The teacher has been described as someone who expresses value-consensus.[2] The conflict of his rôle is clear in a society where such consensus is no longer a reality. Traditionally he represents moral virtues, integrity of mind, honest criticism, tolerance, loyalty, sensitivity, appreciative imagination, consideration for others—but in a society with an intense achievement orientation, with the commercial exploitation of what were once manifestations of personal relationships, these values are frequently under attack. Children are exposed to television and other mass-media for almost as much of their time as they are in school, and generally the values that the mass-media present are not those of the teacher. Frequently, too, these alternative values are presented through agencies which confer significant weight—highly technical media presenting a readily acceptable escapist, type of material, and providing the fantasy of vicarious success by quick methods, rather than by slow hard work. The message of the media is presented by young people, and is frequently presented in terms of the values of youth against those of age—and the teacher is clearly represented as the voice of the past. This circumstance creates conflict in the teacher's rôle, but it is a conflict which passes beyond it, into the very structure of contemporary society.

[1] See the very cogent discussion on the value consequences of social mobility by Melvin M. Tumin, 'Some Unapplauded Consequences of Social Mobility in Mass Society', *Social Forces*, XXXVI, 1st October 1957.

[2] This point is made in a highly suggestive article by Kaspar Naegele, 'Clergymen, Teachers and Psychiatrists', *Canadian Journal of Economics and Political Science*, XXII, 1st February 1956, pp. 46–62.

5

The Writing on the Redbrick Wall
(1962)

On the founding of what is now Manchester University, a journal of the time remarked sourly, 'Anyone educated at Manchester would certainly be dull and probably vicious.' Nowadays, of course, much the largest proportion, some five-sixths, of our university student population is at provincial universities like Manchester. The numbers are growing; the redbricks, answering to the needs of our time, are vindicated. Yet there are moments when, surveying their present expansion, one wonders whether this comment on dullness and viciousness might not increasingly come to contain a mite of truth.

The redbricks will, with expansion, become the standard university experience; but the very process of expansion makes vulnerable the values of an institution like a university, whose task is essentially subtle and humane. Unlike Oxford and Cambridge, which, stablized by their long tradition *and* their partially guaranteed income, periodically make it clear that they do not intend to expand to the point where their traditional purposes and values are threatened, the redbricks have been subject to pressure groups of several sorts, all of whom want expansion even at some cost to traditional university values.

Among these pressure groups are the local corporations of the business cities, with their mixture of business practicality and civic pride; the weight of a public opinion more and more persuaded that every child has a B.A. as his birthright; the Treasury, whose purse-strings are unloosed only on promises of expansion; the Government with its vague assumption that more graduates mean technological advance for Britain; the industrial concerns, who have altered universities by donating money for the kind of research they consider universities should

73

do; and the schoolmasters, interested in getting more success for their school and themselves (and often, to them, getting a boy into university is success in itself, without regard to the way he comes out of it).

Since all these groups, and others, have some influence on the redbricks, the values these universities express are ambiguous, vague and subject to a wide variety of interpretations. They are consequently subject to easy modification and subtle shift of emphasis, and those within them to uncertainty about intentions and values. In these circumstances it would be remarkable if there were any consensus of opinion among the redbrick academics about the university's mission and purpose.

And since as a group they stand to gain much from university expansion—it is one of the ways in which promotion is likely to come for the run-of-the-mill lecturer in a system which has few gradations of status—they too cannot speak easily on the problems of expansion.

Yet these problems can be felt in every redbrick; and their effect has been to make more difficult the permanent problem that every university has of maintaining and sustaining the quality of all that takes place within it. In what follows, we are concerned to indicate that the redbricks show signs of following the trend that one can observe in many American universities—a trend towards formlessness, lack of direction, uncertainty about values.

There can be no doubt of the efforts made by universities to offer the highest possible quality of education in the circumstances—just as there can be no doubt that many students seek to make the most of that education. But, as the Vice-Chancellor of Birmingham University has recently suggested, many current circumstances work against that quality. Our concern here is with the circumstances, with the broad social and institutional changes which tend inexorably to detach universities from their traditional scholarly ethos.

Expansion—the present *kind* of expansion—is in fact the process of change. University education now has great social appeal—though our social and economic system has still not adjusted itself to the accommodation of the graduate, and though ideas of its purpose seem vaguer than ever. In spite of the newly announced cuts, the Government still, it seems, expects the expansion programme to continue—more on the cheap than ever.

The principal objection to university expansion that is usually made has been the 'more means worse' argument—the suggestion that universities now take practically all the candidates of reasonable quality who present themselves, and would have to have lower standards of selection if they took more. Those favouring expansion have often asserted that there is still a pool of untapped ability, an idea that fits in well with their ideological assumptions, and have pointed to the low percentage of graduates to population. The issue is in fact complex, and there is no easy conclusion to be reached even from extensive research —since what is measurable is but one facet among many which enter into a university education.

Perhaps a more significant aspect of expansion is, however, the matter not of student *ability* but of *motivation*, and the consequent problem of maintaining within the university a climate in which the student can be stimulated to scholarly pursuits. There are signs that this climate has already deteriorated in the expansion of the redbrick universities. It is a climate which can persist only where students are intensely committed—where they participate in university values, and have a scholarly end in view—or where there is extensive personal contact between staff and students. Where, as in Britain, students come to the university almost always at State expense, as a matter-of-fact course for the bright pupil, the commitment is not always much in evidence.

Perhaps this was so at pre-war Oxbridge—but we are now passing into a phase where the tutorial system, maintained at least in the better arts faculties of English universities, is becoming more difficult to sustain, and where the easy informal contact of staff and student is diminishing. Student opinion on the subject has been voiced already in many universities, and this expresses a genuine difficulty, though often the staff are blamed for a situation which is structural rather than personal.

It must be evident now that if our redbrick universities are to get bigger, they will become mass universities—and mass institutions of any kind must rely on lower, more manipulated commitment. The feature of the mass organization is apathy and uniformity, with commitment induced by administrative

75

demand. Already these phenomena exist within our universities. One observes the signs—growing administrative staffs with no personal knowledge of the teaching process; a competitiveness between departments and between faculties; a variety of conflicting notions about the universities' mission as not only the number but the *kinds* of discipline within the university increase.

Particularly important are the consequences for staff-student relations. In a situation where students see much more of each other than of anyone else, and this in the mass, where commitment is limited, and the traditions of university experience little known, then university values cannot persist. Students are left rather to socialize each other than to educate themselves. The failure of the old system, where teachers socialized students— and we use the word 'socialize' to indicate the width of the educative task—is evident in the growing dissidence among students in Britain's redbricks, a dissidence more characteristic of Asian and Middle Eastern universities where teachers and students are poles apart.

As expanded universities take on further the character of mass institutions, there will be less possibility of relying on individual student commitment than there is now, and this lessened dedication will require the operation of an enlarged administrative process. More and more it will be formally assumed that if a student has been exposed to so many courses, then education has taken place.

Increasingly student commitment will become 'routinized', and mass administration will provide more and more mechanically for a clientele for whom the personal response of the dedicated teacher to the committed student will no longer be necessary—or possible. In the old situation the good teacher could induce the good student to learn for himself; in a mass university all that can be done is for a general low-level facility to be made available to the students as a whole.

The consequences of this situation are already in some measure evident:

(1) Students become disaffected because they are not being treated as responsible individuals. But in their mass circumstances they do not always behave as such. And since the teacher-student contact has deteriorated it is difficult to induce this

responsibility and use it. Thus the vicious circle continues. So part of their irresponsibility is ignored—as long as it does not actually cause trouble for the administration no one now finds it his business to attempt to induce more constructive responses from students—and part is handled by heavy administrative machinery.

(2) Mass universities also mean that administration assumes an ever more important rôle, and universities find that their policy is increasingly dictated not by what is educationally desirable but what is administratively convenient.

(3) Really bright and highly motivated students may have their commitment blunted because the system relying on mass provision will not really be able to put up with the inconvenience of administering to enthusiasm.

It is not surprising, therefore, that there is in redbricks at present an atmosphere of uncertainty which is communicated to, and reinforced by, the students themselves. It is against this background that there has developed the distinctive redbrick ethos and styles of life—a noticeable set of unofficial values and attitudes that have been formed in response to the discredited traditional values of the university.

At the staff level, too, there is sometimes a casualness, mixed with anti-*élitist* and even at times anti-cultural attitudes. At student level there is a growth of dissident pressure-groups, which sometimes appear to believe that agitation is the student's principal business.

One consequence of this uncertainty is growing student pressure to mould the university into what they would like it to be. Students make demands about teaching methods and, emboldened by the Press, reject the idea of the university's educating and socializing them and, often, seek to impose the values of the youth culture on the university. And universities—compared to the training-schools of the professions (law schools, medical schools and teachers' training colleges)—are particularly vulnerable to this process, because they lack an ideal product.

Indeed, in university education nowadays there are divergent ideals. The old ideal was of the cultivated all-round man: today one popular image seems to be that of the loosely-committed and free-floating intellectual whose insouciance, casualness and marginal nature are, apparently, a perpetuation into society of the student condition as some students experience it.

Before we expand universities further, we should decide whether what we are expanding is all that it could be. We pose the issue on the assumption that there are certain fundamental values, certain liberal and cultural qualities, which are essential to a university, and that if these are dissipated an institution is a university in name only.

At present not even the personnel of the universities, the academic staff, show any marked agreement about what business the universities are engaged in. It is certainly appropriate that such staffs should contain people of diverse interests and commitments, but today there can be discerned two distinctive polar types in whom the conflict of values—which is in fact much more extensive and diversified—can be epitomized.

Among the older staff are those who see themselves as the custodians of ancient university values. These are people who maintain, and are used to, a cultured style of life. Scholarship is for them a gentlemanly pursuit, at best a matter of intense personal dedication, and at its worst an amiable dilettantism. Their leisure and personal thinking is of the same calibre as their university thinking; they epitomize the civilized man, the quality of whose life displays a distinction which, if it were universal among academics, would make the university a distinctive and separate place.

The student coming into contact with them is usually impressed by their all-round urbanity, the diversity and extent of their cultivated interests. He may find them a bit remote and unreal, and they present an elevated (if class-oriented) model, though one which often does not offer a natural development from what the student now is, to what he might be. Yet this type of academic at his best espouses a reverence for liberal and human values which one hopes a student might acquire.

At the other extreme is a group to be found in most redbricks. They are young and represent the professionalizing of the academic life. They come from a more practical generation and a stratum which thinks in terms of 'getting a job', preferably one which is free from the dreary and distasteful constraints of business and school-teaching. They relish the freedom of the university since they feel that their kind of integrity would be compromised in the workaday world. They like the permissive atmosphere without necessarily espousing the self-discipline which traditionally went with it.

To some extent they represent a change in the classes from which university lecturers are recruited. They think of their cultivation as something they have worked for, and sometimes their taste does not overspill the lecture room. Often early marriage, children, and the lack of any imposed standards mean that they live in relative squalor.

They are not, of course, paid enough to maintain their lives in the old university style, which often depended on private income—and the celibate ideal. It is unlikely that they would adopt this life-style even if they were. They 'do' evening classes for 'a bit of extra cash'; often they are waiting for pay day at the end of the month.

At best, they are the inheritors of that nonconformist, conscience-laden tradition, with its emphasis on acting well, making good choices, and putting up with no nonsense; at worst they are fashionable protestors, happy with any new agitation. In their extreme form, they are not only anti-cultivation but anti-culture; they do not belive in the educated all-round man, and although they may emphasize critical standards in their lectures they are not always evident in their lives.

Sometimes they are self-consciously 'the ordinary chap', deflating anything which seems false or phoney or bourgeois. To some extent they demonstrate the malaise of the intellectual condition today. The more intellectual one is, the more cut off one feels. But while the one polar type regards its separation almost as a mark of caste, the other regards it as an evasion of responsibility. Many thus appear to be more contemptuous of culture than they really are, because culture has false associations for them and their standard of living does not allow them to afford cultural appurtenances.

To some extent they oppose traditional university values and the traditional rôle of the university teacher. Because, as intellectuals, they have less direct stake in society, their political thinking is sometimes semi-revolutionary, and their situation allows them to espouse extreme attitudes which would not be feasible elsewhere.

For some students they provide an immediate and recognizable model, and thus the traditional freedom of the university may be used by minorities of staff and students for displays of generalized dissidence. This group of staff is often on Christian-name terms with students, and their estrangement from the establishment of the university allows them to absolve themselves of responsibility for existing university arrangements, and to identify more with students than with the rest of the staff. In the mass university situation, where there is increasing 'us-them' feeling in students about staff, this provides a short-term solution to pedagogic difficulty; but in the long run it is not always in the interest of the co-operative scholarly enterprise, since it lays the way open to extensive mutual exploitation and simply perpetuates 'us-them' attitudes, with a proportion of 'them' having come over to 'us'.

The relations of these two group of academics, and others who stand between them, are matters of strain within universities; and much of this strain comes from the fact that the intellectual pursuit is increasingly devalued, and the influence of intellectual *élites* declines. There is indeed a common attitude of self-denigration, and an increasing feeling that university staff are not an *élite* at all.

To some extent this is a divestment of pretences—but there is often an accompanying divestment of responsibility. And once more this is intensified by the atmosphere of the mass university. As expansion continues, as assistant staff become more conscious of their distance from the centre of things even within the university, and as university decisions are increasingly left to an administrative staff only little influenced by the cumbersome façade of democratic consultation among academics, so disillusionment spreads further, individual responsibility lessens, and the cynicism has more to feed upon.

The universities grow too large and unwieldy for staff to feel the involvement and participation in a shared civilizing enterprise such as is evident in, say, Sir Charles Snow's dons. The young lecturer is much less committed to his university, much more to his specialism. Usually he is looking for a better job elsewhere. There is less loyalty to the community, because it is too amorphous; little loyalty to an intellectual *élite*, because its status is uncertain; and he does not feel loyalty to a liberal ideal of creating by education a rounded and civilized man, because he is, often, not that himself.

Not surprisingly, a similar sense of indirection and uncertainty is felt at undergraduate level. Not only are the overwhelming proportion of redbrick students first-generation undergraduates, but a large proportion are first-generation grammar-school people. They come because going to university is what now happens to the brighter youngsters, because it is part of the processing they undergo, because it is a step towards a good job, and because studentship implies a good time.

From the point of view of the scholarly academic their motivation is unformulated and unarticulated; anyone who has interviewed candidates for university admission knows well this vagueness of purpose and ambition. Only if the university values are clear, cogent and the subject of consensus will this extremely diluted motivation be strengthened and enlarged.

Many modern students are from backgrounds where intellectual pursuits are often limited to working hard and passing examinations, and where it has never been pretended that intellectuality suffuses the whole of life. Some go on regarding intelligence simply as useful equipment in their discipline, and never approach the values of liberal inquiry. Others respond to the intellectualization available in the university experience, but never have the opportunity to live out, after they leave college, the liberal and humane values which go with it. Even within the university, they develop a sense of separation from, and a feeling of cynicism about, the wider society.

The assumption within the permissive atmosphere of the university is that there is an inner discipline in all who are present, a discipline which presupposes a deep personal concern for culture. There are no agencies or mechanisms for imposing university values; they are assumed to underline the university's long-term mission and day-to-day operation. In fact, as we indicate, these values are increasingly vulnerable in the face both of changing circumstances and the new attitudes evident in its personnel, clientele and among some organs of public opinion.

University education is approved of as never before; but it is approved of as a means of providing the staff for large businesses, management and scientific technicians and research officers.

Others of a more political persuasion regard it as a recruiting ground for dissentients—yet while a university obviously has a responsibility to encourage critical thinking about existing social and other institutions, it is not its task to pass on emotionally hostile orientations in the guise of scholarly criticism. Either way, it is less and less assumed that the business of the university is to produce the cultivated and civilized intelligence. And even in the university context these values appear increasingly less relevant to the student.

There are many students who do not really experience the university at all; it is not uncommon to find a strong body of student thought that expresses disdain for art and culture, and that has no conception of the history of their discipline and its social meaning. Many redbrick universities sponsor recitals of chamber music, poetry readings, art and sculpture exhibitions, special lectures, but student attendance (even when normal curricular activities are suspended) is often less than 5 per cent of the student population.

Many student unions are extremely active in putting on plays, debates and the like, but even then support is frequently lacking, or of the wrong kind; debates are sometimes imbecilic, union film shows ruined by noises off, dramatic societies watched by a handful. Sometimes the union as a body is run by a small group of semi-professional students, while the majority of students are apathetic.

Parents who visit university unions in term time are frequently surprised at the overcrowded and shabby facilities, the standards of manners and behaviour, and among a fringe of students—the cult of dirt and dishevelment. Sometimes there is behaviour which would be called hooliganism were it to occur among Teddy-boys. And the overall impression is that unions are not communities, but crowds, with members not of a scholarly society but of bear-garden. And agitation from the few, and apathy from the many, seem the commonplace responses to the university's mission.

It is perhaps in response to this problem that some universities are attaching increasing importance to residential arrangements. But building halls of residence does not automatically revive the educative values of universities at their best; it simply offers the theoretical *opportunity*. No research has been made into the socially desirable size of halls, though a lot has been discovered about the economically desirable size; little is known about the rôle and function of wardens; frequently false formality and imitation ceremony are mistakenly thought to restore quality to university life.

It is commonly supposed that by bringing people of different disciplines together, one enables the dust of culture to rub off one on to another; in fact this occurs only with careful cultivation, and the exposure of students to common experience. Putting them together may in fact only increase tolerance or reduce conversation to the lowest common denominator.

The communications barrier can be broken down only by conscientious and sustained effort by a warden or house tutor. Not all halls are inspired by cultural, intellectual and scholarly concerns. Many have little identity of their own, provide little substantial community allegiance; more often than not they manufacture an artificial identity by pitting themselves in athletic rivalry and in rags with other halls equally impersonal and unstained by university values.

It is not therefore surprising that there has grown up in redbrick universities a distinctive student culture which manifests a number of the disturbing aspects of our modern anomic youth culture. Movements with high ideals become vehicles for young people in search of excitement; already some of this activity has moved into over-excited demonstrations. Much that undergraduates do is inspired by a sense of social duty, and their contributions to such programmes as War on Want, aid schemes for the aged or sick, and the like represent the best response to university life. It is hard to believe, however, that all who join in the marches and agitation that are now *de rigueur* among a certain set of students are directly motivated by high political objectives, for more and more rebelliousness becomes a general attitude, seeking causes to fasten on to.

Youth is rightly critical of the ideas of its elders, and of the institutions of society, but what is disturbing is that rebellion is now accepted as a conventional pose among some sections of the student body. It is indeed an accepted part of the new student culture. Their movements frequently tell us more about the students who are moving than about the expressed objective; and in the void which some students feel because of the un-

83

certain value-commitment of their university, these movements provide easily adopted attitudes which are worn rather than lived.

The philistinism or the social nihilism of some students are facile responses to an anomic situation, in which students experience *en masse* the clash of home values and the challenge of the university. Once the university socialized students; today, with large intakes, *they* amend *it*. And this is alarming because it jeopardizes the university's liberal cultural mission.

Today *Lucky Jim* and *The Catcher in the Rye* are almost textbooks of what the university experience should be like. They are particularly acceptable because they debunk what are increasingly seen as 'phoney' values. To a degree, they may be— but these books do often portray standards which people can easily live down to. Thus the one prevailing self-image, alike among Chelsea beatniks, professional teenagers, Teddy-boys, and some groups of undergraduates, is of the individual at odds with society.

The university takes young people at an age when they are uncertain and insecure; it necessarily detaches them from their home values; yet it has no clear ideals to offer them. It *must* create a radical upheaval in young people, but it should do so by demanding an exacting self-discipline and by carefully developing the quality of their intellect, imagination and sensitivity. If this were always done, there would be less cause for parental anxiety about the university experience of their children; yet for it to be done requires a firm sense of university education as something more than vocational and the acceptance of culture as something more than a marginal concern.

The redbricks' mission is necessarily different from that of Oxbridge, but not on that account less worthwhile. There is an independent tradition on which the redbricks can draw. It owes something to Oxbridge, but it is a different tradition from theirs. At their best, the redbricks draw on the Oxbridge ideal of cultural inquiry, which works together with the tougher-minded heritage which stems from the nonconformist academies of the eighteenth century. The liberal scholarly inheritance could and should prevent the tough-minded search for unpretentious intellectuality from becoming the debased expression of anti-culture which it sometimes is today.

The present authors—reared in, and concerned for, redbrick universities—find themselves deeply disturbed by the casual surrender of that which is best in the redbrick tradition. There is today a common assumption that if social values are changing, nothing can be done about it, since the changes are sanctified by 'social progress'. Universities should be the last places where this type of resignation should prevail.

At a time when the Government, the University Grants Committee, the Association of University Teachers, and the Press are all—for diverse reasons—supporting university expansion, and when towns vie with one another to be the location of new redbricks, it seems appropriate to ask whether the universities will in fact do what is generally expected of them. Will they produce young people who differ in more or less expected ways from their parents by becoming well-educated men and women; or will they be little different from the products of further education colleges, and perhaps display a lower social and cultural commitment than the products of teachers' training colleges and the professional schools?

Students have already voiced their disillusionment—and those who know individual students in their early weeks in university see their bewilderment, their loss of idealism, and their growing cynicism. All too often the teaching process has been reduced to the mass exposure to facts; often there is no concern about what the student 'can make his own' but only for an efficiently administered, impersonal, anonymous and routinized process of mass-education. Especially is this true in technology faculties, where casual *bonhomie* often deputizes for genuine personal concern.

The university experience generally is reduced to the passing of examinations rather than the acquisition of disciplined attitudes of mind, and the awakening of sensitivity and imagination. Universities have still a mission to be the preservers and the disseminators of distinctive cultural values. It would be dangerous for them to become passive mirrors of the values of the world outside.

6

The War of the Generations
(1964)

Mods and Rockers are the latest, British manifestation of the distinctive, semi-delinquent and sometimes riotous, youth culture that has been growing in the industrial societies of the world in the last decade. Conventional history regards riots that had clear economic causes as purposive and comprehensible, those that had not (unless they could be 'explained' as outbursts of religious enthusiasm) as a form of mania. Mods and Rockers appear less excusable because their behaviour has no evident economic motivation: the participants are largely high-wage earners. But they are less articulate than the Luddites. The roots of their problems lie far beyond their comprehension in contemporary changes in social structure and community organization.

The youth culture has taken various forms since the late 1940s,[1] but Mods and Rockers merge more completely with a much large proportion of the juvenile population than did the Teddy-boys or the yobos. The line between Mod and Rocker defiant postures, dispositions to delinquency and even riotous behaviour, and the general standards of other young people, has become much more difficult to draw than was the case with the earlier expressions of the youth culture. From being a minority phenomenon, the distinctive styles of the youth culture are, as they change, steadily influencing bigger proportions of the age group. There used to be strong differences between young people from different social classes: then the youth culture was essentially a working class phenomenon. These differences are being steadily eroded, largely through the impress of

---

[1] See below, Chapter 9, for a more complete analysis.

mass-media. There is some resonance of social class differences in the opposition of Mods and Rockers—in the differences of clothes, aspirations and life-styles—and this is perhaps the first appearance of competing, class-influenced variants in the youth culture. The differences are, however, really superficial. The antagonisms between them function to consolidate group identity, but the real division in the modern world is not between social class variants of the youth culture, but between the youth culture and the way of life of the adult population.

The public response to Mods and Rockers has been highly confused. Their riotous behaviour has been widely condemned: their activity costs large sums of public money in the police action necessary to contain their riotous affrays. On the other hand, the entertainment idols with whom these groups so conspicuously identify themselves receive public honours. Royalty attend their film *premières*; mayors give civic receptions; heads of Oxford colleges offer lavish hospitality; members of the aristocracy provide (at a fee) the places and occasions for thousands to convene decked out in Mods and Rocker outfits. When their entertainment heroes are acclaimed in this way, it is difficult for young people to take police action against their riots and brawls very seriously. When delinquescent styles are given such public recognition in the entertainment sphere, it is not difficult to see why teenage dissidence and violence, which ten years ago was a thing for small groups in shady streets, has now become assertive and self-assured activity for large mobs on holiday beaches in broad daylight.

The rebelliousness of youth is not new, but the resilience, infectiousness and self-confidence in dissidence for its own sake in the face of a hostile, if helpless, public, is new. Mods and Rockers are spontaneous 'leagues of youth' that reject the political, religious and do-gooding objectives for which youngsters were organized in the old-style youth movements—Church Lads, Army Cadets, Boy Scouts and the like. They reject not only the particular discipline, loyalties and traditions that such movements espoused, but they reject discipline, loyalty and organization as such. Organization is already the bane of their lives.

The growing youth problem reflects deep-seated changes in

87

the structure of industrial society. In the past two or three decades the community has ceased to be the natural context in which most people's lives are lived. Solidary communities and neighbourhoods have given place to amorphous suburbs. With more space and more privacy, people have moved apart: 'friends and neighbours' have become neighbours and strangers. Community control of the behaviour of young people has diminished. There is less consensus about how youngsters should behave, and less interaction between people in the same neighbourhood on the basis of which they might acknowledge control of the young as a common necessity. The separation of life activities —work, school, entertainment and home—divorces young people from their families, and families from neighbours. Young people move into contexts where they are anonymous, and anonymity is a splendid cloak for the individual who wishes to misbehave.

The mobility of Mods and Rockers, on their scooters and motor-cycles, has attracted attention. They arrive, congregate in groups, fight and—when police arrive—drive off, swiftly and anonymously. But it is not only they who are mobile. The facility with which they can descend on a seaside town on bank-holidays merely reflects the increase in movement by the mass of the population. The young enjoy mobility most, in getting away from parents who might keep them in check. They move off to into places where relationships are increasingly devoid of personal commitment, among people who do not care for them or what they do, and among some who make a profit from encouraging them to do things and to adopt styles that pronounce their antipathy to the general public of older generations. Whereas, in the past, most young people, confined to particular districts for most of their lives, sought there a stable reputation, today they seek instant prestige among a casually known group of age-mates. Older people have become a less significant reference group for them, and this has occurred as the intensity of particular contacts with well-identified older persons has diminished. In a more impersonal world, superficial and external criteria define those who belong to the group with which the young individual identifies. Age, clothes, hair-style, speech-habits, gestures and among Mods and Rockers the status symbols with which they load their scooters and bikes, are paramount among these—all within the boundary of the age-group. Possessions, new status-symbols, and daring to adopt new 'way out' styles, are part of this process of defining the reference group and cutting a figure with the right set of one's age-peers. This process in itself is a recurrent social phenomenon, but the dominance of the age-group is now greater, and sets itself much more firmly off from the rest of the population than has been so in the past. Equally, the reference group is a much wider, more anonymous category, the members of which are not a group of close companions, so much as a 'class' the members of which 'know' each other impersonally and anonymously and only by external criteria of placement (i.e. clothes and appearance).

The transport revolution, from public to private conveyance, has increased both mobility and the anonymity of modern man. For the young in particular it has helped them to escape social control and to accept the controlling ideas of the age group, but transport has merely been a facilitating factor for this particular type of deviant youth culture. The values of the age group are dictated largely by the entertainment industry. In the latest wave of youthful dissidence, however, the process has gone a stage beyond the mere facilitating circumstance of anonymity. As deviant life-styles have become fashionable and widely publicized in the entertainment world, the search for notoriety has replaced the need for anonymity. Anonymous vandalism has been increasing for years. What is new is the openly acclaimed disdain on a mass scale for the values of the wider society. Although Mods and Rockers, representing super- ficially differing variants of the youth culture, fight each other, the people they are really fighting is the rest of us. The anonymous vandals were also fighting the public, but Mods and Rockers have discovered that in our impersonal society, it is possible to be anonymous and delinquent whilst being con- spicuously on public view. And this is so, because of the mobi- lity of modern society, and because they have discovered some- thing about mass action. The age-group is a more protective context than the shady alleys of the local street-corner gang ever were.

The moral abandonment of other men that has reduced the social control of the individual—most significantly of the young (and therefore unsocialized) individual—has been a consequence of more than a transport revolution, of course. It reflects the trend towards centralization, bigger firms, bigger schools and bigger towns. Face-to-face contacts with known persons who have known moral reputations is less likely in such large institutions. Individuals disappear as rôle-performers become the important point of interaction. Large organizations depend on men performing their rôles, and consequently, in these institutions, concern for the person as such can be relinquished.

As long as this process affected only the middle classes, personal behaviour did not deteriorate. The middle classes had for a long time demanded inhibition and self-discipline in their children. But once the working classes were inducted into large institutions and once their community life became impersonal, vital elements in social control were lost. Control among the working classes was much more a feature of community, and much less a matter of the internalization of a distinctive set of values. When working-class folk-culture was replaced by mass culture, so the least socialized sections of society inevitably passed out of effective control. As the least socialized working-class youngsters were released from neighbourhoods where the observation of parents and neighbours prevailed, their clash with the police, the embodiment of middle-class values and the protectors of property, became inevitable.

The changing organization of school and work organization in our society have done a great deal to create the new gulf between the generations in their understanding of each other. Older people have lost touch with developments partly as a result of the rapidity of technical change, but also partly because of the kind of social arrangements that we have adopted, and especially because so much of our modern organization has struck at the stability of the local community. Formally we continue to act on the increasingly outworn assumption that if people sleep in the same district then they are 'a community'; but in practice our social legislation as well as our technology militates against the continuance of community life. Sixty years or so ago, Graham Wallas, discussed the fragility of society's continuance: if, by some terrible mishap, only a generation or two were to miss their education, man would return to the condition of a Stone Age. If, because communication between the generations breaks down, human values and conventions are not transmitted, the social loss may be as drastic as technical loss would be. The agency might be not so much one great cataclysmic event, as the war of attrition of human culture represented in the conflict of the generations. Although contemporary civilization embodies a great deal of its culture, its expertise, its productive power and its scientific faculties in equipment, the non-cumulative aspects of human wisdom are transmitted only by sustained human interaction. These certainly determine the fineness of the quality of human life, but they also affect much more fundamental, and perhaps even essential, elements for the very continuance of society as we know it.

There is a sense, of course, in which there has always been a war of the generations among men, although it is more conspicuous in some other animals—among deer, elephants and seals. Young bucks displace old bulls. In this sense the war of generations is akin to the war of the sexes: there has always been a struggle for dominance, or for relative placings, and sheer force has not always been more important than subtlety in the process. But the war of generations has now ceased to be a private war, in herds, families or local communities. It has become war in the public arena, in which significant segments of the younger generation identify themselves as something set over against the rest of society. That they use contrasting styles as a way of subdividing themselves, does not eclipse the fact that at least these two styles have a certain relevance for each other: those of the older generation have none. And the styles are not local styles, nor the language a local argot—they are presented as appropriate for a whole generation, and only for that generation.[1]

The agency that has provided a style appropriate to the whole youth culture is of course the entertainment industry acting through the mass-media, which are themselves increasingly devoted to entertainment. The most expensive entertainment, and hence the most prestigious, is that provided for the section of the population with the largest uncommitted incomes, which, being the young, is also the section with the least cultivated taste, and

[1] The term generation is used for a loosely defined age group that covers the span of perhaps those from fourteen to twenty, or thereabouts.

the highest vulnerability to whatever will arouse animal passions. Whereas community recreation in the past used to bring the generations together, commercial entertainment now drives them apart. We pass from a society in which we had films that were unsuitable for adolescents to one with coffee bars unsuitable for adults. The mass-media are not merely the providers of entertainment, but for the young they are also the disseminators of styles, postures and patterns of behaviour.

Television has been particularly important since, in a way that has not been true of earlier agencies of communication, it completely rejects any moral stance. Even radio, in pre-television days, had a philosophy of public responsibility, and, as an agency the goals of which were neither profit nor mere popularity ratings, its directors, conspicuously Lord Reith, saw themselves as participating in the guardianship and dissemination of particular mores and cultural values. Television, operated for profits or popularity (or both), proceeds in a completely amoral way. It has tested the market, escaped the conventions governing printed matter and the theatre and has steadily grown more daring about levels of public decency. It presents all types of attitudes and values without adopting any firm moral stance of its own. It disavows positive values and accepts the yardstick of the market, which, on moral issues, is an invitation to viewers to abandon their own standards of propriety which —because television is technical, prestigeous and clearly identified with the metropolis—suddenly are made to seem provincial if not parochial. Without exerting or seeking to exert direct, didactic authority, television has managed to convey the impression that men who are outside the advanced circles of the semi-literary entertainment people who run television are somehow antequated in their moral senses. In consequence many people, and particularly young people, who are least sure of their values, and least socialized, have aped the manners and styles of television, which is the new authority on acceptable, prestige-conferring behaviour.

Competition for audiences between channels has been the principal factor behind this development, and entertainment has been its principal genre. But this effect has also been brought about because television has adopted the impersonal, detached style of an agency that merely 'holds the ring', 'provides the facilities', for 'all points of view'. Everything is put across with the same sort of authority. Inevitably a Gresham's Law affects what is offered, given the ease with which men readily prefer to indulge gross sensations rather than engage in elevating experiences, or wrestle with subtleties. Letting things find their own level, with a mass audience is to invite the steady deterioration in standards, to let the salacious and the sensational displace or infect other material. Even the interview, no matter with whom, proceeds with the same moral indifference: the interviewer's 'attack' does not represent moral concern, but is only a device to produce the crackle of controversy. The exercise is not engaged in to let a man say what he really wants to say, but rather to goad him into saying what he does not mean, to draw forth emotional responses rather than considered argument.

The ubiquity of television has undoubtedly produced a climate quite different from that of the pre-television age, and one that cannot be adequately measured by the standard procedures of social science surveys. The climate is a social phenomenon, not really discernible in individuals isolated by the questionnaire schedule. As a climate it has affected not merely viewers when viewing, or soon after viewing, but the whole texture of social relations, and the standards of everyday behaviour. Those most affected have been the young, who have received widely divergent ideas about standards from the contradictions between what is taught by parents and teachers and the style that is picked up and the atmosphere that is experienced through the influence of television. Entertainers, indirectly as well as directly, provide the new models for behaviour and the new standards, and this is clear even from the pop-music connotations of the names 'Mod' and 'Rocker'. The awareness of the bankruptcy of parents, teachers and priests in influencing the young, as once they did, is evident when public men say, as they have recently, 'If only the Beatles would tell young people that it isn't clever. . . .' Clearly, this situation is not one that is conducive to the socialization of the young to the received human values of our civilization, nor to the acquisition of those moral dispositions that will sustain them in a routine work-a-day world when youth has gone.

Theoretically the social institutions of the family, education and religion might be expected to provide access to an understanding of young people. These were, traditionally, the institutions that socialized and humanized the young. In practice, religion now has virtually nothing to tell us about youth—and the majority of youth believes that it has nothing to tell them. With education there is increasing uncertainty of control and unclarity about goals. In the family the wrench between generations is felt at its keenest as soon as the young have a sense of their independence and learn to imitate the models of the peer-group, and of the peer-group culture disseminated by mass-media. The social institutions to which attention must be turned, if the condition of modern youth is to be understood, are communications and recreation, particularly as these coalesce in the entertainment industry. The cluster of factors that give entertainment this pre-eminence of influence are worth briefly mentioning.[1]

The redistribution of income, from older persons to younger, that has occurred since the war, has also been a redistribution from people with more responsibilities to people with less responsibility. Whatever the social justice of redistribution between social classes (and this was the only redistribution that was intended as a matter of policy) the consequence of such a process is also to redistribute from the more-educated and more-cultivated to the less-educated and less-cultivated. The effect is reinforced when class redistribution coincides with the generational redistribution noted above. The entertainment industry has grown enormously in the period since the war, in the context of this changed distribution of consumer power. Promoters and producers have recognized the young as their market, and they have been able to sell them commodities of low quality at high prices. They have catered for a new phenomenon—the affluent adolescent in search of excitement and status-enhancement. Young pop-singers, with little training and dubious talents, have been projected by careful publicity in a massive exploitation of the new moneyed but uneducated classes. Inevitably, what they have offered has been progressively inclined to titillate uncultivated appetites: it has often been sensa-

[1] For fuller analysis of these and other factors see above, Chapter 1, and below, Chapter 9.

tional (or presented sensationally) unsubtle, crude and without cultural or educational worth.

Much of what has been provided has expressed the problems of the young: both the heroes of new stories, and entertainers themselves have become much younger since the war. Life, as presented by the media, has become predominately young people's life. Social mobility of the young, the search for glamour, have been reiterated themes, passing into increased presentation of youthful despair and emptiness when success-dreams have failed. The entertainment industry itself has made direct capital out of the war of the generations—using the tensions existent in social life as the basis for a fictional documentation of them. But it has presented them as more powerful tensions than in real life they were. In doing so it has, however, affected real situations, providing them with a new dimension of drama and with an intensity of emotion that otherwise they might have lacked. It has exacerbated the almost biologically determined tension of son and father; in its folk-lore of pop-singers it has induced heightened and exaggerated awareness of easy roads to success, which hardly any youngster will discover; it has pressed home the message of failure which an achievement-oriented society, by the relentlessness of its educational selection system, already communicates to the majority of young people. It has, above all, communicated modes of deviance and defiance as an appropriate mode of response for the young in the modern world. Thus, entertainment has not sought, as did the older forms of recreation, to assuage men's experience of social tension. Instead it has exacerbated the situation and helped to sustain a basically neurotic response towards it, in which action prompted by tension sustains tension rather than reduces it.

Not the least significant contribution of the entertainment industry to the contemporary gulf between generations has been the diffusion to young people of a generation-consciousness. By taking younger heroes, by disseminating standardized life-styles for the young, the mass-media have powerfully affected the self-image of adolescents, and their interpretation of their social relationships. An impersonal, abstract conception of the generation has developed—of the young as a group apart, identifying in an anonymous way with each other, rather than with the rest of the population. (What used to be achieved in part by uniforms for soldiers, has now been achieved by much more pervasive and persuasive agencies, to mould a strong sense of group identification—in this case an age-consciousness.) This sense of identity with all other young people, although lacking an institutional context is undoubtedly a powerful force: Mods and Rockers represent an attempt to realize this vague, abstract media-manufactured sense of identity in real situations and by collective action.

This is its more assertive aspect. It has another consequence, and that is the flight from the family as a group that has social relevance for the young person, or as a context from which he can draw useful intimations about how to conduct himself. As the new form of generational identification grows, so attachment to the family will diminish. A good deal of what has been learned there will necessarily be overturned as the new values are seen to conflict with ideas received in childhood. The movement will be from the affective situation to one that—although promising excitement and involvement—is, in the casual acceptance of anyone in the age group who chooses to manipulate the symbols of group-identity, necessarily impersonal and lacking in affection. Youngsters clearly seek affection, but they seek it without the control that affection implies. Casual associations, perhaps casual sex, come to replace relationships in which sustained care is a characteristic. The strong emphasis on gregariousness among the young indicates, perhaps, the desperate nature of the search for an experience of love that the new situation cannot, in the nature of things yield. Love is personal, particular and discriminatory. The new context of youth is casually impersonal and generalized. The 'party' has become an almost continuous activity of leisure time, but the relationships that arise are often brief, superficial and casual, since commitment is less to persons than to the age-group and the life-style. In the widespread search for real affection in contexts where the symbols of affection are manipulated (conspicuously in pop-songs) but where the actuality is elusive, boredom becomes a persistent condition. From boredom the 'rumble' in the streets or on the beaches of a holiday place provide collective relief.

If, as has here been suggested, the real causes of the persistent youth problem of our times are in the changes in social structure, it is clear that we shall not stop hooliganism, whether among Mods and Rockers, or other young dissidents, by arresting them in large numbers. Mods and Rockers are only a phase of the youth problem, and that problem itself is part of a much wider social malaise. If we have failed to provide social conditions in which youngsters can acquire a responsible sense of social values, we cannot impose such values suddenly by sharp punitive measures, such as some public officials have suggested. We cannot, by punishment 'bring young people to their senses', if we have failed to maintain the social conditions in which they could acquire senses in the first place.

Punishment is not even likely to be an efficient instrument of repression. Only a tiny percentage of offenders get caught, and the most vicious almost certainly get away. In any case, in the deviant youth-culture, punishment might only serve to confer prestige. It also provides vindication for anti-social attitudes among youngsters who have never been unambiguously informed or educated about what a well-ordered society expects of them. Punishment in such a situation makes criminality part of the logical response of the young dissident's situation. This is not to suggest that punishment has no place in dealing with the young, but only to suggest that it can in itself achieve nothing unless other, much more radical, things are done first, and that, unless those things are done, punitive measures merely create the idea of a repressive state.

Evidently our public policy towards young people is bankrupt. To rehabilitate youth would mean radical modification of contemporary social organization on a scale that politicians have not yet contemplated. Yet, if society is not to progress to increasing disorder among young people, it is something that must be contemplated. We have accepted economic planning: it is now imperative that we take steps to restore social health, whatever the economic costs. What traditional society did spontaneously we must now do consciously, in particular we must seek to re-establish spontaneous agencies of social control and to re-establish the superior status of adults. As work demands less time and, in large plants, becomes de-personalized, agencies of social control to do what work used to do become particularly important. In creating them we might also counteract these de-personalizing tendencies of modern life.

Since the redistribution of income to the young has coincided with the intensified expression of boredom among adolescents, it would be appropriate for an official commission to explore the income structure of the young. It would not be impossible to legislate for the restriction of adolescent earnings, so that only at twenty-one could a boy earn a full man's wage in his own trade.[1] This was one of the unintended effects of National Service, which has been so widely canvassed as a remedy for Mods and Rocker hooliganism—although it was canvassed as a disciplinary measure rather for its pecuniary significance. Such a measure would also require the effective restriction of credit facilities and the hire-purchase opportunities of young people. The hire-purchase of a variety of items used as status symbols by the young might be prohibited, and perhaps this might help to restore the saving habit.

It would not be impossible to raise the age at which car, motor-cycle and scooter licences might be obtained. The suspension of vehicle licences could become automatic for any offence against public order in which it could be shown that the use of a vehicle was even indirectly involved. Measures of this kind, however, must be seen as merely deterring particular patterns of behaviour among young people, they do not centrally address the fundamental problem, which is more a matter of the dissemination of values than of transport facilities.

Since increasingly the dominant 'official' value of our society is achievement, especially in the educational system, it might be possible to take steps to diversify the opportunities for achievement in many different spheres. The real inferiority of so many contemporary teenagers is not, certainly, in income, but in education for their rôles in society, and for their leisure. We might seek to emphasize criteria of success in the world other than those that depend solely on academic and technical educational performance, and it might be well worth doing this, even at the cost of some economic progress.

Schools themselves have grown large and have been centralized. It would not be impossible to reduce them in size to a

[1] This was written before the recommendations of the Latey Committee recommended eighteen as the age of majority!

point where personal relationships would be restored, and to reallocate them so that they were again part of the local community. We should thereby reduce at one point the type of mobility that so much destroys social control, and we should restore some degree of common experience for teachers and parents in dealing with youngsters. Recent American research has shown the superiority of the small school over the big one in the realization of individual opportunities for involvement and responsibility,[1] and these may be the most important aspects of education.

Teacher mobility obviously reduces the effectiveness of teachers as models from whom children can learn standards; it also reduces the amount of loyalty to the school that can be elicited from children. It might be possible to offer salary differentials in favour of teachers who stay in one school over longer periods. The teacher's task must be seen as work that implies long-term commitment, not merely day-to-day operation.

If our society is really concerned about its youth, the social consequences of all types of legislation will be scrutinized. Thus, as an example, the act to end resale price maintenance may pose an oblique threat to important elements in social life, and break another fibre in the fabric of the local community by replacing small shops with supermarkets, thus encouraging that impersonal style of social organization, in which morality deteriorates.

The re-education of our architects is vital. Housing estates policy has led to increasing loneliness and the breakdown of community life. We cannot, certainly, re-create 'Coronation Street', but we might persuade architects to keep buildings 'man-size' so that men can exert an influence over their environment and make it their own, rather than living helplessly against the monotony of featureless pre-stressed concrete in urban areas which local people cannot, no matter what they do, create any sense of distinctive locality.

The examples of issues on which an alert public policy would seek to exert influence on behalf of the young could be multiplied. What has to be learned is that the mere manipula-

[1] R. G. Barker and P. V. Gump, *Big School, Small School*, Stanford: Stanford University Press, 1964.

99

tion of economic benefits has little relevance to this problem. Long ago steps were taken to prevent employers exploiting youth as labour. What is now needed are measures to prevent manufacturers, entertainers and impresarios from exploiting youth as consumers. Has not the time come when the entertainment industry ought to be placed under public examination, and its values, policies and organization revealed? We carefully control, in the school system, the credentials of teachers, and we move closer to a system of licensing. But children experience as much television as they experience schooling. Ought we not to consider licensing producers, and providing them (if they cannot provide for themselves) an ethical code, and a system in which licences could be endorsed and revoked for violations?

Measures of this kind appear drastic. But without positive action to restore community control, the law will come to be administered through an increasingly impersonal machine. Without the restoration of spontaneous community control in support of and prior to, the operation of the police, the law itself will fall into disrepute as a repressive and coercive instrument, at least among the under-socialized sections of society. The police—already suffering from lack of social support for their function of maintaining that framework of order necessary to protect men in their everyday life—will be seen as oppressors, devoid of the humane, personal and moral qualities that have long characterized the vast majority of their operations. To allow society to develop in this way would be to deprive young people of the possibility of acquiring the values of civilization, to the utter impoverishment of their generation and the utter disinheritance of the one that will follow.

7

The Changing Universities
(1964)

In canvassing the expansion of universities, politicians—more in ignorance than in cunning—have failed to mention that expanded universities will necessarily be different from universities as we have known them. The public supposes that expansion means that they will get more of the same. They will get nothing of the kind. More there will be, of something passing by the name: it will be something of a very different nature.

This can be asserted without regard to the pool of ability. We have no finally reliable way of knowing whether in terms of ability 'more does mean worse'. Academics differ in assessing direct experience. Tests of intelligence remain inconclusive. Percentage of degree results is clearly inadmissible evidence, since there is no common standard between universities, between faculties, or within one faculty over time.

But even if there is untapped high ability, this will mean less if student motivation is lower, or is less easily mobilized and-because of larger numbers, this is likely to be so. University operation will rely more fully on impersonal procedures; the whole context will become one in which the individual is increasingly anonymous. Teaching methods will change—closed, circuit television and teaching machines may be part of it—and people will persuade themselves that new techniques are even more 'efficient' than the old, if only because 'more people can be put through'.

At present, universities are not very effectively organized to deal with very large numbers. They lack residential accommodation, and their teaching methods emphasize frequent personal student-teacher contact in tutorials or supervised laboratory work. Academic policy and administration is largely in the hands of professors. But just as academics are untrained amateur teachers, so professors are amateur administrators and policy-makers.

One much cherished item of university ethos preserves the amateurism which has given British universities so much of their distinctive character—the assumption implicit in the whole enterprise that undergraduates come to university already committed to intellectual inquiry, largely for its own sake. It may never have been wholly warranted, but as long as undergraduate numbers were relatively small, and universities were governed and run by those who held such values, the system could work on this assumption. But universities can no longer function as if such motivations dominated their clientele or could readily be communicated to them. Differential enthusiasm is hard to administer; it spoils routine operations. Mass universities will work with mass manipulative techniques.

Voluntary student commitment has been sustained by the non-professional character of academic life. Teachers did not regard their work as 'a job'; their wide-ranging intellectual interests, sympathy with students, and willingness to devote time to them in informal relationships were perhaps more important than marginal differences in professional competence. With increasing pressures, and more students, much of this amateurism has disappeared. It is no secret among undergraduates that some academics half-resent teaching, avoid informal contacts, give 'short measure' in effort, and even in time, in order to concentrate on the research which will—as excellence in teaching never will—bring recognition and promotion.

As the academic rôle is professionalized, personal concern for students will be replaced by impersonal manipulation. Registers of attendance at lectures, and allocated numbered seats, so that absence can be more effectively noted (since numbers can be known, whereas individuals can no longer be recognized) become the order of the day. We shall perhaps hear a new ideology in praise of the elimination of idiosyncratic, potentially discriminatory and wasteful personal elements from the educational system. Sooner or later university administrators will become administrative specialists, trained in institutional organization for work in hospitals, unions, schools, universities. . . . Their values will be those of administration, shared within their own profession, rather than university values, shared with the academics in the organization in which they work.

The growth of knowledge brings increased specialization even at undergraduate level, with more pressure on the time-table, particularly for technologists. Universities which, on educational grounds, resist the trend to specialization will risk losing their places in the academic hierarchy, and become mere 'liberal arts colleges', with teachers frustrated at the restriction of their opportunity for more specialized work and its higher status.

The social demand for technical specialists will mean that universities will produce more technically-informed but fewer culturally-educated people. At a time when society faces the prospect of increased leisure, it is paradoxical that the specialist technical education which makes that leisure possible increasingly unfits its recipients for the use of leisure, except as non-university men—catered for more by a specialist entertainment industry than by culturally enlightened minds.

Expansion has made universities more competitive. Glossy brochures project a new 'public image' with full attention to just those subtle irrelevancies which have become familiar in the advertising of commercial products. All the non-educational amenities receive special emphasis. The new universities, in locations more evocative of medieval romance or Regency decadence than of Victorian graft and grime, have been able to choose distinctive gimmicks from the outset—from yet shorter M.A. courses to mixed halls of residence and (or so the Press has had it) the elimination of all rules.

Universities are as vulnerable as other institutions to the demands of their clientele—in some ways more vulnerable. The students who entered university just after the war, many of them ex-servicemen, were often said to be interested in a university education only because they wanted a vocational training. But a decade and a half later, students are much less committed to any particular vocation. University teachers themselves are not worried because students do not have definite careers in mind: indeed, they often prefer candidates for places who admit to unformulated ideas on this subject, as long as they have a wide-ranging intellectual curiosity and interest in the subjects they wish to study. But increasingly students come to university because this is where success in the classroom leads them. Many do not particularly want to undertake three years of further study: they want a university place, a degree, and, eventually the higher salary and the greater independence that these things will ensure. For some, there is no doubt that the university succeeds only in blunting the enthusiasms that have already been awakened. Attending university is justified— sometimes quite openly—because a youngster 'likes the life', wants a good time, and is saved from making a decision about a job for a further three years.

Residence has undergone a quiet revolution. At one time everything which a university undertood was infused with its educational mission, halls of residence conspicuously so. With expansion lodgings have become a major problem, and now in some places nineteen-year-olds are turned loose into flats, as administrative convenience displaces educational concern. It is presented, of course, as a response to the 'changing needs' of young people: but some who do not believe that the real needs of young people have changed very much, see it as a failure of educational nerve, as evidence of the nine to five professionalism of an education which no longer sees itself as having any implications for every-day life. Expanded universities are touching more people, but touching them, it appears, rather more lightly.

Technology is increasingly represented in universities, even though it makes very different demands of students from those made by traditional university disciplines. Lectures, labs, and drawing offices crowd the time-table from nine to five, but much less outside reading is demanded of technology students. In the vacation they are often directed to work for several weeks in some approved firm, or to do a survey course. They do not do tutorials: 'What is there to talk about?' as one professor plaintively put it. The technologies have different rhythms of work and study, and different conceptions of education.

One might ask why—other than for the prestige of association, and the sake of qualifications called degrees—the technologies were ever fitted into university structure at all. But in social organization there is a tendency to use any existing institutional structure for new functions, regardless of how they diverge from existing functions or whether they might be mutually detrimental. There is a curious paucity of imagination —still evident in the Robbins Report—about the range and diversity of possible institutions of higher education. The university becomes the common mould—no matter how ill-suited.

Application of industrial technology to human relations presents a new threat to traditional university studies. The appropriate education to fit a man for an executive post, the liberal professions, for an understanding of public life, has hitherto been the cultivation of the mind and its critical faculties. Now more specific qualifications will be demanded: in business management, traffic control, organizational behaviour, computer science, productivity consultancy, perhaps even in public relations. Amateur concern for human values and the discussion of moral issues, in which the student is supposed also to become morally informed and morally engaged, will be replaced by disciplines which take pride in their scientific detachment, technical precision and their intrinsic ethical neutrality (even though they rest on assumptions and will be part of activities which are far from ethically neutral). These will be educational manifestations of what is now called 'modernization'.

Will traditional arts subjects—even traditional social science subjects—be able to resist displacement? School boys already resist being pressured into science; perhaps because science has become routinized, and remote from excitement at the level at which it must be taught. Or perhaps boys seek the wider freedom of arts faculties at a time when youth is in rebellion against the growing institutionalization of every-day life. But the real long-term hope for the arts may be girls. The wives of all our new technological 'J.B.s' will occasionally have to make dinner-table conversation with top executives. Perhaps for this, in a technocratic age, the arts will be preserved.

8

The Needs of Students
(1965)

The needs of present-day students cannot be understood without some regard to the changing character of universities themselves, and the changing circumstance of young people in contemporary society. I shall try to look at these needs from these two perspectives. To say this is not to abandon the belief that there are certain abiding needs of youth, and some values which must persist both in the changing university and in a changing world. My own consideration of these matters has been informed by seven years spent as sub-warden, and later as warden, in a small hall of residence in a redbrick university. In this circumstance I was able to spend almost every term-time evening, and many evenings of vacation talking to—and listening to—students. I was able to maintain sustained relationships. I state this circumstance at the outset by way of presenting my credentials for the provocative discussion which follows. Some may consider my conclusions wrong, but I am not prepared to believe—on the strength of my particular experience—that they are wrong because I am misinformed about students. Their deeper needs are, today—paradoxically and despite—perhaps because of—the extraordinary concern with university expansion, society's need for technologists and the educational rat-race with other countries, the increasingly forgotten element in the educational situation.

THE FUNCTIONS OF A UNIVERSITY

The minimal functions of universities are the advancement and the transmission of knowledge. It is predominantly in terms of the need for greater dissemination of knowledge that the expansion of universities has recently been canvassed, on the assumption that our society needs a vastly increased proportion of knowledgeable people, who will help us to keep up with the Russians and the Americans in the maintenance of scientific advancement and the improvement of our living standards. The demands are mainly for the technologically educated, and one might suppose the launching of the Russian Sputnik of 1957 to have been the beginning of the wave of intensive pressure for university expansion. There are a variety of contestable value propositions in this argument for expansion, which must here be left aside. What is more to the point is the fact that university education, as we have traditionally known and valued it in our society, has always been very much more than the mere transmission of knowledge. In England the universities themselves have regarded their distinctive mission as the dissemination of human, liberal, civilizing values. They have sought to introduce students to the richness of our cultural inheritance, to provide access to the cumulative aesthetic, literary, philosophic and scientific resources of mankind, and to stimulate intellectual discussion and critical assessment in a context in which young people have leisure and opportunity to savour all the best that our culture has to offer. Thus information alone has never been the concern of English universities—it has been merely the basis on which an educated understanding and a cultivated attitude could be developed.

The ideal has, of course, often outstripped the reality, but the ideal has been there, and has in itself, even if only as a myth (and often as myth with a good deal of substance) been of importance to the activities and ethos of the universities. It would still find widespread assent among academics, as a formulation of the business with which they are engaged: nowadays there would undoubtedly be dissenting voices to maintain that universities were properly concerned only with the transmission of specific skills and specific know-how. The voices are those of the new professional men of the academic world, whose interests are often confined to their own subject, who despise the wider cultural concerns which still persist in universities, and who describe them in pejorative terms as 'frills' or 'goodies'. The expression of the ideal is, however, to be found heavily emphasized in the speeches of vice-chancellors—more fully by the older scholarly type of vice-chancellor, perhaps less so by the more modern money-raising vice-chancellor, who sees his rôle more as a conductor of public relations rather than as a custodian of scholarly values. But the ideal may also be found in the charters of universities, and in the activities which universities sponsor, such as, exhibitions, concerts, lectures, demonstrations. It is still true to say that these activities are sponsored primarily for their own sake, and have not yet been reduced to mere goodwill gestures towards a public from whom donations, grants and contributions from the rates are being actively sought. There is, then, a body of easily available evidence about the values which have been built into the functions of British universities.

My concern is with the university in this rôle as an agency of intellectual and cultural transmission and dissemination. I leave aside its functions as a research institution. My premise is that as an educative agency the university is an organization with certain distinctive value-commitments, its primary responsibility being to produce the educated man in the wide sense of the word. That universities embody certain distinct values is evidenced by their welfare orientation, and in their widely manifested concern for students. Education operates on the assumption that there are certain objective values which older and more experienced persons can transmit to younger and less experienced ones in a university context. The tutorial system and the residential arrangements of our universities are an example of this welfare orientation which amounts to more than merely providing lodging houses, health facilities and refectories. It is 'welfare' in terms of the cultural and intellectual well-being of the student, who is being introduced to the traditionally highly valued aspects of our civilization. He is being given the opportunity to grow into another kind of person, and not merely to pick up notions which he can regurgitate at examination time. This, at least, is the assumption of the types of provision which universities make.

PRESENT THREATS TO UNIVERSITY VALUES

In course of time all institutions tend to suffer an attenuation of function and a dilution of values. Commitment may diminish, especially as there is compromise between original intentions and subsequent pressures, both internal and external. New purposes are added and old ones are (often involuntarily) surrendered or relaxed. High officials become preoccupied with the merely mechanical operation of the institution, particularly in periods of expansion, and lose sight of the values which institutions are supposed to embody. New disciplines, with very different requirements and different demands, are accepted, and these have consequences for the whole institution, for the conception of the institution which is held in the minds of personnel and clientele alike. Whenever new functions or new purposes are grafted on to an organization which was not designed for them, this dilution of value commitment, or confusion of goals, must occur. Under pressure to expand, the universities become especially vulnerable to threats to their values. A number of such threats might be listed:

(1) There tends to occur distinct competition between institutions. This is likely to be particularly acute when they are seeking to establish what is nowadays called 'an image' and what used to be called a reputation. (An image is a surface presentation intended to elicit favourable responses, whether these are justified by the actual reality or not; a reputation was related to the actual and enduring characteristics of an institution, not merely to its façade.) Obviously new institutions cannot enjoy a reputation immediately, so they tend, especially in a society in which publicity values dominate over reality values, to succumb to the temptation to project an image as a substitute for building a reputation. The tendency of new universities to find a gimmick, and to 'put themselves over' with every device of publicity seeking, is especially evident. The search for publicity and the concentration on public relations illustrates the extent of the underlying competition between university institutions. Publicity is clearly a significant deflection of the purposes of a university. In terms of the received values of university education, a university in the news ought to be an object of suspicion.

Competition is also evident in other aspects of university development. The struggle for finance from the University Grants Committee is a struggle between universities and between departments within them. Universities also struggle not only to expand but also to avoid contraction when certain specialized departments exist in too many institutions and when greater concentration is demanded (as in the case of departments of Mining in the recent past). There is competition between departments in terms of the take-over of ancillary departments. Professorial imperialism is a common phenomenon of academic life, as professors seek to increase their students, staff, equipment and living space in a way which is not uncommon in the business world. But in the case of business such aggression is at least consonant with the ethics of economic activity; in universities it is a form of aggrandizement alien to the values of scholarship and of culture.

(ii) Institutional values have suffered dilution in the growth within universities of new types of discipline, particularly of applied disciplines, from business management to fuel technology. That these subjects should be taught somewhere is not in dispute; the only point at issue is that their introduction into universities has had consequences for these institutions themselves, altering them in unintended, unforeseen, and—in terms of commitments to their primary values—undesirable ways. These subjects are more instrumental, more confined to set skills, with less use for initiative, judgment and argument, than the traditional subjects. Learning in these disciplines is less a matter of reading, essay-writing, tutorial work and discussion, and more a matter of work done in drawing offices and laboratories. Thus, when away from the university and its nine-to-five curriculum, students in these subjects have very much less to do. In vacations they are not expected to read but rather to take jobs which are useful, and which are sometimes obligatory for their courses.[1] These time-dispositions differ radically from those of the arts, pure sciences and social sciences, and yet the existence of students with this type of time-table has an impact upon the rest. The technologies have affected ideas about study among students in other faculties, who would also like to be free in the evenings and to earn money in the vacations. These others also tend to develop a more instrumental attitude to their studies (not only as a consequence of this association with

[1] See the evidence presented in the University Grants Committee report 'The Use of Vacations by Students' (H.M.S.O., London, 1963).

technologists, although this is one factor at work). Increasingly they, too, see the university as training them in specific skills—however inappropriate this approach is to their subject.

(iii) A third circumstance of institutional vulnerability is in the change of personnel. As universities grow, so there must be an induction of staff who would not previously have been appointed. Narrower criteria of selection are likely to be applied, and the specialist who is not interested in learning and culture outside his own field, grows more common. The intensification of specialization itself promotes this result, unless deliberate steps are taken to mitigate the consequences. The attitude to academic life becomes more highly professionalized—teaching becomes just a job, in which commitment is to be defined and delimited. Lucky Jim becomes a reality, and narrow specialization sometimes appears to result in anti-intellectualism. Such personnel are more difficult to socialize to the values of particular institutions. They take the institutional framework for granted and accept and intensify its impersonality by their own professional responses to it. They do not see that their loyalties need be engaged towards the university itself. With the increase in number of this new type of academic man it is not easy to see how the values of the university community can escape dilution. As universities expand so the staff grows more mobile, becoming a migratory *élite*, sinking no roots in the life of the community but only in the profession which offers them advancement and career-opportunities.

(iv) The clientele obviously affects an institution. Today there is an alien youth culture which plays on the university through young people who are not primarily committed to the ideals of education. In some measure the youth culture draws its values from the entertainment industry. 'Work' becomes a bore, to be got through, and there is often resentment against lecturing which does not seem to be specifically useful for examination purposes. The pressure of the clientele can be made very evident even in the actual lecturing situation—by passive resistance to discussion of the wider implications of particular points (regarded as 'waffle') or even by extensive noises off and interruptions of lectures when dissatisfaction is more acute. Once the lecturer leaves the strictly 'examinable' items, particularly in the more factual subjects, he is often exposed to very emphatic pressure by his clientele, which can even lead to complete disruption of a lecture, especially at the beginning of sessions. All this reflects two characteristics of the clientele: the demand for a qualification and the demand for a good time. The qualification is the passport to a better job, to be gained without necessarily becoming committed to a subject and without acquiring a more cultivated mind. Mechanical processing, and a certificate of exposure to it, are what are demanded. Because education can be reduced to the time spent in lectures and labs., with intense 'swotting' in the weeks prior to examinations, there is plenty of time for the 'fun ethic' of contemporary society to be brought into the university, the permissive atmosphere of which has no defence against such importations. There is sometimes hooliganism, damage and injury.[1]

(v) The public—as a clientele at one remove—also imposes pressures on the university in a variety of ways. The anxieties which a few years ago, were induced largely by the Press about the selection system at 11 +, have now shifted to anxieties about

---

[1] The incidence of hooliganism is not, of course, recorded by those who undertake research on universities (who are themselves usually employed by universities and therefore sometimes somewhat involved in seeking to project an image not unfavourable to expansion). Newspapers (especially student newspapers) often reveal the surprising extent of student hooliganism. I quote only two examples. In the autumn of 1963 the students of Leeds University Union contemplated banning all students of the Manchester College of Science and Technology from the Leeds University Union after sports teams visiting Leeds from Manchester were alleged to have indulged in 'an orgy of hooliganism' in which glasses, bottles and microphones were broken and cigarette machines damaged. The police were called in when 'students started to tilt concrete mixers'. So strongly did the Leeds students feel about the matter that they took the unusual step of a letter of protest to the Principal of the Manchester College. My quotation is from *The Yorkshire Post* report which was written by a former President of the Leeds University Union. In Sheffield, on 14th May 1963, the following incident is recorded, not without a note of pride, in *Darts*, the newspaper of the Sheffield University Students Union: 'Thursday night proved an eventful night for three of the Halls. . . . Inebriated members of Stephenson Hall visited Halifax (Hall) and Crewe (Hall) . . . (where) windows were bombarded by plants uprooted from the garden. The reason for the celebration was the Foundation Dinner at Stephenson, where gallons of free beer were flowing in such

social selection at 18 +, with the inevitable accompanying demand for a wider distribution of success. The public at large is unconcerned with the maintenance of standards and the intrinsic quality of educational and university experience: it is interested in the distribution of prestige, pay and access to better jobs. Status inflation, in a society in which rapid social mobility is possible and expectable, and for which demand grows, is not unlike monetary inflation: the end result is the devaluation of the commodity concerned, prestige and academic standards in the one case and specie in the other. The intrinsic quality of education is affected (and later its social evaluation) just as currency is affected in monetary inflation—a consequence of the over-distribution of a commodity the supply of which is easily increased on paper but the value of which rests on some much less easily expendable reality. The search for status in our society successively devalues particular status symbols. The brightright B.A., if ever we succumb to the demand, will obviously be of no use as a claim to status, as a criterion of income distribution, or as an objective assessment of ability or academic achievement. Nor, for other reasons, will it be an evidence of all-round education. The supply of a commodity which is scarce (perhaps because of limitations of ability, and certainly because we do not have the means to increase the supply whilst maintaining its character) and which is socially valued less for its intrinsic content than for its instrumental use and for the status which scarcity itself provides, cannot be increased without destroying both the extrinsic basis of its value and its intrinsic character. But in a democratic market-society these demands are hard to withstand: inflation and devaluation are the Achilles' heel of democratic systems and the pressure of demand

---

quantities that the residents were able to prime themselves for an evening's heavy drinking in one of Sheffield's many public-houses. When all the food and drink was gone, Stephenson, dressed to kill in dinner jackets and gowns, rode into town *en masse*. . . . As they strode along, they left clear signs that they had passed by. The times of all the "No Waiting" signs had been altered, the University Car Park sign had disappeared, and several women, met *en route*, were molested. . . . Hearing a din outside Crewe, the Warden of Stephenson hastened to the scene, only to find his charges deflowering the grounds and hurling plants at the windows. . . . His answer to their behaviour was to ban all free beer on subsequent occasions.'

falls on the quality of the commodity. Yet, as has been remarked, inflation is a disease which is enjoyed—in the short run—by its victims. Universities, as public institutions, are sensitive to criticism, sensitive about their 'image', and feel this, perhaps, more acutely in the short run than they feel the longer-run consequences of succumbing to demand. Freedom of action becomes difficult in this circumstance and the unpopular commitment to the maintenance of values and standards surrenders to the demand for increased distribution.

The consequences of pressures of this kind—and doubtless there are others—is uncertainty of purpose and conflict of values within universities. Expansion is apparently the easy and popular solution of all contemporary difficulties: values alone suffer. Expansion has an appeal because it offers improvement of personal circumstances to almost everyone. Some academics are attracted by the prospects of new posts as universities expand; the A.U.T. sees higher salaries and the increase of membership; vice-chancellors see growth of the enterprise with which they are identified; the public sees more opportunities for their children; and the political parties rejoice in an easy electoral gambit, distribute the new political largesse, and bid up the number of new universities at the rate of a public auction.

One contemporary evidence of failure of nerve in the universities is the new willingness of university authorities to respond to the demands of its clientele—as if the academics themselves were no longer certain of the appropriate content and methods of education. Students have never been listened to as much as they are today, but the use of elaborate questionnaires and market research techniques may be little more than a publicity gimmick for universities which feel the need to demonstrate their 'progressive' approach. There is no reason to oppose consultation with students where their interests are affected—but it must be a sustained and natural process, reflecting joint concerns, and in the context of shared values; it must itself be an educative process, and the commitment to the educative ideals of universities must be an unchallengeable first premise. It is, in the curious condition of modern large universities, easier to 'buy students off' with a survey than to establish human relationships in which teacher and administrators *really* talk to students in a continuing discourse. Questionnaires have all the appeal of democratic measures. But they canvass opinions out of contexts, and simplify the complexities of the issues at stake. They often illustrate the prejudices of the investigators, but do so in a concealed way, and they respond to the limitations of their computers, missing the richness and diversity of the texture of real-life relationships. It is particularly alarming to find the results of this type of inquiry seriously regarded as the basis for the formulation of policy, when the research techniques which produce such results are open to such misuse.[1]

[1] The limitations of this kind of research and the biases, conscious and unconscious, which it permits might be illustrated by three examples. (i) Robert Peers, *Fact and Possibility in English Education* (London, 1963), appears not to be aware of the extent to which a question 'framed somewhat differently', throws into doubt the significance of his results. I quote: '. . . an overwhelming proportion of those who expressed an opinion welcomed liberal studies as part of their professional education—at one of the institutions 84·4 per cent. . . . The question was framed somewhat differently at the second institution and here 51·5 per cent regarded liberal studies as helpful for their specialist professional education' (p. 111). It becomes evident that results sometimes hang on an almost incidental choice of words. (ii) Mr. Peter Marris investigated student preferences for different types of accommodation among final-year students at Leeds and Southampton (final year is, of course, the year when preference for hall is likely to be lowest, since more students have either left halls, come to terms with the fact that they cannot get into halls, or are beginning to seek a more independent arrangement as they get older). He shows that 27 per cent and 33 per cent of final-year students at these universities preferred accommodation in halls. Mr. Marris ignored in his presentation (*New Society*, 33 [14th May 1963], pp. 8–10) a 1961 survey for Sheffield University in which 44 per cent of students in all years (finalists showing no special difference from those of other years) stated a preference for hall from a choice of eight types of accommodation (P. H. Mann and G. Mills, 'Living and Learning at Redbrick', *Universities Quarterly*, 16, 1 (Dec., 1961), pp. 19–35). He preferred instead a 1957 survey of Birmingham, the results of which were rather more in accordance with the case he was making. Mr. Marris, like many of the investigators into university accommodation, does not himself favour halls. (iii) The Report of the Committee on Student Accommodation at the University of Leeds preferred the response to questionnaires about the type of accommodation for which students had applied to the actual documentary evidence of the filed application forms. They preferred retrospective rationalizations to actual evidence of behaviour. The committee noted the discrepancy in the case of the women's hall particularly, where 'all the women in hall (in their sample) . . . when asked whether if they were

What one must ask is whether there are no implicit values within university education which can provide the basis for consultation and for decision-making? Ought these not to be changed, when necessary, as a result of deliberate decision, not as the unforeseen consequence of fashionable but dubious 'fact-finding' procedures? The problem is particularly acute in periods of expansion, when universities are threatened not only with the attenuation of values by internal adjustment to mass-education, but also by the reduced commitment of a less fully socialized clientele.

The conception of the university which I am propounding is both expensive and selective—not for the sake of expense and exclusiveness as such, but because these conditions appear to be necessary for the maintenance of the educational values of universities as we have known them. These values in themselves have not been disapproved of, or there would be no demand for the expansion of university education; instead, there would be a demand for education of a distinctly different sort. But only a minority can profit from what a university can do—not because only a few have the intellect (a matter still open to dispute) but because the system cannot operate at the mass level and because few develop a genuine commitment to this educative experience. Its expansion will merely over-extend its resources, destroying its value for all. Despite the popular pressure for university entrance relatively few are prepared for the intellectual commitment which it demands. The present pressure is not a sudden conversion of the population to a taste for scholarship but only a demand by parents, and in some measure by students, for access to job opportunities and—for some would-be students—

---

starting university life again from the beginning they would choose to live in lodgings or in hall, said they would prefer to be in hall' (p. 81). From girls in lodgings they again had almost unanimity in favour of lodgings. From the tone of the report the committee was loath to come to the conclusion, on the strength of this evidence, that the selection procedures employed by wardens were so startlingly satisfactory. But curiously they failed to draw the other conclusion, that actual data of behaviour from documentary sources (the application forms) is more reliable than questionnaire responses on which they were so heavily reliant. From these illustrations it becomes apparent that market research techniques must be regarded with some suspicion even on technical grounds.

a desire to experience the permissiveness of the university life. Expansion, because of the mass clientele which it implies, will make more difficult the task of winning the commitment of young people to the university's mission. Furthermore, increase of numbers as such threatens the contexts in which this educational experience can be created. It is an education which, to be of maximum value to those who receive it, and to the society which will enjoy the influence of those who receive it, should be intensified rather than extended. Expansion jeopardizes university values, and in doing so it reduces the value of university education to students and to society. It thus creates an elaborate deception of the public.

OLD EXPECTATIONS AND NEW RESPONSES OF STUDENTS

This is the background against which we have to see the student experience at the present time. They often arrive at university with two distinct and contradictory, indeed unrelated, sets of assumptions. In the first place they expect an elevated intellectual atmosphere and look forward to a mysterious experience which will result in intellectual transformation: they expect to emerge with new power. They are vague about how such transformation will be accomplished and temperamentally ill-disposed to the idea of its imperceptible gradualness. They have little idea of what might be entailed in the process, but there is a vague hope of increased articulateness and heightened understanding. It is a set of assumptions to which disillusionment is an almost necessary consequence; unless, from the outset, someone with time and sympathy is prepared to give this aspiration realistic dimensions, the strength of this pristine aspiration will never be harnessed. The mere experience of university routine will otherwise be enough to destroy it. The other assumptions are those of the youth culture —that the university is the confrontation with an alien and somewhat suspect world, that it threatens the individual's tastes, attitudes, life-habits and values, and that this threat is to be resisted.

Clearly these assumptions do not have this degree of precision and articulateness in the minds of those students who hold them. They are not conscious responses. They appear to be more clearly manifested in those whose subjects of study allow them to think in terms of a set of skills to be impersonally acquired and carried off—without the need even to breathe the atmosphere of the place in which learning has to take place. At their worst, they represent a refusal to grow up or to surrender the advantages of being young, and in particular a refusal to be educated. The desire to be transformed without having to undergo the suffering of change implies a resistance to academic commitment: the personality remains free of obligations, and the university experience is detached and impersonal—as compartmentalized as are the activities of work in contemporary society. There is little conception of the need for an investment of the self in the process: university obligations are a routine, to be kept at a minimum. To get away with a good result without actually having to be involved in the process of learning is more important than to understand or to be educated. There is a widespread mistrust of intellectuality and contempt for those who cultivate the intellect or devote themselves to cultural concerns. The union newspaper knew the situation well, when in its well-meaning way it directed an editorial to freshmen, and told them that 'Culture is not really a dirty word'.[1]

Disenchantment with the university is by no means an uncommon experience for students. There is the deadening routine of mass institutions; the queues, the inevitable overcrowding; the extensive petty pilfering.[2] Refectories are frequently more reminiscent of London street-corner cafeterias—but less

[1] The foregoing paragraph and, in somewhat amended form, several other paragraphs first appeared in my article 'Youth Culture and the University', *The Cambridge Review*, vol. 85, No. 2059 (26th October 1963), pp. 50–2, which I reproduce here by kind permission of the editors.

[2] Thefts from students of valuables, clothing and even lecture notes are a commonplace in universities. Sometimes these matters reach such proportions that, despite the reluctance of university officials to risk publicity which might tarnish the university's image, matters are placed in the hands of the police. Thefts occur not only from students, but also by students from the university. *Redbrick*, published by the students of Birmingham University (a journal interestingly reminiscent in style of the *Daily Mirror*, which, rather than *The Times* or *The Guardian*, appears to be the model for student journalism) reported on 20th November 1963, that 'pilfering from Catering Department had soared to an all-time high. . . . Since the beginning of this term 40 per cent of the knives—£62 worth—over 25 per cent of the forks, and

clean, less efficient and often offering less attractive fare. The
lavatories are liberally decorated with *graffiti* which would be
quite in tone with down-town public conveniences. The quickly
deteriorating furniture of common rooms and lounges, sometimes speeded on its way by deliberate acts of vandalism, is
over-used and completes the depersonalized institutional atmosphere. But in such institutional contexts young people have
to live. It is not surprising that much of their behaviour reveals
little sensitivity to others, when others are just part of the institutionalized mass. So one finds that essentially private types
of behaviour are indulged in in very public places. Parents on
casual visits are sometimes shocked to find so much 'snogging'
in the public parts of union buildings and even of university
buildings. Obviously no one finds it his business to interfere:
and the much-prized 'university atmosphere' for some appears
to stimulate neither self-discipline nor social constraints. Young
people in the mass often appear to be out of touch with the
established values of the universities they populate.

In the mass university, too, there appears to be a heightening
of *Us-Them* responses. The bigger universities are, the more
likely it is that two cultures develop—not Snow's two cultures
of arts and sciences, but the more tragic separation of staff and
students. Students increasingly associate only with students;
from them they acquire their categories of norms and values for
interpreting their social situation. The facile dichotomy *Us-
Them*, helps students to regulate their responses to a strange new
world. It provides ready-made stereotypes of behaviour, and it
is buttressed by all the paraphernalia of the contemporary
youth culture. The *hip* and *square* categories, the generational
lines of cleavage which they imply, are readily applied in the
university context—and more especially since intellectualism,

---

more than half the spoons, worth £17, have been stolen from the Union's
seven service points. The figures for cups and other implements are similar. . . . The refectory has also has its troubles. Over £800 worth of cutlery
and cups have been borrowed . . . since the refectory opened last year.' The
same issue of this journal reports: 'Third-year student S . . . L . . . reports
having a wallet containing £15 stolen from his case in the Library cloak-
rooms.' There is also a story that money from the student newspaper
collecting box in the Medical School had twice been stolen. Loyalty to the
University and even to the Union appears to be lacking.

civilized values, good manners and cultural concerns are precisely the hall-marks of the stuffy fuddy-duddies as the entertainment leaders of the youth culture depict them. It is probably only a minority of students for whom these categories have firm meaning and who are not at times ambivalent in their responses, but the pervasivenss of the youth culture tends to define and structure social situations for young people in these terms. The extent of the *Us-Them* response is the extent to which young people are insulated from the values of the university, into which the teaching staff is supposed to socialize them. In fact the young socialize themselves, drawing little from the university experience except as a specially permissive context of the youth culture. Apathy and loutishness, periodically condemned by the Union officials themselves, become widespread responses, while there is a strong belief that 'academics are not much interested in us'.

The *Us-Them* response is conditioned by ignorance—a complete absence of information about the nature of the university's mission, its wider concerns and its traditional values. Many students learn very little about the university to which they belong (indeed the very idea that the 'belong' sounds almost quaint). Except in the context of games, their loyalties to it are low. Universities characteristically lack channels of internal information. As they grow and diversify, so they become too many-sided for students to feel that they *know* the university, and can become committed to it. Yet often there is no effective smaller unit with which students can become strongly involved, except in some cases, the department. But departments are themselves often too specialized, too narrowly instrumental to take on the community functions which strengthen allegiances and summon loyalties. Some departmental heads—viewing their function in professional, intellectual terms—prefer to maintain a certain impersonality within these units. Finally, in the sense of the university's values and its mission to introduce young people to a wider intellectual culture, the department is ill-suited to be the sole unit of identification for the student. Nor do all students respond very readily to the idea of committing themselves to the university or its mission. Increasingly used to the impersonal character of institutions from their now enlarged or comprehensive schools, they reach a point where they merely use the facilities rather than become involved in an intellectual community. Often they do not want the university to impinge much upon them. They are not realistically prepared for any challenge to the values they have brought with them, nor for any inducement to develop a critical faculty towards them. Often when the first millennial dream of transformation is over, they settle for a mechanical relation to their studies and disengagement with everything else for which the university exists.

As the disillusionment with the prospect of painless transformation grows, and as university life is increasingly revealed as merely a shoddy extension of life-patterns learned before, in a context where (compared with school and home) people care less about you, so the trumpeted claims for the university (by Vice-Chancellors at Freshers' Conferences, for instance) grow more hollow, and the inarticulate disinclination to commit oneself to academic pursuits, beyond the strictly necessary and the mechanically routine, grows stronger, Disillusionment is frequently expressed—about the crowded time-tables; the dreary routine lectures with blackboards covered with formulae; the impersonality of relationships with academics, and the fact that students never meet lecturers outside the classroom, or when they do, the lecturers do not acknowledge them. Obviously this process does not occur in all cases, but it appears to be of widespread incidence in redbrick universities.[1] Some students meet inspiring tutors; some come with higher commitment from their schools, if they have been lucky enough to have had sustained contact with a master who has transmitted values and enthusiasm to them; some discover really absorbing things in their

---

[1] The phenomenon is not, of course, confined to redbrick universities. An unidentified 'Oxbridge undergraduate' began his substantial article in the *Sunday Times*, 13th October 1963, 'While there has been much talk recently about the structure and organization of universities, little account seems to have been taken of the life and problems of students themselves. . . . They are either regarded as having the happiest time of their lives, or just raw material for whatever production line the experts feel is best for the country. Yet, anyone who has come into close contact with undergraduates must be struck by the sizeable proportion who seem ill-adjusted, bored and frustrated. For many of the most intelligent and imaginative students, university has apparently not provided the intellectual stimulus and all-round education that it claims.'

subjects (but how many others discover that what they thought would be fascinating turns out to be drudgery?). Where inspiration is derived from the university context, it appears to be derived from personal contact—a type of contact which grows less common, and is less sustained, as universities grow bigger. One must, of course, be aware that those who later complain that they never meet lecturers outside the classroom, may not display much enthusiasm to do so, nor show much civilized receptivity to such encounters when they do occur. But this in itself merely illustrates the rôle which academics must play in regard to students. They must recognize both the complaint and the causes of the diffidence which make it all the easier for complaint to occur. It is they who must break into the cycle of disillusionment-frustration-criticism-diffidence. This paradoxical situation corresponds to the desire for transformation whilst yet retaining one's personality and values unscathed in the university encounter.

It is for the university to recognize this reluctance on the part of its clientele and therefore the need to be more active in the socialization of students. The university must provide a total environment in which intellectual interests, regard for cultural achievement, liberal values and critical discernment are a natural context for the student. The business of civilizing is to make what are regarded as 'artificial' circumstances (the charge which students often make against universities) into natural circumstances. The university must carry this concern well beyond the lecture-room, and this, indeed, is the only justification for universities setting up as lodging-house keepers. The need is not to provide places for students to live in, but to provide places in which young people are educated and acquire university values. It may be that over-lecturing (and many academics complain that their students are over-lectured) is a half-conscious acknowledgement in redbrick universities that the university must provide a more total context for students. The lecture-room is one of the few agencies which universities have discovered for the stimulation of the intellect and the transmission of scholarly concerns. Since these universities make little other provision, they try to deal with the general *malaise* of the university through the one procedure which is already well established, ill-adapted as it is to treatment of the disease.

But, in general, universities do not give much heed to the lack of commitment in many of their students. Indeed, they operate on entirely contrary assumptions—the assumption of a self-disciplined, committed clientele, which, given a high degree of freedom, will avail itself of the intellectual and cultural facilities provided. These assumptions are evident in the permissive atmosphere of universities and it might be argued that they are assumptions necessary to education itself. But students do not—in the main—arrive at university prepared for the rigours of an academic involvement to which they are completely dedicated. For many of them university is simply what follows from success in school—it is a prize in terms of a freer atmosphere, independence, a good time, and a necessary processing towards the attainment of a better job. Academic motivation has, for most, little part in it, yet it is exactly this which the university in conducting its operations assumes to be present. It assumed intellectual and scholarly self-discipline—two qualities against which the contemporary youth culture militates most trenchantly, even if they had been acquired in any measure in school. But although there is little reason to suppose that undergraduates possess these qualities at the outset, the university does little to inculcate them. When lecturers find that students are not highly committed they often shrug their shoulders and disclaim responsibility. One has heard them say such things as, 'Oh well, if they haven't sense to give their minds to it, it's their own funeral'; 'If they don't want to work, they shouldn't be here'.

But shouldn't they? The argument is one scarcely considered by the Robbins Committee, but that committee was hardly concerned with the education of the individual. These responses by academics are, of course, a divestment of moral responsibility just at the point at which their obligations to students are most vital. In the present situation, the responsibility of academics is not only to teach students, but also to induce them to want to be taught. (But the very word *taught* takes on an archaic ring—since many contemporary young people dislike the inequality implicit in the idea—they do not mind discussing, even on the strength of brief acquaintance with the subject, but they are less patient about learning how to explore it.)

It is still vaguely assumed that scholarly values should be inhaled from the atmosphere of universities. But the atmosphere has changed: the clientele itself has radically affected it. In the past it seems that people brought with them to the university values which were much less dissonant with the university's business than is now the case. At the time adult society was *still* respected, and the accumulated knowledge of society was esteemed, so that those who entered universities, even if not always desperately keen to learn themselves, were not root-and-branch opposed to what learning stood for. There was not then a generational sub-culture, promoted by mass-media, with values largely alien to those of the academic and cultural tradition of our society. The universities had less need to concern themselves with socializing their intake, with transmitting an appreciation of scholarly values to them. In addition, they could claim less responsibility than they can legitimately claim now. People came at their own or their fathers' expense more frequently and their education was seen as something for their own personal benefit, or as a personal accomplishment, in which society at large was not really involved, certainly not in the way in which society's supposed needs for university-educated people are now emphasized. Universities were not asked, as they now are, by grant-awarding authorities, to give details of the progress of particular students in receipt of public money. In the welfare state the universities have—or should have—new responsibilities, not the least of which is that of ensuring that they have done everything possible to win the commitment of their increased clientele to the educative process in which they are to be jointly involved. But as numbers have increased and deficiency of commitment has become more pronounced, so the tutorial system, which is perhaps the best systematic method of winning this academic response from students, has been placed under greater strain. It often exists more fully on paper than in reality, for the satisfaction of vice-chancellors and others sufficiently 'far-up' the hierarchy to know relatively little of the grass-roots experience of the students. In universities, no less than in other institutions, information is corrupted as it goes upwards, as successive ranks of the hierarchy justify themselves in their reports, and rationalize and formalize 'available information'.

The failure of the universities to evolve an appropriate process of socializing students has been all the more accentuated because the prevailing social and cultural context supports university values less than it used to do. To say this, at a time when pressure to get in to universities has been so much increased, and when universities make daily headlines for the Press and television, may seem paradoxical, but it is precisely this popularization which threatens the universities most. Their mission proceeds best when it proceeds quietly—its real concerns are not news or newsworthy, and the consciousness of newsability is itself a corruption of their purposes. But today universities are reliant on a public which is less informed about them and their rôle in society and less committed to the maintenance of their distinctive values. This is expressed, at the simplest level, in the failure of parents to appreciate the need for young people living at home to do academic work in the evenings and in the vacations; in the general public's mistrust of the permissiveness of university life, especially when students flaunt their leisure on sunny days and appear not to work. (This mistrust, interestingly, now gains more substance as permissiveness is misused and scholarly commitment declines.) The very popularity of universities jeopardizes their character, and the persistence of their endeavour. But the character of the wider society has altered in other ways, ways which particularly affect the clientele which the universities recruit. They are now more alienated from the values espoused by universities than ever before.

THE PERVASIVE YOUTH CULTURE

In contemporary society young people live in a much more segregated generational context than they did. No doubt youth has always, and appropriately, expressed its rebellion, but it has never before existed in a circumstance where the gestures of rebelliousness have been manufactured for the young as they now are. Mass communication and mass production have made possible the dissemination of what might be termed expressive postures and expressive products. These products are highly profitable to their producers and distributors, but we are still quite unaware of their 'social costs'. Today we have an industry concerned with the canalization and manipulation of youthful rebelliousness, which it succeeds in transforming into delinquescent, anti-intellectual defiance. Prospective undergraduates are as involved as consumers in this market as are most other youngsters—intelligence alone is no protection against compulsive generational behaviour which is, on the one hand, astutely exploited, and on the other, insufficiently inhibited by older generations. Had distinctive class patterns of behaviour prevailed among young people, middle-class youngsters would have been insulated from the growing conformity of the youth culture by the class values learned in their homes and schools. Generational segregation, the enormous increase in real income among young people (earned or given as pocket-money), the replacement of parental and scholastic values and tastes by those of more aggressive and less disinterested agencies—all this has meant the increasing conformity of styles and values within all classes of the younger generation. In this situation education—necessarily transmitted from older generations—appears to have less and less to do with attitudes, tastes, standards and morals, and to be reduced to skills which leave unaffected the character of the individual who has acquired them.

The present youth culture does more than give organized expression to what might be classed as 'natural' youthful rebellion. The postures of the youth culture constitute a generational defence-mechanism against the charge of failure in a society which places a high premium on educational success. The response is that 'we never accepted success in those terms, anyhow'. But the rationalization for failure, which the vast majority need in some form or another, is accepted as a cultural mode, even by those who succeed—or who are succeeding—partly as an insurance against future failure, but also because in the youth culture this type of success has been devalued, and other sub-cultural goals have been substituted. An alternative reference group has been established: instead of parents, teachers, elders and mentors, there are contemporaries, and their judgment matters more, since more of life is lived with them. It is nothing new for young people to debunk the values of their elders, but the process of debunking appears to be more serious and systematic; it has been transformed into ready-made attitudes and commodities which the young individual *must* possess. Those who exploit this market—journalists, entertainers, manufacturers—naturally go on record as being liberal, progressive and on the side of youth (as if teachers and parents were in some curious way always against youth). Their concern is not for the young people—who will one day be not-so-young—but is a form of social discrimination in which generational divisions have merely replaced class or racial divisions.

All of this means that students today are very much less differentiated from young people outside the universities than they used to be, and that many bring these manufactured generational values with them into the universities. Although at an idealized level these youngsters are motivated to come to university by the prospect of obtaining social power and income through education, the university also has an appeal as a permissive context in which a good time can be had. The culture in which these young people participate is not only different, but also hostile to the values of the universities, and thus, because of their permissive atmosphere, the universities are themselves vulnerable. The heroes of this youth culture illustrate this point. These heroes are socially mobile 'stars' of the entertainment world, and their accomplishments are often imitated at the cost of considerable effort. Their social mobility has not depended on training, intellect, civilized values or liberal education (nor, be it noted, on competitive examination). Indeed, these would be positive hindrances to the 'discovery' of those native talents from which success springs. (There is at least one celebrated case of a 'student' who gave up his studies for the prospect of stardom in the entertainment world.) Success in this case owes nothing to what the star has been able to make his own of the accumulated cultural tradition, and not much even to hard work.

But rapid and glamorous achievement are the very antithesis of success in the university, where close acquaintance with accumulated knowledge and its development are vital to proving one's competence. The myth of easy, overnight, untutored success is part of the entertainment ideology of the youth culture— and it is success which can be intimately appreciated by a very wide audience, the whole generational reference group. Academic success is hazardous; subject to frequent hurdles, each of which is the preparation for a higher one to follow, and with an audience which, in terms of intelligent appreciation, grows ever smaller and less easily impressed. And it is all hard work, all the way. Nourished on the values of the youth culture, there is less willingness to postpone present gratifications for future benefits than once there was. Marriage is earlier, and, egged on by the mass-media and by some academics, sexual experience is earlier still. University education assumes the self-discipline of its students as a necessary concomitant of the permissive atmosphere it provides; it assumes willing postponements of alternative activities and ends. Marriage, money and the pleasures which money can buy, and time-taking pursuits such as motoring (and motor-making) are ill-adapted to the university context. But for those brought up in the contemporary youth culture the demands of the university, and the circumstance of learning are in themselves acute threats to pleasure. Learning imposes a sense of deprivation. It means, if the rules are followed, less money, less time for pleasure and less opportunity for extensive social contact. Study is largely sedentary and solitary, but the youth culture is active and gregarious. The social pressures on young people, from which we do so little to insulate our students, make it more difficult for them to sacrifice time, money and pleasure for the sake of cultural and intellectual enrichment—two commodities rapidly losing value, and no longer regarded as rewards in themselves. The demand for fun and money is such that one has met students who wanted to rearrange the times of graduate seminars so that dances might be more easily attended, and others who, though in receipt of a full grant, have surreptitiously undertaken paid employment in term-time, or less surreptitiously when the paid employment has been with a dance band earning quite 'big money' several nights a week.

The pressures of the youth culture make the retention of scholarly values more difficult even among those who are more committed to them. Gresham's law operates, and more comes to mean worse—not necessarily because of the lower intellectual quality of students, but because the universities have devised no way of protecting their values in the face of a large new unsocialized clientele. The permissive context itself militates against 'doing anything about it'. It is easier for academics, if they perceive these trends, to seek refuge and solace in their own work: moral responsibility is not readily accepted and in a situation where the rewards and prestige go for published work or for participation in university politics, or work on public

committees, it is easier to disregard the wider implications and
obligations of teaching, for which, no matter how well it is done,
there is little recognition and small extrinsic reward. If the personnel can avoid the implications of this situation, the clientele
clearly prefers a situation where it is less troubled, even if,
from time to time it resents the lack of interest shown. There is
a prevailing mood which favours non-interference in student
affairs—'it's their life', it is said. But education is necessarily an
interference, a moral commitment to the well-being of students;
since education implies interference, re-structuring of orientations and values, the circumstances in which education takes
place have also to be subject to interference. To use the word
'interference' is to accept the word of the *laissez-faire* theorists
in universities; as 'help' and 'participation', 'interference' is an
implicit necessity of the system.

THE NEED FOR THE IVORY TOWER

If I am right in my foregoing analysis, then it seems to me that
universities, if they are to maintain their mission, must take
radical steps to insulate young people from influences which not
only distract them from education, but create conflicts about
the values which they should accept. It is frequently asserted
that the universities must not lose touch with 'real life'. Just
what is meant by 'real life' is somewhat elusive. In an age of
mass communication it is hard to see how knowledge of the
main social activities, of political, social and educational debate,
and the changing course of fashion, can be avoided, wherever
one is. Frequently the argument is that halls of residence protect
and cloister students too much, that there is something more
vital in roughing it in digs. As a warden of a hall for some years
I found it a curious idea in colleagues that they should believe
that a landlady was more real or more relevant to students than
I was. The argument sometimes had a curious class overtone—
that working- and lower-middle-class life (and most digs were
of this type) was more robust than that of other classes—an
assumption which, true or false, merely reflected a preference.
Whatever else, there was no doubt that the facilities of such
digs did not participate deeply in the distinctive traditions of
English universities. A great many of the students themselves

I   129

were from these classes and needed no deepening of insight in these respects, but rather the enlargement of horizons which a more pervasive university atmosphere alone could provide. The 'real life' argument sometimes came from technologists, who found in it their counterpoise to academicism, and revealed in it their anxiety about some of the university traditions for which they felt themselves ill-adapted. Their demand for 'real life' as they chose to call it, was merely a further evidence of the pressures which these disciplines impose on the universities and which militate against distinctive academic traditions.

When the argument for the exposure of students to more 'real life' is used in support of the location of universities in cities, one can only suppose that it means that students should be exposed to the horrors of the motor transport situation and parking, and should go to town dances.[1] In fact our incoming freshmen have never been so worldly-wise as they now are, never so completely indoctrinated with the values of the wider society (and I do not exclude the ex-service generation in which I was a student). They have heard and seen and imbibed much more of the world's values. Only a few years ago students were much more favourably disposed to a whole complex of cultural values

[1] It is somewhat difficult to understand the attraction of siting universities in industrial areas, except for the political appeal of showing that they do not belong exclusively to the snob environment of cathedral cities. Mr. Harold Wilson said at the Labour Party Conference (*The Times*, 2nd October 1963): '. . . let us try and see that more (universities) are sited in industrial areas where they can, in some way, reflect the pulsating throb of local industry and work in partnership with the new industries we seek to create.' But apart from the less congenial atmosphere for study, the problem of digs, parking, traffic, noise, dirt, unavailability of local labour, absence of cultural facilities, there is also the important fact that most academics do not like to live in industrial environments, and that in a period when their specialized labour is certain to be scarce, universities in industrial cities are unlikely to attract the best staff. Mr. Wilson's point was perhaps not really made for the sake of universities, but for the sake of industrial areas, since, according to *The Times*, he went on to say that 'not enough thought has been given to the establishment of the new universities which could help to revitalize areas.' This statement reveals little concern for education. It reminds one of the claims of Stevenage when, some years ago, it sought to attract a university and advanced as grounds the significance of a university for local trade and the opportunity it would provide for local architects who needed to have something big 'to have a go at'.

than they are now. A decade ago popular music was not nearly so much a part of student culture as it has now become. Students then were conscious of the expectations of others that they should aspire to things more consonant with university values. Partly as a consequence of the expansion of mass-media with all the prestige of its curious techno-demagogic authority, the values of young people have considerably altered, and their readiness for the challenging context which a university at its best should provide, has diminished.

The university now has to begin a process of 'de-indoctrination' of young people before its own mission can be begun, since its clientele is probably more alienated from university values than any previous generation of students. It thus becomes vital for a university to extend and intensify its influence over its students and to create a pervasive atmosphere in which its own values are dominant, unequivocal and resistant to the values of the wider society. The extraordinary increase in the influence of commercial and entertainment values in our society has as yet met no positive response from the universities, except perhaps in the emergence of the television-don, doubtless single-mindedly seeking to raise the tone of public discussion. It is true, of course, that universities lack the apparent authority of the mass-media, lack their technological slickness, their evident efficiency, conspicuous wealth, and capacity to create fashions. They cannot enter the public lists in a conflict over values. But ought they to accept the values of these media; ought they not to maintain a mission to transform by education, the wider society which the mass-media now so dominate? To do this, the university must re-immerse students in precisely those ideals and values which in 'real life' have become, so often, sullied. The university needs to be a place apart, transmitting the values of academic integrity, sound scholarship and cultural achievement and, for all these things, winning the commitment of students. Its weapons in the struggle for the minds of students must be insulation from the wider society; the intensification of academic values in university life; the infusion of these values into every area of its activity, no matter how ancillary. There is no reason why the lodgings office, the bursar's department and the refectory should not be as fully imbued with humane, academic and cultural values as other branches of the university—and it is most vital that this should be so in halls of residence. Nor need the universities fear the response of the clientele, as they now so manifestly do in their pusillanimous temporizing on basic issues: if they can but grasp the millennialist dreams of the freshmen, their more positive confrontation is likely to be both understood and accepted by students themselves.

To make evident the nature of the precious shared commitments it is offering, the university needs to take these young worldlings out of the world a little and into the ivory tower. It must given them other ideals than those of the dubious jazz-musicians, the popular press, pop singers, TV commentators, women of easy virtue and the contemporary satirists, whose sayings and doings so dominate the mass-media, and about whom youngsters know so much more than they know of philosophers and scientists. If the universities are to have an impact on the wider society it must be when their undergraduates *return* to it, after an adequate education, and after making clear to them the nature of the commitment which is implicit in their decision to become students. It means, of course, the acceptance by academics of much more work and personal concern for students, but if the universities can return people to the world who have acquired critical eyes, whose values are not automatically those of a conformist (sometimes, of course, conformingly non-conformist) mass culture, they will probably achieve more towards remarking our society than they will ever do if they confine their rôle to that of mere institutes of instruction.

EXPANSION AND 'BIG UNIVERSITIES' AS A THREAT TO EDUCATION

The student's experience of the university is threatened by two internal phenomena—departmentalization and expansion. The civic universities in particular tend to be structured as collections of departments—and all too often a student's total university experience is conditioned by this circumstance. His understanding of the wider concerns of the university is undeveloped, and his loyalties to those wider concerns is unengaged. Only the Union and the halls of residence mitigate this pattern of cleavage, and the Union tends now to be too big an organization to offer really good facilities of an educational kind to any except the tiny minority of the politically active. In large institutions dominant patterns of cleavage are not counteracted by centralization but rather by the establishment of alternative lines of subdivision, which create unity in diversity by the creation of many small cross-cutting associations.[1] Departmentalization is clearly a consequence of specialization, associated with increasing emphasis on learned skills, but its consequence tends to be that no department is much concerned with the maintenance of the more general values of the university as a whole. The results can be seen in one especially cogent example though it has other applications: students often gain a narrow impression of their own subject, fail to see any connection between disciplines, are not introduced to wider questions, and take as a *natural order* of objective categories the breakdown of subjects into departmental concerns.[2]

Expansion will alter the nature of the university and will diminish what students can derive from it. Much has been made in the Robbins Report and elsewhere of the maintenance of the staff-student ratio. The elementary fallacy is recurrently committed of assuming that a ratio of 1 staff member to 8 students is the same thing in an institution of 10,000 as it is in an institution of 1,000. In fact little is so irrelevant to the texture of social relationships as this artificial ratio: the total number is

---

[1] The importance of this principle has been appreciated at York where the authorities have rejected the idea of one central Union in favour of a plurality of smaller student associations based on residential colleges. There can be little doubt of the superiority of this arrangement in the modern large university in terms of its value for the individual. The Unions elsewhere are, of course, likely to persist, despite their declining value to individual students as universities grow larger. They continue simply by force of institutional persistence and the automatic receipt of income collected for them by the authorities as an obligatory part of student fees. Much of the money is spent on relatively few student athletes. The Unions are, of course, supported by the equally small numbers of politically-conscious students who use the mass-organization as an arena in which to test their political strength and discover power. Even within its first term of operation the decision against a central Union at York was the subject of bitter comment by the Presidents of other university Unions.

[2] Some of the newer universities have been well aware of this problem. The University of Keele has, since its inception, insisted on studies spanning three faculties, and the University of Sussex has deliberately abolished departments in the attempt to 'redraw the map of learning'.

more significant in determining the atmosphere of an institution. The ratio is a typical piece of quantitative misinformation about the qualitative. When staff reach a certain number they form a society of their own, self-sufficient and gaining all they need for social and intellectual intercourse from among themselves. They have less impact on students, and two sub-cultures develop within a collectivity in which the interests of the two groups stand in ever less clearly understood relation to each other. Among a hundred staff and a thousand students there is a possibility that everyone can know everyone else—the contours of the community at least can be discerned. But when staff number five hundred, it is likely to be the experience of each individual that he actually knows *fewer* people even among the staff. Many surface contacts replace a smaller number of more significant associations. The university acquires an impersonal atmosphere, men become anonymous to each other, and this circumstance dictates social relationships. Communication —the vital business of universities—is reduced, information is increasingly confined to the instrumental, the sense of shared participation in a meaningful enterprise disappears, sometimes for academics as well as for students. The ideal of the impact of mind on mind is surrendered, occurring only randomly here and there. The basis of confidence of students in staff, and respect of staff for students, diminishes. The academic increasingly finds himself 'doing a job' for a university which increasingly expresses its regard for him in strictly material terms, communicated through bureaucratic administrative procedures. As the university grows in size, he is less involved in its decision making, less committed to it as an investment of personal goodwill; the manifestation of goodwill may, indeed, be regarded by the more completely bureaucratized as eccentric behaviour. As the two sections of the university live in increasingly impersonal relationship—which I have underscored by calling them 'personnel' and 'clientele'—so the academic absolves himself from moral responsibility for students. They cease in the strict sense to be regarded as persons with personal claims. For some this circumstance permits judgments that 'what is wrong with this place is the type of students we get'—without much commitment to doing anything about altering that type.

Yet the current advocacy of bigger universities goes virtually unchallenged.[1] Bigger is assumed to mean better. The case of larger universities appears to rest on a variety of rather curious associations.[2] Bigger universities, it is said, alone justify the expense of cyclotrons and computers and other expensive scientific equipment. The argument might have force if universities were profit-making organizations, dependent on mass sales to justify technical innovations, but since universities are so overwhelmingly supported by state funds, either as direct grants or through the fossilized remnant of an earlier system, as student fees, the connection is meaningless. The state could supply equipment for selected institutions, which could be of any size. Since undergraduates do not work at the frontiers of research, the relevance of their number to the provision of expensive equipment is hard to understand. It is hard to see why a university has to have 1,500 or 2,000 arts and social science students before the physics department merits consideration for

[1] Thus Professor P. M. S. Blackett asserts that 'the advantages of a large university over a small one are becoming increasingly recognized. In many ways they are certainly more efficient and provide a better education because of the breadth of knowledge found in a large staff' (*The Times*, 9th October 1963). We are not informed what is meant by efficiency in this context, nor how it is related to the individual's educational experience. Or is the 'increasing recognition' merely a euphemism for saying 'it is becoming increasingly expedient to believe'? Professor Blackett continues: 'In my youth the absolute pre-eminence of Oxford and Cambridge lay not nearly so much as some think in the college system and spiritual effects of medieval architecture and green lawns, but . . . (in the fact that) they were so big; this meant they had a lot of distinguished staff.' But how big were Oxford and Cambridge when Professor Blackett was a youth? In 1923–4 Oxford had 4,163 students. It was thus little more than half as big as present-day Manchester or Leeds—even before the expansion which Robbins demands! He continues: 'In general any university which wants to be distinguished in learning and research will have to plan for a large number of undergraduates, for only so will they get from the Government the money to buy distinguished staff.' This emphasis on the mercenary quality of academic incentive reveals the fact that it is not *bigness* which attracts staff, but the persistence of the absurd relationship between size and income, which is today a hang-over from an ancient system of income distribution in our universities.

[2] The argument for larger universities which I seek here to refute, point by point, has various advocates whose assertions are essentially similar. I take them here in the order in which they were put forward by Godfrey Hodgson in 'Wisconsin Shows the Way—a commentary on the Robbins Report' in *The Observer*, 27th October 1963.

the provision of special facilities for its two or three score graduate research students.

It is said that a big American university offers a greater diversity of subjects and teachers. This is in itself true, but what is the significance of this point? How specialized do we wish undergraduate education to be: how many divisions of subjects are necessary to equip young people of this age, and in what degree of refinement? The supermarket approach to studies appears to have little to commend it, except to allow undergraduates to seek 'soft options' and bizarre combinations without anywhere acquiring anything basic. Our own recent developments, fortunately, see the need for broadening the range of student experience rather than for multiplying the courses of narrow specialization. One might doubt whether many specialized fields were particularly suitable for undergraduate study. If this is so, size merely means larger numbers of people doing rather similar courses—and in this circumstance size becomes a disadvantage on other grounds. Graduate students, who may need specialized supervision, can always move to institutions where this is available. Students rarely get a choice of teachers, except by choosing specialized courses, where this is allowed, and this is choice of course rather than of teacher. On the other hand, in small universities students often get the benefit of informal association with tutors and lecturers—which amounts *in effect* to a larger range of association with academics than they are likely to experience in the mass institution.

The other assumptions about big universities are of a similar type. It is argued that in a larger institution there are more people with whom scholars can discuss their work. But this assumes very much more academic discussion than can ever in fact take place. It would be interesting to know in just how much distinctly tehnical discussion academics actually engage with each other: in most fields the number of people with whom such discussion is possible outside one's immediate department (and sometimes even within it) is probably relatively few. Cross-disciplinary fertilization is a fairly rare phenomenon, and it seems doubtful whether big universities would really very much facilitate its increase. Specialization in most fields means that scholars must seek out those with whom they can profitably discuss their research. In a small island with (still) reasonable public transport facilities, frequent conferences, visiting lecture-ships and seminars which often bring scholars from different universities together, there seems little case for the establishment of larger universities on these grounds. Associated with this argument is frequently one which suggests that undergraduates also benefit from the more extensive mixing with students of more diversified backgrounds and of different nationalities. The argument may have some relevance to the smaller type of American state college with largely local intake. It is hard to believe that it has the same relevance in England, where in even the smallest universities there are radically diverse social types. The argument is naïve about the nature of social contacts, and the number of meaningful social relationships which the indi-vidual can sustain. It seems altogether likely that people of other nations are better known, and better cared for, in a com-munity of a thousand, than in a community of ten thousand, where they are likely to form national or regional cliques. If a university is large enough to provide people with an interesting choice of friends, from a community the periphery of which can be known, so that choice at least has meaning, then the opti-mum position from this point of view has been reached. Increase of size beyond this simply implies greater superficiality of most relationships and ultimately the absence of any relationship with the vast majority of one's fellows. Those who will be rejec-ted are those of divergent social, racial or national type, since the basis of relationships in this impersonal context will most probably be on the basis of initial similarities of values and background. Big universities impede effective social mixing.

The advocates of large universities tend to see the problems associated with them in administrative terms—they are, after all, universities in which the administration is likely to grow in power and in influencing the atmosphere of the institution. The problems they acknowledge are those of congestion, over-crowding, rebuilding and parking space. Unfortunately they tend also to assume that once they have solved these problems they have solved all problems, and that by providing good material facilities they have administered into being a university. Those problems which cannot be administratively defined, such as the maintenance of a texture of relationships, are, for the administrators, non-problems. They have been eliminated by a restatement of the university's business, by the surrender of its distinctive values. The university has been made over on the model of the business corporation. Like the business corporation profit and loss are calculated in essentially money terms—even in educational institutions, the idea that *educational* losses (as distinct from financial losses) should be entered in the ledger becomes a curiously alien thought. This, however, is the uncounted social cost of the so-called economies of scale.

One has seen some of the consequences of growth even in our own civic universities: students who, being unidentified within the university, fail to identify themselves with it; professors who have to be introduced to their own students, when, after three years in the same department, they chance to be brought together for some social occasion; halls of residence in which invited guests become an embarrassment to students who do not want to entertain them and 'slope off' as soon as possible. Of course in these universities there are professors who pride themselves on knowing all their students. But some manage to know them only by a twice-a-year handshake and a cheery word expressing in this gesture their touching faith in human contact in the university. There are others who specialize in concern about student problems, but who never really meet their students till a problem arises, and who imagine that a problem can be dealt with independently of knowledge of the man whose problem it is. This is perhaps a common fallacy about the value of mental health facilities in universities, too. Mental health provision is itself largely a symptom of the sickness of the universities, of the loss of genuine human contact between academics and students.

The weakest argument for the big universities is that if one is lecturing (soon it will be 'if a teaching machine is lecturing') to 20 students one may as well lecture to 500, and that thereby a tremendous saving is achieved in *per capita* costs. But this argument assumes that mere exposure to information is what constitutes university education. It assumes that size can be determined by the economics of exposure. The good teacher knows that 'what can be said' is much less significant educationally than 'what the student can make his own'. Slowly we move to a position in which routinized, impersonal exposure, without human contact, will provide students with the knowledge ('the notes') of which they should be in temporary possession in order to pass examinations. It has nothing to do with the tenor of their lives, it is unassociated with the spirit of inquiry, critical discrimination, broad cultural perspectives, unless these are derived from somewhere else. But if the universities are not to provide these things, where shall they be provided for the student? Where, indeed will they be maintained in the kind of society we are going to get?

Already in the older redbrick universities the routinization has advanced a long way. It is not uncommon for students to regard the material provided in lectures as the actual material which will constitute the body of knowledge to be examined. The assumptions of the clientele influence the personnel, who find it increasingly difficult to set questions which give the student opportunity to exercise his judgment or to display the width of his reading in matter not specifically included in his lecture notes. Lecturers even say, 'I can't ask a question on that because I haven't lectured on it this year.' The pattern which develops is a process of feeding information to students in lectures so that they can feed it back in examinations. Even in departments in which tutorial work is done (by no means all in redbrick universities), so dominant is the lecture course-examination nexus that the function of tutorials often appears to be as much custodial as educational—simply to keep students 'at it'. Reliance on the lecture course as the main staple of education has other consequences: it permits students to assume that vacations are free of all obligation to do academic work.

Thus the pattern of instruction becomes a 'feed-in feed-back' system. Notes are 'learned up' for examinations—answers are frequently copy-book recollections of what a lecturer said, or what he is thought to have said. Notes are sometimes passed on by those present to those absent, and some manage to perform quite well in remembering a lecturer's notes, without ever having met the man who has lectured and who marks the papers. This would not matter, of course, if the result were achieved on the strength of wide reading displayed in well-argued answers. But the system as it stands permits smartness to replace both wide knowledge and genuine ability. The occupational skill of students ceases to be intellectuality and becomes the ability to pass examinations without being exposed to a mental discipline. Passing examinations becomes remote from education as students learn the inbuilt disjunction in the system, and how to operate its mechanisms without expenditure of real effort. Being 'smart' and getting a degree whilst avoiding getting an education becomes a more-or-less approved procedure within the student reference-group. In the highly routinized large university this approach becomes the clever way to 'play it'.[1]

Clearly when teaching machines replace teachers, this abbreviation of the educational experience will not only become easier, it will become almost necessary. Our educational pundits will, of course, ignore incidentals of this kind in their bigger concern with statistical evidence of the amount of education which is taking place. As universities grow in size and as the teaching activities are routinized and mechanized, so the examination alone will reveal what the student 'knows'—however notional his knowledge, and regardless of what difference its brief retention makes to him as a person. With continued expansion students who have been 'educated' in this system will be those from whom newer teachers are recruited. Clientele and personnel will now be committed to the smart operation of the mechanized procedures: students will spend their three or four years copying notes, swotting up periodically, sitting examinations, without being very much 'stained' by any educational experience.

THE TUTORIAL SYSTEM

The tutorial system is one feature of English education which commands widespread acceptance in England.[2] Criticisms are usually made only on grounds of expense or 'waste' of teaching

[1] The system comes to resemble that observed by Malcolm Bradbury (to whom I am indebted for this point) at the large University of Indiana, where fraternities and sororities keep highly-rated essays on file, so that when the theme is set again, students need neither read nor think but simply copy up the essay which made the grade before. For a more general set of impressions see Mr. Bradbury's article in *The Twentieth Century*, vol. 161, no. 950 (February 1957), pp. 116–24.

[2] Students appear to value the tutorial system very highly. This has always been my own experience of student opinion, although they have often found individual tutors deficient. A survey of Manchester University students, directed by Salvino Busuttil (Manchester, 1962), reports: 'Some 65·2 per cent of the sample were in favour of having more tutorials, and we

resources. In the expansionist case it is a feature which tends to be ignored, or it is assumed that tutorials for five or six might easily replace tutorials for one or two. Given conscientious tutors, the system appears to be the most effective agency for the inculcation of critical discernment, and the transmission of intellectual and cultural concerns. The system is by no means universal in English universities. Thus in Sheffield in 1961 a third of the students were reported to have had neither tutorial nor seminar experience.[1] The technologists, in particular, find no use for tutorials, and again reveal the remoteness of their conception of the needs of the student from that of the university tradition when they say of tutorials, 'In our subjects there is nothing to talk about or to write essays about.' They claim that the associative aspects of the tutorial and the contact of mind with mind are gained in laboratories and drawing offices. But the differences in circumstances is apparent: the association of the tutorial of three or four people (the usual numbers in red-brick universities) with a tutor is a very different experience from the tens of students who work in a laboratory. The whole texture of relationships in the two situations is utterly different.

But even where the tutorial system is in operation it is often under strain. There are doubtless many conscientious tutors, but students I have known well often provide gloomy reports of their tutorials: 'He comes late every week'; 'He seems to be just waiting to get through the hour'; 'He isn't interested in us'.

---

have reason to believe that a good many of the 22·9 per cent who gave no answer shared the same opinion. . . . Tutorials, we were told time and again by students, were considered to be the most valuable part of university training' (p. 29).

[1] The 'Memorandum to the University Grants Committee' of the Students' Union, University of Sheffield (March 1961), expresses, though curiously written, the strong appreciation by students of the tutorial system: 'An overwhelming majority of students express the desire for both an increase in instruction in the form of seminars and individual tutorials. In our opinion the seminar and tutorial systems are essentially complementary to the lecture system: the latter being solely a one-way process. Only in either a seminar or tutorial are members of the teaching staff able to judge the individual needs of their students and therefore teach accordingly. We therefore recommend most strongly that such methods of instruction should be implemented at the earliest possible time, as apart from its obvious merit on academic grounds, these systems make an invaluable contribution to staff-student understanding.'

The moral tutor is even less meaningful than the academic tutor. Some see their students once a term when they summon them to an interview. They make no pretence of getting to know their students. The 'Any problems?' approach is common: or the question: 'How's the grant? How's the digs? How's the girl?' are a matey technique meant to reveal a 'knowing' awareness on the part of the tutor. Instead it is a technique which imposes superficial *bonhomie* on to a situation where it serves only to guarantee that the student will say he has no problems, or none which, in this context, he is prepared to discuss with his tutor. It is an approach which does much to salve the conscience of the tutor without doing much to solve the problems of the student.

THE PRESERVATION OF UNIVERSITIES AS EDUCATIONAL AGENCIES

The present condition of our redbrick universities, and their vulnerability in a period of further expansion means that we are faced with a situation of immense wastage of educational resources. Wastage occurs not only when those of high intellectual ability fail to get into university, but when *universities themselves fail* to educate those who do get in. The real issue of the times is not whether we shall have more university education, but whether we shall maintain university education at all. Or shall we maintain the name for something which becomes intrinsically quite different? To expand university education without recognizing the changes which such expansion must entail becomes a piece of political deception of the general public, whose children are promised something which in fact they will not receive.

The consequence of egalitarianism in educational matters is that unequal abilities must appear to be treated equally. Yet education and our whole system of social selection must, to be efficient, rely on discrimination. Democracy and education exist along an uneasy frontier. One can be sure that when education is represented as being democratic, in fact certain concealed manipulative processes necessarily occur in order to maintain the façade of democratic organization. As in the Dodo race everyone must win and everyone must have prizes—so that a subtle manipulative process of redirecting the aspirations of the less able, by counselling, euphemistically-described alternative soft options, and 'gradual disengagement', becomes necessary. The circumstances have been well documented in the case of the American junior college system, where the 'open-door' admission policy entails reliance on 'cooling people out', if any sort of standards are to be maintained.[1] As the apex of an educational system, universities must be discriminatory, must ensure the maintenance of a climate conducive to scholarship, must socialize young people, and eliminate all extraneous threats to their values. Educated men cannot be produced on a crash programme; our most elevated values cannot be entrusted to or transmitted by machines.

From these discussions the following conclusions emerge:

(i) To maintain university education at its best we have to be prepared to accept it as a selective, expensive and discriminatory operation. We have to recognize that there is a size beyond which universities become institutionalized at the top and out of control at the bottom. We have to demand heightened dedication from staff and their willingness to give more time to students. Lecturers must face the fact that their rôle is not a job but is a commitment to a way of life in which human values are centrally entrenched. It may be argued that to demand that more time be given to students (not necessarily to be spent in, or only in, teaching) would be to jeopardize the research work of academic staff. So it might, within the context of the university itself. But then we must have the imagination to establish separate research institutes—centres like Ottawa for the sciences and like Palo Alto for the arts and social sciences. We must be prepared to arrange generous secondments of staff for two, three or five years, according to need, and to ensure graduated promotions between these institutions and universities proper. In return for facilities of this kind, we must demand a much higher commitment to students from these privileged classes during the normal course of their university careers.

[1] See Burton R. Clark, 'The Cooling Out Function in Higher Education', *American Journal of Sociology*, LXV (May 1960), pp. 569–76; also reprinted in A. H. Halsey, Jean Floud and C. A. Anderson, *Education Economy and Society* (Glencoe Ill., 1961).

(ii) We must also be prepared to place in separate institutions those disciplines which make demands which can be ill accorded in universities. The technologies have different requirements, sometimes even appear to espouse quite alien theories of education itself. Ought they not to have institutions where they can develop with minimal tension, and with facilities specifically designed for their needs? They may argue that such institutions would lack the prestige of universities. One has yet to be convinced that in contemporary society academic learning commands such high social prestige—the pay and social standing of academics suggests otherwise. The lack of imagination in the Robbins Report is that it failed to envisage the multiplicity and diversity of possible educational provision. It seemed stuck with the university model and assumed its universal applicability to all forms of social training. One would have liked to see proposals for many types of institutions of higher education, all organized for the needs of particular types of discipline. The opposition to the expansion of universities need not be, and in this case is not, the opposition to the expansion of higher education as such. The final argument of the technologists (and of others) is that the technologists gain something of the general culture from being in association with the arts and the natural sciences. One assumes that the argument applies mainly to students—that technologist lecturers do not at this stage feel still the need to pick up gleanings of culture from their arts colleagues. Yet the assumption that the dust of culture falls from arts students to technologists is highly questionable. To put the historian and the civil engineer into one room in a hall of residence is to see that they talk of things other than the academic: often reciprocal disdain is increased by such contact, unless there is someone in the situation who is prepared to discover a common language and a set of common interests. That can be done only in the context of a community—a relatively small hall in which individuals can be well known, and their particular interests, needs and experience be taken into account.

(iii) The tutorial system seems indispensable to the maintenance of the values of English universities, but it is something which must exist at more than the paper level. One is impressed, as a newcomer to Oxford, by the thoroughness which is induced when reports have to be made in detail about students by tutors to the colleges to which those students belong. The divergence of allegiance, the separation of the examining and the tutoring agencies (and sometimes of the college responsible for the student and the man who actually teaches him) appears to provide a machinery which ensures that a tutor gets to know his pupil. This is something which does not always happen when the relationship takes place within a department, where the difficulty of colleague-relationships prevents effective checking and criticism of each other's work, which would of course be contrary to the spirit of the university system. In Oxford the cross-checks appear to operate more naturally: there is, too, a multiplicity of tutors which has advantages for the pupil, and provides the tutor with some incentive to do his work more conscientiously.

(iv) Halls of residence can be a context in which the cultural and intellectual concerns of the university can be sustained. The halls of residence have recently been under attack. On the one hand they are expensive, and on the other they imply a moral responsibility for students which not all in universities are willing to undertake. Blocks of bed-sitters are recommended as being both cheaper and 'more popular with students'. Popularity with students chances to coincide with expediency, and so the university prepares to surrender the educational commitment of its concern with residence for something which is justified as 'more in the spirit of the times'—whatever that may mean. In fact it means the abandonment of concern for students, and the replacement of cumbersome and difficult regard for their welfare as individuals by something which is administratively more convenient. Administration begins to replace educational concern, and this, of course, is the trend once organizations accept a policy of expansion into mass institutions. The new blocks of bed-sitters and the very big halls of residence (the skyscrapers) are themselves a surrender to the institutionalization even of living conditions. The hall, as a place in which people broaden their educational experience and learn to make education part of life, is one of the facilities of universities which has been suddenly almost abandoned in the past few years: quickly it has become 'old fashioned'. It projects no image, being committed to abiding values rather than to modern gimmicks. This is not to suggest that all halls have ideally fulfilled their possible functions. Some have been too hierarchic, maintaining status-divisions, initiations and the dominance of cliques—either with or without the approval of wardens.[1] Some have an imposed unnatural and forced formality on public occasions, without realizing that high formality of the authoritarian kind invariably leads to high informality of the rebellious kind. There has sometimes been a failure to realize that an even level of appropriate formality has more dignity and more value for students—in revealing to them civilized habits which can be maintained in daily life—than has the occasional high formality of the parade.

But the hall *can* be a community of a unique kind, in which university values can inform a way of life, in which individuals can express individuality, acquire personal dignity and experience security in an assured context. Tensions will inevitably exist, both inter-personally and institutionally, but halls can be places in which individuals learn to contain tensions and to deal with them. Young people can be treated as adults and induced to make adult responses; they can be induced to live up to their own best pretences and aspirations about themselves, so that these become natural to them. The concerns of the community can become the shared concerns of warden and students, from decisions about domestic details to wider ranging community concerns. This is to encourage student participation—but not to sell out to the demands of the youth culture. Individual liberty can be provided in a context of sustained concern and shared involvement. People must be free enough to learn by making fools of themselves, but in the secure context of a community this freedom is valuable rather than deleterious. There must be a high degree of formal and informal communication which occurs within a clear structure of relationships, in which wardens never cease to be wardens, never try to become 'one of the boys' or to gain confidence by undue familiarity. They must

---

[1] For an account of a system which one has seen with variations elsewhere, see the revealing article by Anthony Giddens, 'Aspect of the Social Structure of a University Hall of Residence', *Sociological Review*, 8 (July 1960), pp. 97–108.

get beyond inviting people in for sherry once a term on a rota system, but they must also know how to draw the line at accepting invitations to go to the pub with particular groups. They cannot afford to become identified with particular cliques; nor must they be remote, status-conscious individuals; they must wear authority lightly if, ultimately, firmly. Their business is to support students in coping—academically, administratively (and this becomes an increasing problem for students who find it difficult even to understand the administrative operation of the university) and socially.

A hall should be a place where learning can proceed and liberalize the specialisms of the university; it should promote activities which are consonant with the university's purposes—hikes, concerts, talks, poetry reading, music, exhibitions, as well as the dances, social occasions and sport which students will largely organize for themselves. It must provide a context of shared enterprises in which the various talents and skills of its members can be drawn into use. All of this makes it easier for engineers to talk to historians, the more so if equally new cultural experiences are being presented to them from time to time: conversation in 'living groups' gravitates quickly to banalities unless someone (a warden or his deputy) constantly works at it, introducing new ideas and opening up new vistas. In this context there need be no establishment of what we shall no doubt soon hear canvassed as an inevitable consequence of mass institutions—a counselling service. In a good hall the warden learns about a student's problems almost before the individual student himself. Counselling is simply a part of the free flow of discussion between warden and individual hall member, without there being much need for formal interviews. Knowing the problem means knowing the man, and only sustained interaction can provide that knowledge. This is the basis on which counselling can take place, and on which proper testimonials can be written (one wonders how the teaching machines will manage that, but perhaps these, too, will be routinized into a series of three or four standard forms of letters of recommendation!). All of these facilities are, of course, part of the *small* hall —only there can meaningful inter-personal relationships operate throughout the community; only in small pools can each individual have the experience of being the big fish. The hall must be a distinctive institution, and its operation cannot be conducted on the model of a hotel, a hostel, a hospital, a hostelry, a sport pavilion or a holiday-home. The small hall can be more than a mere ancillary service to the university, it can and does become a most valued and meaningful part of university education: 'You know, Warden, if I hadn't been in Hall my time at this university would have been pretty miserable.'

The small hall might be the relief from the big university, if we *must* have big universities.[1] It could be the place where individuals are not reduced to punch-cards, are not manipulated by increasingly mechanized devices. The demands of administration become necessarily dominant in large institutions, but education is a subtle, complex and highly individuated experience which surrenders reluctantly to administrative imperatives. As administrative pressures grow, so the human considerations in education, to which I attach primary importance, will be gradually reduced and perhaps eliminated. One wonders whether this is a legitimate development in an educational context, whether it is not ultimately the betrayal of the values of education. Might one not hope that in a mass society universities

---

[1] The attitude of students towards large universities, and their appreciation of small units with which they can more readily identify themselves, can be seen in Ferdinand Zweig, *The Student in an Age of Anxiety: A Survey of Oxford and Manchester Students* (London: Heinemann, 1963), pp. 98–101. 'At least half of the sample [of the students at Manchester] had only praise for the university... 53 out of 103 students "enjoyed", "enjoyed thoroughly" or "enjoyed very much" their university life. . . . *Those who had only praise for university life were often in residence in Halls* . . . or were students in small departments with a more integrated social life. . . . There were 34 other students who were critical of the university. . . . "It's too big and impersonal"; "Too large and overcrowded"; "Too cramped and restricted"; "Drab and dirty with nothing to take you out of yourself"; "Too formal, there is little personal interest on the part of the staff"; "Too much concentration on getting a degree instead of getting culture and education"; "The teaching's impersonal, a gulf exists between staff and students. In my department you can go right through the course without ever speaking to the professor". . . . There were 16 other students who voiced their criticism very strongly, disapproving of this type of university altogether. . . . "A depressing place. No bond, no pride, no sense of belonging." This criticism often came from students in big departments where the personal contact with the staff is often lost and which give an impression of overcrowding.' (My italics.)

should remain small enough to permit personal relationships
to exist and the shared experience of intellectual and cultural
concerns to become the radical alternative to administrative
expediency?

9

The Social Context of the
Youth Problem[1]
(1965)

There is a general tendency among those who express themselves on youth problems in this country at the present time to
pass very quickly from a discussion of what young people do,
and are like, to pronouncements on moral issues. Young people
are discussed in something of a vacuum outside the general context of the social structure in which they live. Those who do
discuss the youth culture, tend, in moralizing, to fall into two
distinct groups: those who suggest that young people's morals
today are not what they were; that young people have never
been less moral than they now are; that this is a situation to be
deplored and that young people are themselves to be condemned
for this. And there are those who take an opposite point of
view, and who assert vigorously that today's young people are
splendid, have never been more public-spirited, more socially
conscious and that those who condemn them are simply Jere-
miahs and killjoys. I do not want to discuss young people in
these terms at all. I do not want to condemn them or to condone them for the things that they do, to excuse them or to
accuse them.

If we examine what goes on among young people today in
the wider social context, in the context of an industrial society
undergoing a rapid process of social change, we shall avoid
moralizing although I do not even want to condemn moralizing
as such. One might say that moralizing itself fulfils certain
important social functions; after all the moral fabric of the law
and of our traditional customs provides a basis for moralizing
even though that word itself has now become somewhat pejora-

[1] The Charles Russell Memorial Lecture for 1965.

tive. What we need to recognize is that neither those who condemn nor those who praise modern youth avoid moralizing. They speak and write within the common framework of discussion. It is not the perspective from which the sociologist begins, but he may appropriately take received moral standards as data: it is in their terms that commentators make their judgments.

The sociologist's business is to analyse, as dispassionately and objectively as he can, the trends which he sees occurring in the society around him. But to discern trends does not mean, as some popular sociological publicists seem to think, that one must applaud them, or to suggest that every change is for the best in a world that will soon be the best of all possible worlds. Nor does it necessarily imply condemnation of those who adopt new behaviour patterns. Given the distinctive patterns of youthful behaviour which have become a matter of public concern, the sociologist's business is to look at the social circumstances in which this behaviour arises. Public concern is itself a matter of importance, and the assumptions of the public ought not automatically to qualify for that contempt that some sociologists accord them. New disruptive behaviour—and new types of behaviour tend to be the behaviour of new, i.e. young, people— *and* the public attitude towards it are both responses to processes of more fundamental change in social and economic circumstances. Public concern proceeds from the assumptions of received traditions and values, and these are also the only objective starting point for sociological inquiry. These, after all, are the existing customs and mores, opinions and standards— not merely the prescriptions of reformers (however enlightened) or the desiderata of libertines who, seeking divestment of responsibility for themselves, are not above elevating their own penchants into principles. Values change, of course: they may receive criticism and undergo change for either high-minded reasons, or through the impress of mindless social pressures. But in the present case the changes in behaviour are seen generally as manifestly disruptive. From the base-line of received values one may appraise the youth culture and its life styles. Only by so doing will public concern be explicable, and only so will the motive forces for youthful unrest be understood in the context of the shared expectations of older people in our time.

Clearly young people display certain behavioural dispositions in any society: animal high spirits, abundance of energy, lack of formulated standards, lack of taste, incomplete socialization characterize the young in all societies. In a rapidly changing society like our own, these phenomena become more noticeable and more evident for a number of other reasons, to which I shall turn shortly. In an industrial society young people experience uncertainty of status: the boundary between childhood and adulthood is ill-defined and confused. There are diverse standards of social expectation not only among different people, but our social institutions themselves establish rather different criteria by which to judge adolescents. The differing ages at which society expects social responsibility illustrates this. The age at which young people may marry with parental consent is still sixteen. At seventeen they may start learning to drive, at twenty-one they may vote, at eighteen they may be conscripted, at fourteen they may pay full price in cinemas, at sixteen they may see adult films, and so on. There is a wide diversity in the presumed age of adult responsibility in different sorts of social activity. I do not suggest that we could easily remedy this situation, but we need to recognize that our institutional arrangements destroy any unitary conception of an age of adult responsibility in our society. We can no longer solemnize the meaning of growing up by appropriate community recognition. Instead we expose young people to a series of hurdles which leaves them in continuing uncertainty about the stage of adult responsibility which they are supposed to have attained at any particular age.

All of this, of course, is made much worse by the changing technical practices and the changing social habits of our society. All of us know that the moral precepts with which we grew up are no longer quite adequate to the increasingly complex situations in which we find ourselves in everyday life. We find ourselves involved in personal decisions about highly institutionalized processes and in situations so complex that personal responsibility is often hard to determine. Clearly it is very hard to impress firm moral standards in a society which has grown as complex as ours, and very difficult indeed to suggest the appropriate area of personal discretion to young people who are facing these complexities for the first time.

It is all too easy to emphasize the universality of the youth problem, and very easy to find parallels with other societies, or with our own society at different periods, and from that to go on to suggest that what young people do in Britain today is what young people have always done; to affirm that young people always behave in similar ways and evoke similar responses from older generations. One would be saying that the current youth problem was just a particular manifestation of a general phenomenon, and that nothing can be done about it. Evidence in support of this thesis of the universality of the youth problem comes from the writings of Fynes Moryson, travelling through Holland and Germany in about 1595. In commenting upon the lack of good comedians in Dutch society and upon the relative success of an English troupe of players, he wrote:

'So as at the same time when some cast players of England came into those partes, the people not understanding what they sayd only for theire action followed them with wonderfull concourse. Yea, many young virgines fell in love with some of the players and followed them from citty to citty till the magistrates were forced to forbid them to play anymore.'[1]

There is a contemporary ring to this commentary which might easily be describing contemporary pop singers, such as, P. J. Proby or The Rolling Stones—except that our 'magistrates' pay less attention to the effects of entertainment.

Clearly, there *are* some constant factors in the situation. Or if we turn to the work of Charles Russell, we find that he wrote in a passage which has been partially quoted by a previous memorial lecturer, this commentary on the youth of three hundred years after the time of Fynes Moryson, the youth of the late nineteenth century:

'. . . it was not until the later decades of the nineteenth century when the ruffianism of youth had reached such a pitch as to become an absolute danger to the community that attention was thoroughly roused, and men who had the welfare of their city and country at heart grew apprehensive and began to cast about for some means of checking so alarming a development. They asked whence came these hordes of young blackguards

---

[1] Fynes Moryson's *Itinerary* (ed. Charles Hughes), London: Sherratt and Hughes, 1903, p. 373. (I am indebted to my friend, Robin Briggs, for drawing my attention to this quotation.)

who showed little promise of growing into anything better than vagabonds or criminals, what occasioned their frequent conflicts with the police, their brutal assaults, not only on enemies of their own class but on inoffensive persons who had not attempted to interfere with them.'

Russell believed that the causes were to be found in the actual limitation of the life circumstances in our large towns and cities:

'. . . where little or no attention was paid to the provision of decent dwellings, open spaces, facilities for amusement, health for body and mind, cleanliness, much less beauty. Production, rapid and cheap, and production alone was the be-all and end-all of life. Production meant work; pleasure had to take care of itself.'

Russell wrote of the narrow streets and the squalor where men were herded together, where,

'. . . the eye is never cheered and the imagination never stirred by diversity of form or colour, where fields and parks are so far away that they are but rarely seen. The conditions exist which when realized made it unnecessary to search further for the causes which filled the streets by night with bands of unruly young savages. There was in fact hardly any direction in which a boy even with the best intentions, could look for a pleasant way of spending his leisure time. The day of dreary monotonous labour over and the evening meal finished, the problem before him was what use to make of the few hours between tea and bedtime.'

Apart from drink-shops and music-halls, only the streets remained:

'Nowhere else could nature's physical energy find an outlet for surplus steam to be let off . . . but the streets are not fertile in resources, so it is not surprising that the boys should often have given play to their cravings for excitement and violent exercise by indulging their more combative instincts. Since they could not play football, what more natural than to fight each other or anyone who dared dispute their right to the pavement. . . . A party of lads from one street would band themselves together and constantly be fighting similar gangs from other streets on absolutely trivial pretexts. . . . Occasionally the police had to interfere to stop really serious rows in which hard and even dangerous blows were given not only with the fists but often with the buckle end of a heavy belt and sometimes with an earthenware mineral water bottle.'

The less rough and the less unscrupulous, Russell tells us 'gloried in the name of "scuttlers" and wore the peaked cap, hair curled well over their forehead, white neck-scarf, bell-bottom trousers with sharp-pointed clogs with heavy brass nails which formed the uniform of their class.'[1] Russell's 'scuttlers' bear a remarkable resemblance in their dress and hairstyle to the very latest styles even to the pointed shoes—apart perhaps from the brass nails. Their activities would also fit fairly well the modern scene. But these are essentially superficial similarities which conceal important differences. To cite some of the instances which have come into the Press in the course of the last few days makes evident the differences. Russell's 'scuttlers' did not do hundreds of thousands of pounds worth of damage to public property in a year (quite apart from the damage done to private property of which we have, of course, no full assessment). The public were still safe from hooligans on excursion trains or on football 'specials'. Certainly, there was not damage to trains and to rolling stock amounting to over £100,000 a year. There was not loss of life from the activities of young people on railway tracks. People could still go to the beach in the popular resorts without feeling that they would be involved in a 'rumble'. The Corporations of industrial cities did not contemplate suspending public services, as Glasgow has recently threatened to suspend late-night bus services because of rowdyism, or as Leeds has threatened to remove telephone kiosks from housing estates because of the high rate of destructiveness. Street lighting was not wantonly destroyed on the scale which is reported today. One has only to read the provincial Press of industrial areas to see how extensive this damage is as revealed in the proceedings of city corporations. Schools were not broken into and made unfit for use perhaps for several days after the depredation, so that the activities of the 'scuttlers' did not involve in cash or in the human cost anything like the cost of present-day hooliganism. Nor was the work of the agencies of public welfare, the police service, social services and the educational services, so massively frustrated.

[1] Charles E. B. Russell, *Working Lads' Clubs*, pp. 9–12.

The scale and intensity of the problem have changed, and so have the causes. One could hardly say that the life of modern youth was all production, 'the be-all and end-all with pleasure left to take care of itself'. Indeed, it might not be too exaggerated to say that almost the opposite is true for many young people in our society—that life is all consumption, which for some appears to the the be-all and end-all, with work as a residual claimant, as a dreary round, the way of obtaining money for leisure-time activities. The social context of the youth problem has in fact changed dramatically. The streets are not the only place of recourse either for vigorous exercise or for vicious activity. There are now a whole host of amenities from the educational and recreational to some which almost avowedly cater for what we might call the more animal appetites of young people. Our young people are not the social outcasts that Russell's 'scuttlers' were. They are indeed a section of society which commands widespread public attention and which commands an increasing proportion of public expenditure and on behalf of which a growing body of public servants is kept in employment.

A Charles Russell working today would need to examine rather different social causes to explain a rather bigger social problem. It could no longer be seen as a problem confined to one social class or to one group; it could no longer be seen as arising from unadjusted elements among the lower classes of society. The contemporary youth problem appears to know no class boundaries. The equality of opportunity which our society has established has extended to the field of delinquescence— those styles of behaviour which if not emphatically delinquent display every potential of becoming so. Nor could a Russell working today assume that the society in which he worked had a stable and uniform moral order which might be set over against the amorality of young people in the slums. That circumstance has gone. The immoral and the criminal are less clearly defined activities than they were; they constitute behaviour less sharply distinguished from the social expectations about the normal activities of the young.

Russell explained a great deal of the youth problem of his day in terms of economics, but explanations of that sort are manifestly inappropriate for the youth problem of today. We have, of course, become used to accepting economic explanations of behaviour and if we find that riots, defiance, rebellion and strikes occur because people are without food or without work, or because their conditions are deplorably unhealthy, then we regard their behaviour as defensible, if not excusable. We are as yet rather unready to accept social explanations. That is to say we are rather more puzzled by behaviour which has no economic motive, and which from the rational perspectives we employ—the very perspectives which make economics motivations intelligible to us—appears senseless or meaningless, wanton, or abandoned. The very fact that we say 'senseless' means that we are saying *un*understandable—not to be justified in any way. And since our teenage dissidents themselves cannot adequately explain their anti-social behaviour, it becomes so much easier for the rest of society to castigate what they do in these very terms as simply immoral, silly and wanton and to make no further attempt to explain it. Yet, we must be prepared to recognize that man's social needs are not simply economic, and that hitherto our social legislation has been too narrowly economic in character.

A great deal of what we have tried to do as social welfare has often been little more than cash payments. We have lost the sense of the importance of human relationships and we have not discovered methods of social legislation which help to support them. We have hardly begun to look at the roots of disenchantment and dissidence among young people in terms of their sources in the structure of society itself. Action to meet these problems will have to be very much more fundamental than that which amounts to merely economic action or alterations of the educational system on strictly ideological grounds (evident in the introduction of comprehensive schools). We need an assessment of the social cost of economic progress, an examination of the consequences of the process of economic and social change which—with little regard to the human consequences —have been set in motion in our society.

Since the war we have seen a teenage revolution, the growth of a youth culture as a separate and distinct phenomenon. It is not confined to an outcasted minority but is increasingly the way of life of the larger part of a whole generation. The youth culture comprises a range of distinctive attitudes, postures, life-styles and patterns of action. In response to its development there has been a growth of public anxiety, most particularly, of course, about the delinquent aspects of the youth culture, but in part also about some of the more general and less delinquent elements of the youth culture. There has been a succession of fashions. Russell's 'scuttlers' of the last century might have been the spivs in the war and post-war years; they became successively the yobos, the cosh-boys, the teddy-boys and the beats, the mods and the rockers and the greasers over the course of the last decade or so.

A number of tendencies about these styles are worth noticing. They have extended to larger groups among the younger generation; the people adopting the distinctive styles have grown younger; they have grown more gregarious; they represent more overt and more open subcultural expressions, and they are less afraid of public disapproval. Scuttlers were confined to one social class; spivs—coming to our own times—were isolated individuals battening on to society with largely economic ends in view. Cosh-boys moved about in relatively small groups, and sometimes pursued economic ends as well as indulging in violence. Teddy-boys moved in rather larger coteries. Mods and rockers congregate in mobs bigger than the forces of law and order available to control them. (With fairly vigorous repression of the mods and rockers movement part of the youth culture has now diffused itself: there are now many centres for dissident young people. There are coffee bars, clubs and dives in which the youth culture is commercially catered for.)

Each style has been increasingly successfully projected as the image of a group different from the rest of society. The names have become less pejorative, have in fact come to be both socially accepted and accepted by young people themselves, sometimes as proud labels to be worn on the back of a leather jerkin. Boys would have denied being yobos or cosh boys. Although their dress proclaimed the teddy-boys, it was always asserted that the dress did not necessarily imply any sort of anti-social behaviour. Beats chose the name for themselves, and mods and rockers— the names are derived from musical styles originally—are badges of identity. The new youth culture groups are accepted in some way as social entities; the names are used in the press, and the groups acquire objective recognition by the amount of social attention which they arouse.

What is perhaps more important is that each of these successive styles has increasingly blurred the distinction between purely delinquent forms of behaviour and normal youthful behaviour. What is avowedly delinquent and what is merely the behaviour of young people enjoying themselves has become less and less clear. The word 'delinquescent' coined by Professor W. H. J. Sprott, is not a bad one to describe the tendency of much of the mass behaviour of young people. Finally, young people's behaviour has become less and less economic in its motivation—from fraud and sharp practice by the spivs, to destructiveness, hooliganism and rowdyism on the part of mods and rockers, who congregate not only on bank holiday on Brighton beach but quite frequently in many other towns and cities.

The youth culture, then, is a distinct, identifiable social phenomenon which has now acquired the objectivity of large-scale public recognition. As generalized anti-social behaviour has increased in scale, so a minority of young people have become more frankly delinquent. Yet to say this is not to explain matters in terms of saying that young people have become more immoral. Anti-social tendencies are evident in the younger generation in all periods. What has happened in the last decade is that the social forces which normally control youthful behaviour have become less effective. The agents who control and socialize the young have become less confident of themselves, and less effective in their operation. The common morality of society itself has become more uncertain and more ambiguous in this period of rapid social change, and young people have been very much exposed to exploitation as a social group, and have become very much more vulnerable to pressures.

But although these changes have certainly occurred—and one can point to considerable objective evidence—it is also the case that the change has become *more visible*. We have become more aware of young people's behaviour than we used to be. Young people have become more observable partly because they have become more mobile, and enjoy the increased freedom which mobility confers. The middle classes in particular have had it very forcibly imposed on their attention that young people move about in the mass more and more. They increasingly invade middle class suburbs and resorts, and bring very different and very conspicuous values with them. The middle class have assumed—not without justification—their own morality to be the public morality. They might claim, and they often tacitly assume, that a great deal of our civilization rests on the moral standards which the middle class embraced in the last century. But new classes with new affluence increasingly move into prominence, and their most energetic groups, namely their young people, become especially evident in modern society.

Many of these young people have never been extensively socialized to middle-class values and there are forces of growing strength in our society—the mass-media in particular—which retard that socialization process. Thus although the youth problem has grown in size it has also increased in observability. Although large numbers of the young people who impress themselves on the attention of the middle classes do come from some of the lowest classes in society they are not, as they were in Russell's day, exclusively drawn from that stratum: the youth culture is not a class phenomenon, indeed it becomes a generational phenomenon. The youngsters from middle-class homes are involved too: the middle classes see just the same evidences at home as they see when they go into city centres. Class differences, that at one time would have protected their own young people, have now been so far eroded that there is in fact no immunity even for the children of the middle class.

In a mass society we must expect to have a mass youth problem of a generational rather than of a stratificational kind. Russell was working before the first world war essentially with youngsters from the less respectable working classes. The slums were then confined in what we might term working-class ghettoes, and the middle class did not need to know about the behaviour which went on in those ghettoes. It was only the Mayhews, the Booths, the Rowntrees and the Russells who pointed out just what went on in those parts of their own cities to middle-class people who never saw the reality of working class social conditions. Even the police did not always penetrate into those areas. When they saw fights and brawls going on they were often all too happy to see a process of social control at work which they felt was the appropriate way for 'those sort of people' to settle their problems.

Today the ghettoes and the slums have virtually gone; but

although some of the behaviour has gone we cannot assume that all of it has gone. It has simply been spread more widely and perhaps more thinly over the rest of our society. The assumption of a common morality has been shown to be false and indeed the very conception that there should be a common morality has been challenged. The mass society relies on a more naked form of institutionalized demands for conformity than existed in the communities dominated by the middle class in the last century. In this sense the personal communication of values is very much less effective than it was. We rely, and must rely increasingly, in the kind of society which we are now becoming, on the naked operation of the law for the communication of the sense of right and wrong to some groups of our young people. These age groups, mobile, affluent, liberated from home, move into city centres, move into holiday towns and spas, and display their delinquescent behaviour to the general public at large. And the general public, through organs which have been forged by the middle class, expresses shock and alarm at the consequence.

Adolescents in fact are insecure, frustrated and according to their own account, often bored. In a very impersonal and institutionalized society they communicate this insecurity, this frustration, to others. They have the money and the equipment that allows them to become a new vagabond class, vagabond in the sense that they can uproot themselves in their recreational activities if they so wish, and move anonymously—as mobile, leisured, energetic young people—to wherever the kicks are available. Since they are not fully socialized, they are a prey to those who wish to exploit them, and to exploit in particular their unformulated tastes and their awakening appetites.

If we turn to the social factors in this situation we may put them into an analytical, sociological framework. First, there is the breakdown of the spontaneous agencies of social control. The extent to which the family and the community are the immediate environment for a young person has very much diminished. This has been a consequence of the mobility which has so much increased in our society. Living arrangements are less personal; family members are more separated in their day-to-day lives. Tenements and housing estates constitute more impersonalized groupings than work-ingclass neighbourhoods of old. Children and parents move off to school or to work in different directions. The tendency is for housing and work to become more widely separated. Increasingly the context in which individuals lead their lives is impersonal and the people among whom they move are anonymous people. They are much less likely to be those who have a continuing, personal interest in their personal behaviour, no longer people with whom a sustained reputation has to be acquired.

What has happened in the separation of community and family from school and work has also happened in the area of recreation. For pleasure, as well as for education and employment, people move about more each day: for their careers they tend to move farther in the course of their life cycle. In both ways they sink fewer roots, and society is increasingly dependent on more superficial impressions of individuals than it used to be. Even as a matter of public policy (by centralizing schools, slum clearance and zoning) as well as in consequence of the economic forces at work in our society we have undermined those spontaneous agencies of social control which existed in the past. One particular consequence has been the separation of the generations and the emergence of separate life styles and separate life activities for people at different ages.

Our society is increasingly divided into age-groupings, each with its appropriate behaviour patterns, and these divisions have largely replaced the old class divisions. This means that children pass out of the control of those who really know them over a long period and who care for them as people and increasingly into the control of impersonal institutions. Other circumstances reinforce the consequences of this process. Teacher mobility in schools is one such circumstance. To know people well it is necessary to know them over time, and in a sustained way, but as teachers change jobs more frequently in some areas this becomes less and less possible. The more teachers move about, the less likely it is that schools will act as an effective agency of social control over young people. They may do so by strong-arm methods, or they may abandon the attempt.

There has also been a change in the methods of production. New techniques, new education, new qualifications have meant that older people have increasingly found it difficult to win respect among the young. The young know the latest most improved techniques. On the other side of the economic process there have been changes no less important in consumption patterns. Affluence and the redistribution of income has meant the redistribution not only between social classes but also between generational groups. It has meant that even young people not at work now share in very much larger affluence than would have been conceivable in Russell's day. We can read commonly in newspapers that sixth-formers sometimes have spending money of £3 to £4 a week. Young workers often have much more than that. But affluence combined with uncertainty of status has meant that young people are even more in need of confirmation of their social status—hence their search for power and prestige. They become victims in a competitive system of prestige-seeking, as they demand respect from those whom they come increasingly to value more, namely those from their own age group. The age group now becomes the crucial 'reference group' in which each individual seeks reassurance about his own identity. Thus young people become the victims of novelty and fashion and sensationalism in the search for prestige-conferring objects and behaviour.

But all of these things are extremely unsustaining experiences. The addiction to novelties and sensationalism provides no satisfaction: they must be perpetually renewed. Novelties have no use at all once they cease to be novelties. The search for prestige in the peer-group thus becomes a tension-maintaining activity for young people. Tension is sustained by the very surrender to fashion, since each new fashion is of only limited duration in conferring the prestige which the individual seeks. Worse than this, the addiction to novelty and sensationalism is also a disposition which makes it more difficult for the individual to acquire a stable sense of values. Buying the fashionable and the novel is an extremely uncumulative activity; the individual gains his experience only very slowly from participation in the race to be up-to-date in which his mistakes contribute nothing to his education in culture or taste. The steady transmission of more stable values to young people is thus undermined.

All of this is not without its institutional aspects—in the development of an industry which grows up to feed the youth culture, to titillate the emotions and basic appetites of the young by keeping going the supply of novelties and sensations. The entertainment industry has grown in enormous proportions in this country since the war and a large part of its growth has been in response to the discovery of the new market. Young people are the new rich with uncommitted incomes who can buy entertainment at high prices. The trade in the symbols of power, prestige, sex and aggression goes on, and the youth culture has become an in-built part of the economy. To attack it might soon become as difficult as attacking the motor car industry since so many jobs will perhaps depend on these 'services' to young people. We see then, a society in which enhanced technical knowledge increases, and is put to a particular use on behalf of the youth culture. But this also means that young people acquire new knowledge, new techniques, without necessarily acquiring education of taste or the sustained control of the emotions. They acquire high productive skills and large incomes but have not yet opportunity for the acquisition of social, moral, political or spiritual wisdom from their social experience. In instrumental societies in which knowing how to do things, and knowing the skills for particular jobs, is what matters, wisdom becomes a very much devalued commodity, but it is this type of wisdom which young people probably find that they need in later life when they have missed the opportunity of acquiring it.

In contemporary society achievement stands at a high premium. But if success is the universal goal, it is clear that only a few will ever attain it. In terms of the high demand for success most men will feel themselves to be relative failures, unless there are other goals and values which reassure them of their social worthiness. As we have moved from a society in which the stable community was the context of life for most individuals, to a more mobile, more impersonal and more institutionalized social system, so we have ceased to assess merit in terms of stable character, and have come increasingly to measure it by the appearance of success. Thus the image—which is a superficial façade—becomes a more important determinant of status than does character—the enduring dispositions of the individual. Those who do not achieve, those who cannot manipulate success symbols in a competitive system, inevitably experience frustration. But in a highly selective system, which operates by inducing high aspirations as widely as possible, most men cannot attain to that which they aspire, and many fail in even the limited ambitions which they entertain, or which parents and teachers entertain for them.

So the system undermines, in the young person, the capacity for self-respect by creating in the majority the strong sense that in some way they have failed. Yet if it appears that they fail in terms of society's values, young people are sufficiently resilient to reject this judgment: they deny the legitimacy of these values, and they set up counter-values of their own. They find some other system of reference, other groups which offer prospect of self-respect, success and achievement, in other terms. This, then, is what the youth culture provides for the young—the opportunity for prestige and power, the confirmation of status. Any group, community or stratum which provides these things for the individual, becomes his major point of reference—the only collectivity which he really values and this because it is this collectivity which values him.

Intrinsically, the youth culture's values are more animal, and its activities are nearer to unsocialized primitive appetites, and this, too, gives it a relative advantage over against the values entrenched in established social institutions. Since it offers any young person a chance of success and status in terms of these values, it becomes a pervasive generational sub-culture. It offers success in spite of educational failure, in spite of the judgments of the social selection system. Even those who do not fail in educational terms find it difficult to dissociate themselves from so compelling a sub-culture, and from the alternative confirmation of status which it provides.[1] But it is essentially for the majority—and the majority have a sense of failure borne in upon them—for which the youth culture operates most fully. Since success is at such a premium and failure such a widespread experience, there is strong pressure to succeed illicitly, in terms of the values of the youth culture, and in terms which are increasingly delinquescent. Violence and hooliganism are ways in which young people can display power and win respect in their own group. But they have other functions. They provide a way of kicking back at society at large, not so much at people as at impersonal institutions which have in effect, denied one respect

[1] For a discussion of this point, see Ch. 8, 'The Needs of Students', pp. 125 ff.

in a system which has made one a failure. Those shut out of the educational race seek other criteria of achievement in other activities. As society has emphasized intellectual and academic ability increasingly, those who lack these attributes, or who lack the motivation to cultivate them, reject the system which emphasizes them.

The growing 'anonymity' of our social life facilitates this development, not only as this circumstance is experienced at school and in the community, but also as it develops in the work situation. As industrial concerns become larger and the division of labour becomes more extensive, the work task becomes, for many, less meaningful. Tedium becomes the common experience of work. And yet the modern worker is frequently condemned because he shows no loyalty and no attachment to his job. But loyalty must be evoked in relation to other people rather than to machines and conveyor belts. And even beyond the machinery of modern industry, where are the people to whom the worker might be loyal? Many of our industries appear to have no permanent owners. Who can say, at this moment, who, for instance, owns the shoe factories? Shares change hands all the time; take-over bids may be in progress any day. In the modern investment process there is no investment of loyalty by those at the top. Can we reasonably demand an investment of loyalty at the bottom? What is there in the structure of the contemporary work order to win the commitment, concern, respect of the worker? Our industrial system is less and less characterized by person-to-person obligations except in the informal groups of workers themselves: institutionally it supports no moral cohesion. Loyalty, when reciprocated, helps an individual to feel personally needed, to feel that he is of some consequence. But the work-order into which most of our young people are thrust offers no return for loyalties exacted from them. At an age where they often quite desperately need reassurance of worth and status, the system vouchsafes them nothing of the kind. The pop-songs, if we take them seriously, and the pop-films, make evident their need—the need of the young person who, as they put it, wants to be 'a somebody'.

The teenage life-style, then, is largely a response to the needs of adolescents which are not fulfilled elsewhere in modern society. That it is a spurious solution to the problem, is evident. Like a personality neurosis, it offers solutions at a level which only sustain the tension of the situation. The teenage life-style has grown up within, and been legitimated by, the entertainment industry, which gives the values of the youth culture a certain objective reference. Entertainment provides the model for teenagers—a model which is more effective than the model which was provided in the eighteenth and nineteenth centuries by clergymen and school teachers. It is more effective partly because it is more ubiquitous and has better and more prestigious technical means of communication; partly because it has no educational aim; and partly because it appears to belong to young people themselves (although it is clearly manipulated by adults, teenagers remain unaware of this) and to be an autonomous expression of adolescent values. But the industry is a dollar earner, since British entertainers can earn money overseas, and for this civilized values are surrendered and pop values are commended and endorsed by, for instance, the inclusion of pop-singers in the Birthday Honours List.

The values of popular entertainment—now so dominantly adolescent entertainment—are not avowedly delinquescent values. but they do converge at times on the clearly delinquescent. A record sleeve which was issued for a pop-group which calls itself *The Rolling Stones*—although later withdrawn after questions in the House of Lords—illustrates this point. The message on the sleeve was:

'Cast into your pockets for loot to buy this disc of groovies and fancy words. If you don't have bread, see that blind man, knock him on the head, steal his wallet and lo and behold you have the loot. If you put in the boot, good. Another one sold.'

One could hardly summarize the values of delinquescent youth culture more aptly, or more adequately illustrate their convergence with contemporary entertainment values. 'Another one sold' is simply the commercial punch-line on which the whole fun-ethic of modern society rests. The values, even expressed as a joke, stand in sharp contrast with the inherited values of human civilization—but they are values now widely disseminated through the mass-media, with the apparent blessing of organizations like the B.B.C., which, as a public corporation, has not even the excuse of commercial interest.

167

The rôle of the teenager entertainment idol in our society is what might be described as the 'scapegoat in reverse'. He becomes the totem of the tribe, the emblem who expresses vicariously the pleasures of quick and easy success, with money, kicks and sex as the prizes. He represents the achievement, the upward social mobility, which teenagers have been taught to want but which they will never enjoy except by fantasy identification with him. The less cultivated, more unschooled, he is, the more effectively he represents the rejection by the young of the over-institutionalized society, which for all its institutional and economic provision, fails to compensate for the social and moral abandonment of our young people.

Our contemporary young people have been socialized in a child-oriented society in which the child has come to be recognized as a supremely important being upon whom parental affection is lavished. But although our teenagers are urgently keen to grow up, they want also to cling to the advantages of early childhood. Our society has somehow concentrated familial love into the early years of the child's life, and leaves little over for the still only half-socialized adolescent. Small children, we know, feel themselves to be the very centre of the world from their earliest days. Socialization and education are processes which should steadily disabuse the child of this illusion, and help it to learn the need for reciprocal respect among men. But in our society we encourage indulgent patterns of child-rearing, perhaps allowing the child to go on believing himself to be the centre of the universe, with inadequate processes of progressive discipline which will allow him to win the balance of loving and being loved which he will need in later life. It is the adolescent who suffers both from the continued illusion and from lack of preparation for exposure to a society which proceeds institutionally rather than affectively. The teenager experiences the shock of shifting from affective indulgence to affective abandonment. We ought not to be surprised if he continues to claim indulgence and if, when no longer indulged by others, he indulges himself.

Part of the social and moral abandonment of the adolescent is evident in what is now called 'the permissive morality'. The permissive morality is put forward as a positive and progressive approach, embracing tolerance as a much canvassed virtue.

But modern tolerance is often merely the product of uncertainty, of the fact that it is easier not to bother. It may leave young people very uncertain and insecure, particularly when it is combined with the anonymity of modern life. In this circumstance, moral reputation matters less to people. What now counts is 'personality'—the swift, superficial responses and the immediate sociability, rather than the long-term commitment to a set of values. Sustained commitment implies the acquisition of a basic discipline by the individual, and, failing the stability of community life, at least certain prevailing conditions in which disinterested public goodwill is given frequent expression in social institutions and the media of communications.

But these conditions are hardly maintained in contemporary society. The 'private affluence and public squalor' which economists have noted in modern society, is matched by private hedonism and lack of public and community sentiment. Private morality is, today, frequently and widely attacked, whilst community sentiment has lost many of the social and political supports which it used to have. In consequence, the spirit of disinterested good will is less readily transmitted to the young in the mass society than it was to at least the majority of middle and working class youngsters before World War II. As our society has shifted the emphasis from moral, to intellectual, criteria of excellence—hence restricting the proportions who can attain (and who will even aspire) to excellence—so the old moral basis of public order has been eroded. Nowhere has this occurred more markedly than among young people. The permissive morality has become the rationalization for this development, justifying adults—perhaps especially teachers—who have, understandably, no wish to become sergeant-majors, and parents who have been indoctrinated by the American misinterpreters of Freud who write baby books.

A society which is extensively institutionalized and routinized, as ours is, squeezes out a great deal of man's spontaneity. We suffer from an increasing 'disenchantment with the world' and teenagers now suffer it at a time when their natural energies are greatest and their social aspirations are highest: the experience cannot but be galling. There is progressively less which—pop-singing apart—natural enthusiasm and native ability can achieve. The world has fallen into the hands of 'experts' and technocrats. It is a bigger world and even the local community is no longer a context for achievement, since its standards, too, have been exposed to the professional standards of the mass-media. The growth of knowledge means that more and more areas of social life are controlled by specialists. The individual's life is increasingly influenced from remote centres: less can be decided spontaneously, locally or from native conviction. Democracy itself appears as an illusion because the individual feels that what he can do in the context of a mass-society matters less, and has less impact. The individual feels impotent to do much about the conditions in which he himself operates. Our lives are increasingly governed by mechanical devices: traffic lights, electronic devices, conveyor belts, all of which make inner moral conviction seem increasingly irrelevant to the processes in which, in daily life, we are engaged.

The youth culture, given these circumstances, becomes something of a rebellion—a protest against the machine age. At a higher intellectual level, the boredom, frustration and powerlessness are expressed in political idealism. Boredom becomes momentary excitement, frustration is replaced by stimulation, and the sense of powerlessness is eclipsed by sudden, if evanescent, power, in the modern marching movements of youth—C.N.D., Anti-Apartheid, the Vietnam Protest and the Oxfam movement. Clearly there is goodwill involved, and some of these are causes which moralists might applaud, but there is, in the form which support for these causes takes, something else—the prospect of excitement and power of a generational movement when young people come together in a spirit of moral commitment. There is an echo of the revivalism of Moody and Sankey, and the incidental functions which they fulfil seem not essentially dissimilar. Young people may not understand the real causes of the malaise they suffer, but they organize against recognizable symptoms of the ills of the world.

In protesting, their real target is the routinization of society, and their demand—momentarily fulfilled by the movements themselves (and by the dissident sub-cultures which sometimes persist after the marching is over)—is for the personalism and the moral commitment of the past. The demand is for something to which the individual can attach himself, a shared loyalty and personal involvement. In many a self-styled revolutionary with a banner, there is something crying out for the benefits of a social order which has largely disappeared. The march provides the excitement, the spontaneity and the personal association, the traditional expressions of which have been almost systematically destroyed. They, of course, have their own terms for their diagnosis of the things they protest against, and would reject commentaries such as this which are not expressed in the ideological slogans familiar to them.

The tendency of the technocratic society is to coerce men by institutional and mechanical means, which replace the human associations in which social control sprang from moral and affective values which mediated imperative discipline with care, concern and affection. In reducing the rôle of human association modern institutionalism reduces the spontaneity, sensitivity, critical concern which characterize the context in which self-control was acquired. The abrasiveness of institutional arrangements recreates the demand for human association, status-reassurance, excitement. These things are what the youth culture provides. But in the process sensationalism destroys sensitivity, novelties destroy spontaneity, material abundance destroys spiritual richness, and young people, lacking real cultural excitements, are driven back on whatever caters to untutored animal appetites—in the extreme cases to violence, hooliganism, easy sex and drugs. They might, if they were articulate, justify their recourse to these things given the type of society in which they live. As that society changes and 'progresses', so the human cost, in frustration, in aggression and dissidence will increase.

We have largely controlled the evils of which Charles Russell wrote—the overcrowding, the poverty, the squalor, the dirt and the disease—but we have not solved the youth problem. Ironically, in the affluent society, some young people really rather want to return to the squalor, the overcrowding and the dirt, and even to expose themselves to the disease, for the sake of the excitement and the human association which are to be had with these things. But given the enormous influence of our mass-media, and the willingness of these media to exploit the young; given the anonymity and the institutionalism of our society—it is surprising that the incidence of hooliganism is as low as it is. We are still benefiting from the remnants of the old middle-class morality and the recollection of stable community life (even though it was not always much of a reality for some) as the presumed basis for moral behaviour. We still benefit from the relative humaneness of our police force, and from the extensive exercise of self-control and personal restraint which— although British decency, reserve, sense of propriety and fair play, appear to be very much under strain—are still considerable when Britain is compared with some societies. These things are largely the inheritance of the past. It is by no means sure how long we shall be able to rely on these moral reserves into the future.

10

An Approach to Delinquency
(1966)

Any understanding of delinquency must take account of approaches developed in a number of disciplines. The emphasis here is sociological—delinquency in the context of changing society.

Psychological explanations of crime centre on the imperfections of the socialization process: the causes of delinquency are related to deficiencies of family organization.[1] Although this approach may have value in explaining and treating the individual case, it tells us little about the incidence of crime or the circumstances in which defective socialization is likely to become more common. Psychological explanations become more important when they can be fitted into a wider understanding of society and its development, in which context alone is the changing *incidence* of crime to be understood. It is the incidence of crime which is of public and political concern.

Dispositions which society labels as criminal are recognized as widely diffused among men. Indeed most men could gratify some of their desires by criminal activity—had they not been otherwise conditioned. In seeking explanations for crime, therefore, it is necessary also to inquire how the non-criminal individual becomes conditioned or adjusted to the expectations of the society in which he lives.

Children are socialized to a set of values which delimit socially approved ends; they learn also the approved and legitimate means by which such ends might be attained. (In that respect is it worth mentioning parenthetically that such are the contra-

[1] Robert Merton, *Social Theory and Social Structure*, Glencoe, Ill. Free Press, 1957, provides (in Chapters IV and V) the basic statement on which these points rest.

dictions in contemporary social legislation that at the very time in early 1969 when the government was enacting legislation to lower the voting age to eighteen, they were also preparing legislation concerning juridical processes in respect of people up to the age of seventeen, which implied that up to that age they were not even to be regarded as responsible for their own criminal actions. The only explanation of this implied contradiction is that, in a remarkable convergence of view with the attitudes of the pop-culture, the government were prepared to say young people be both responsible or irresponsible according to whatever expedient issues affected their own popularity.) These values are sustained by the individual's induced appreciation of the need to stand well in the sight of others. He is steadily conditioned by 'good' parents to forego the gratifications of escaping his obligations, of getting his own ends at the expense of others, of 'getting away with it', and he is induced, as moral instruction on issues of this kind is reinforced by threats of withdrawal of affection, to feel guilty about his own tendencies in this direction.

In traditional and simple societies there is a much higher degree of general conformity about the process of upbringing. There is less diversity of values and less divergence of life experiences, both at a given time and between generations. A more extended family system provides parent-substitutes and support for parents in their control of children. But since the individual is under more continuous surveillance from a larger number of adults, the process so conspicuous in advance western society in which the child internalizes social values, acquires a highly sensitive conscience and a fund of personal guilt, is less evident among simpler peoples. The experience of public shame, rather than the growth of a private sense of guilt prevails in such less advanced societies, where social control has been so much less superseded by self-control.

Industrialization in western societies relied on a more intensive socialization of at least the new middle and managerial classes. They dominated the new work order and the moral order, and communicated their values to the industrial classes, partly by changing the patterns of socialization and education, partly by inducement, and partly by coercion. Regional, class and urban/rural differences (and in America racial differences) were adapted in greater or lesser degree to the common values required for general social cohesion in a society constituted by new types of relationship among men. But industrialization also caused kinship and community association to decline, and so affected the very agencies on which re-socialization depended. Paradoxically, the process which made a high degree of internalization more necessary for the maintenance of public order, also rendered its achievement gradually more difficult. Instead of adaptation of different sections of society to more or less common internalized values, new agencies of social conformity develop. Institutionalism begins to replace internalization, and those social activities which can be influenced by technology and rational organization—production, marketing and communication—are made more uniform by essentially external constraints.

In this context a more self-conscious demand for a wider freedom of private values occurs; but these values are not now supported by distinct class, regional and ecological differences. (That the new basis of social cleavage appears to be increasingly generational itself indicates the changing tension between the social structure and the socialization process.) Uncertainty of the range of permissible private non-conformity gives rise to various patterns of deviance, and to simultaneous demands for relaxation of the law (for instance on homosexuality, abortion and censorship) *and* for its greater effectiveness (local licensing of coffee bars, control of drug addiction and vandalism). The United States has experienced a more pronounced association of conformity and deviance—partly because of the long-standing preoccupation with the assimilation of immigrants to 'the American way of life'. Europeans often regard America as a highly conformist society; at the same time it has the highest rates of crime and delinquency of any country.[1]

Very generally put, as Britain became an industrial society there was a gradual shift from reliance on social control to enhanced reliance on socialization and the internalization of appropriate motivation and responsiveness to social obligation.

---

[1] See the interesting discussion in John M. Martin and Joseph P. Fitzpatrick, *Delinquent Behaviour* (New York: Random House, 1964). On Britain, *see* Nigel Walker, *Crime and Punishment in Britain* (Edinburgh: The University Press, 1965).

The new diversity of social rôles, and the new reliance on private motivation demanded this development. The new social system offered increasing prospects for those who were appropriately motivated. Aspiration was increasingly—albeit often unrealistically—encouraged, and as the class system gradually become more open and social mobility more of a reality, so the social emphasis shifted from 'knowing one's place' to 'making one's way'. The new emphasis was—little as it often meant in fact—on free labour and liberty of contract, as the crucial elements in the process of remotivating man for industrial society. Methodism, the Evangelical movement and the Salvation Army played their part in providing the transcendental sanction for the re-socialization of the lower orders, and the diffusion of ideals of self-discipline and orderliness, and—in some measure—of self-expression and democracy.[1]

But other changes made effective socialization more difficult, and they became increasingly pronounced after the Second World War. As society has become more mobile and impersonal, and as relationships are increasingly between 'anonymous' people, so the influence of socialization is less effectively reinforced by the agencies of social control—particularly outside work. Thus there occurs a breakdown of the wider social context of support for socialized behaviour. The burden of making the child a responsible citizen and inculcating those values which are meant to become part of the individual's 'mental set' towards the world falls increasingly on parents, rather than on more extensive social groups. Education, which had earlier disseminated moral and religious values, became—though extended in its operation—increasingly instrumental, concerned more narrowly with imparting skills and teaching techniques. Its support in the socialization of children diminished. If the parents themselves are unsocialized or under-socialized, or the process of socialization is irregular, disrupted or inconsistent, then the child's chances of discovering an approved *modus vivendi* are slimmer in modern society than they have ever been.[2]

[1] For a more extended discussion, see Bryan Wilson, *Religion in Secular Society* (London: Watts, 1966).

[2] See John Bowlby, *Maternal Care and Mental Health* (Geneva: World Health Organization, 1961); J. C. Flugel, *Man, Morals and Society* (Harmondsworth: Pelican, 1955).

What particular changes in social conditions have been responsible for the diminished effectiveness of socialization processes in offsetting the natural biological or psychological disposition towards crime? It is to the values embraced by our social arrangements that we must turn for an answer. Society offers men the prospect of certain 'goods', and induces them to want more of them than they are ever likely to attain. These 'goods' have steadily been 'privatized'—have less to do with the community (itself broken down and anonymous) and more with the individual. The consequence is the use of illicit means to attain these ends, and since society has become increasingly pragmatic and instrumental, and less concerned with the sanctity of means, so the individual is induced to adopt similar responses. Man's growing anonymity in modern society and his enhanced social mobility cause there to be less spontaneous social control of individuals who seek their ends by illicit means.

Although all types of crime—including violation of traffic regulations—might be seen in these terms, it has special relevance to the growing incidence of violence, hooliganism and theft. All these types of crime have grown rapidly since the war, but whereas we have a fairly reliable picture of the pattern of theft, since it is normally in the interest of the property-owner to report it, we have far less satisfactory estimates of the number of crimes of hooliganism and wanton damage, which are certainly much more widespread than criminal statistics suggest. (The extent of hooliganism against private property and individuals is certainly under-reported.) Most of this type of crime is the work of adolescent boys, but it would be wrong to assume that people who commit crimes of this kind become criminals in later life. At the same time, it is also evident that the normal 'high spirits' of youth are today much more likely to find expression in strictly criminal behaviour than used to be the case.

Although other types of crime follow a pattern different from that of vandalism, violence and theft, certain common elements persist. Even murder is the expression of ineffective socialization —an incident in the use of illicit means for gain, or the consequence of uncontrolled rage. At the other extreme, even serious traffic offences are found to be committed in disproportionately large degree by those who have been law-breakers in other connections. Thus although social scientists do not generally accept the idea of a 'criminal type', it does appear that there is a distinguishable pattern of criminal response even for different types of crime.

The effect of the induced achievement-orientation of contemporary society has been to reduce the importance of community loyalty, the strength of kin group, neighbourhood, village, regional and national identity. Mobility and impersonality have led to a different style of inter-personal relationship. Thus one of the factors which supports the moral order—personal obligation—has been reduced in its effectiveness. The same emphasis on achievement induces indifference to the means by which the goals are sought. Finally, the same orientation leads to a widely diffused sense of discontent and frustration, for not all who are induced to want to get on, will in fact succeed in doing so. For them the system will appear bogus; and as has long been recognized, they tend to feel more resentment at this state of affairs than do men in a society where opportunities are fewer and the emphasis on achievement lower.

The Sherifs, in an American study, found that, relative to the accomplishments of their parents, lower-class young people were *more* ambitious than middle-class youth.[1] The disparity between aspiration and real opportunity was probably greater, since lower-class people have fewer opportunities for advancement and are usually less well-informed about how to make use of the opportunities which are available. The fruits of achievement are emphasised, but opportunity for achievement is limited. Where success is scarce and at a high premium, failure becomes a widespread experience.

The limitation of opportunity is not simply a matter of persisting inequalities between classes, it is also the relation of reality to over-stimulation of aspiration. Obviously young people are most affected by all this, since achievement-orientation is most strongly induced in those at the threshold of their careers. One example of its consequences is seen in the type of entertainer who has become fashionable with them—the boy, or the group, which has got to the top without formal education, without training and without the advantages of birth, name and class position (those who possess these advantages

---

[1] Muzafer and Carolyn W. Sherif, *Reference Groups: Exploration into Conformity and Deviation of Adolescents* (New York: Harper & Row, 1964).

even have to disavow them to become pop idols). These entertainers are inverted scapegoat symbols: they represent the induced demand for success among large groups of young people who have no chance of attaining it. The fantasy and the vicarious pleasure they provide are not necessarily simply sublimation: like other neurotic responses they serve as a further stimulant to frustration, and hence a further demand for fantasy response. Certainly it is not a response which creates a realistic moderation of the values which society presents to the young: it expresses certain elements of the success ideal, without the ethical emphasis on the appropriate and institutionalized means.

The emphasis on achievement and stimulation of aspiration in an open class system appears to have distinct consequences for crime: the creation of frustration, which may feed violence and disorder; the pressure to discover new means of achieving, which may often be semi-licit or illicit; the reduction of loyalties to family, neighbourhood, work groups, school and so on, as the individual prepares to move on; and the search for neurotic fantasy solutions.

Merton has characterized two responses to blocked opportunity—the tendency to innovate which is frequently innovation of delinquent means; and the tendency to retreat from the effort to achieve, which is characterized in the youth culture by addiction to pop music, alcohol, drugs and substitution of sexual goals for goals of social attainment.[1] It is in this social context that we have seen an increase of crime, both of acquisitive crime, and crimes of violence, vandalism, and drug addiction. Youthful violence and vandalism, and the inconvenience of the general public, provide young delinquents both with relief from frustration, and the occasion for stabbing back at the society which has frustrated them. The whole syndrome is supported by the approval which prevails for behaviour of this kind within the adolescent sub-culture, which defines the traditional moral values of society as 'phoney' and as something to be kicked against.

Delinquent behaviour is facilitated by the growing impersonality of society. The increase in physical mobility—on both

[2] R. K. Merton, *op. cit.* See also, R. A. Clinard and L. E. Ohlin, *Delinquency and Opportunity* (London: Routledge, 1961).

a daily basis in the now much-increased distance of home from work and from school, and from increasingly-centralized recreational facilities; and on a longer-term basis, of journeys for holidays, week-end travel, the willingness to move house— all add to the impersonality of society. As long as they move among unknown people individuals no longer need to worry about their reputations. Thus, in complex industrial societies, there is a growing tolerance for widely divergent styles of behaviour, even delinquent behaviour, as long as the individual himself does not find others' behaviour inconvenient.

It is in this context that the police find themselves with less social support in their activities; they cease to represent a generalized public conscience, and they cease to represent even local feeling, since the local public have so often ceased to be really local. In a society of strangers, men refuse to be their brothers' keepers, refuse to become custodians of the social order on which they themselves depend. Despite the decline of local loyalties, many of our social institutions—local government, parochial organization, voluntary organizations—operate on the increasingly unreal assumptions of their existence.

Perhaps the most important aspect of this development has been the breakdown of the nexus between school and home. Once the school ceases to belong to the community, parental moral training is much less reinforced by school training. As education is shorn of its moral concerns, and as teaching becomes subject to greater professional specialization, so the personal knowledge of particular children by teachers becomes less intense. As school size increases, so this context becomes increasingly impersonal. The individual child learns to look out for himself: if he acquires independence, he also learns the ropes according to the values of the peer group and—increasingly evident—of the entertainment-dominated youth culture. The creased mobility of teachers enhances the effect: today it is not uncommon, even in grammar schools, for a child to be taught one subject by two or three different teachers in the course of one year. With teacher loyalty to the school so low, the loyalty of children cannot be summoned either. If a high proportion of teachers are preparing to move on to a better job, a better district, there will be less care, concern and commitment on their part. The reputation and their success will rest less and less on their sustained rôle in the community, as locally respected people, and more and more on their ability to manipulate a fluid job situation in their own interests.

Associated with the growing impersonality of social contexts, is the increased institutionalism of modern life. Growth in the size of firms, public corporations, schools, universities, recreational establishments and the media of mass communication, give a new institutional character to society. These agencies grow more routinized, formalized and rationalized in their operation. In many ways men in modern society are themselves more rational, but much of their rationality stems not from their own more rational processes of thought (as naïve nineteenth-century thinkers often supposed would be the case) but rather from the increasingly rationalized procedures of the organizational structure of society. Rationality and routine is less an expression of the ordinary man's intellectual conviction, than a constraint on the freedom of his emotional and aesthetic impulses.

Delinquency is, in some senses, rebellion against specialism, professionalism and institutionalized order. In the new social context the individual loses occasions in which to feel his own significance: the scale of operations in which he is involved is so vast that he finds few personal satisfactions and few occasions for self-expression. Individual purpose, personal feelings, are puny in relation to the harsh external reality of an institutionalized society which operates without human warmth and without personal regard. Even the scale of the buildings which house institutional facilities (and housing itself increasingly becomes such) enhances the process.

As modern society has accepted the technical and economic rationality of pre-stressed concrete and synthetic materials, so it has reduced the local and personal sense of purpose and meaning of life for the individual. In these circumstances vandalism and beatnikism have arisen, perhaps in unconscious protest against the over-organized, over-determined, over-routinized environment in which young people must now live. Deviance becomes intrinsically satisfying as an evidence that one has defied the whole complex of social organization—an expression in the fight for emotional freedom and survival against the meaningless complexity of institutionalized society.

Although 'the establishment', as a social remnant of the past, is nominated as scapegoat, there can be little doubt that the real if unrecognized cause of unrest is the rational, centralized, institutional apparatus of the modern world. Against all this the young individual has had to reassure himself of himself.

Thus there has been a search for extra-routinized experience, in particular for excitement. Even the private sector of social life has become increasingly subject to institutionalized provision, and the surfeit of entertainment has meant its rapidly diminished capacity to excite its audiences. Thus it is that one important element in delinquent motivation appears to be the demand for real excitement and real danger. The demand for 'kicks' is a consequence of boredom as well as frustration—and the means whereby real 'kicks' are to be had are widely advertised by the mass-media. The diminished personal investment in social situations and the institutionalism of contemporary society stimulate what has become a widely accepted goal of the youth culture, and what represents an expression of alternative values from those entrenched in traditional morality.

Not all the activities of the youth culture are delinquent, but the way of life has been aptly described as delinquescent—the acceptance of standards prescribed within the age-stratum, but at variance with the behaviour patterns demanded in society. This delinquescent sub-culture is relatively classless and widely diffused throughout the age-group. In the mass society, differential class standards of behaviour are eroded, especially among young people whose common generational situation is more dramatically evident than their class circumstances (a fact apparent with the growth of equality of opportunity and the cult of age-specified models of entertainment and recreation, from pop music to the bowling alleys). The generational divisions of society become increasingly marked by a variety of external symbols, and a new generational consciousness replaces the old consciousness of class. The vast majority of criminals are people under thirty, and a great deal of the undetected vandalism in modern society is surely the work of young people. It is impossible to separate the development of the youth culture in the past two decades from the growing incidence of crime.

The influence of mass-media has as yet scarcely been assessed, and one might seriously doubt whether any research methods yet evolved are adequate to measure their influence. That they do influence men is evident from the millions spent on television advertising alone. The mass-media present a diverse range of values, but the direction of their influence is determined by the fact that they compete for audiences. There are few checks on them as they compete in ever more sensational, ever more titillating, ever more daring presentations. As long as the media are concerned with winning an audience, there is an inbuilt tendency to social irresponsibility: they appeal to private amusement and not to the public good, and the two are often at variance.

Since children watch television for almost as long each day as they are exposed to teachers, we must calculate its moral effects to be potentially as great as those of our very expensive and elaborate educational system. We can hardly be surprised that the youth culture is dominated by entertainment values, and we must recognize that these values are often antithetical to those of social order. We have thus permitted a rival agency to develop which in general influences young people in directions very different from those of home and school. It presents the fun ethic, the easy way to the top, the fantasy of pop success—to leave aside the more obvious emphasis on sex-violence and cynicism.

As crime flourishes, so, both through fictional presentation and factual evidence, it is borne in upon many that dishonesty pays. Obviously those who are delinquent in one context may behave with perfect decency in another—may, indeed, invoke the forces of law to protect themselves from the delinquency of others. Delinquents need not have completely criminal 'mental sets'; they respond to circumstance, and in particular to the dictates of the youth culture as and when they are involved in it. But as delinquent behaviour provides gratifications, and no untoward consequences, the effects of moral education are likely to be of diminishing significance. Even if the individual ceases to be delinquent, he is unlikely, having seen that crime pays, to become a model citizen in protecting social values and his fellow men. He is more likely in some measure to identify with criminals and to think them simply lucky 'if they can get away with it'.

Although broken homes are principally significant in the

183

explanation of psychological dispositions to crime in the individual case, in the inadequacy or disruption of the process of
socialization of the child, the sociological aspects of this phenomenon depend on the incidence of family disruption, and
families can be disrupted without actual separation of spouses
taking place. The broken home becomes merely an extreme
case of the home which functions inadequately, perhaps partly
because of the separation of its members in divergent life activities. Even circumstances not attended by quarrels may exist in
which parents fail to reinforce ethical attitudes by the use of
emotional relationships, simply because family interaction is
too limited.

The broken home and the inadequate home, however, may
be regarded as another symptom of more far-reaching social
disruption. In this instance, as in others, it is evident that increased incidence of crime is not merely a consequence of other
phenomena which are themselves recognizably evil, but rather
that increased incidence of crime tends to be associated with
social changes which in themselves are not necessarily regarded
as evil at all—that crime is in some measure the cost of certain
sorts of social development and certain sorts of 'social progress'.
Whether the cost is too great is, of course, another matter.

11

In Defence of Oxbridge
(1966)

The educational paradox of our times is the growth in popular regard at all social and political levels for university education, accompanied by a new uncertainty about the appropriate style and character of that education. While almost any institution of advanced education now has a claim to the title of university, those which have been longest so-called, and on the example of which university education is so much demanded, find their methods, their operation and their life-styles under attack.

It began most noticeably with the comments of the Robbins Report, whose authors found it inconvenient to have to except Oxbridge from generalizations made about British universities, and who disliked the slowness (in fact, the very considerable democracy) with which those universities made their decisions. Remarks in a report designed to be monumental echoed in magisterial tones some of the less informed criticism of Oxbridge arising in other places—the sour grapes, the emphasis on equality even at the cost of quality, and the thirst for sensationalism which have marked social commentary in a society dominated by the mass-media. The response, at least in Oxford, has been growing uncertainty and self-doubt—a type of mild, but widely pervasive, neurosis.

The idea that the two universities 'need looking into' is almost as recurrent in British public life as similar demands in regard to the House of Lords and the trade unions. And both universities, in characteristically different ways, have set up bodies of inquiry for the contemplation, of the institutional navel. 'The time has come', the committee said, in an Oxford memorandum in 1964, 'to take a long hard look at ourselves.'

185

That was the response when the one telling paragraph of the Robbins Report reverberated round the dreaming spires.

With just a few years' experience of Oxford, and rather longer experience of redbrick universities, I wonder what all the uncertainty is about. In national, and international, terms there can be no doubt that Oxford and Cambridge are remarkably successful institutions, and particularly so in their undergraduate teaching, which is probably unparalleled in any other university in the world. The Oxbridge don in an undergraduate college apparently does more teaching, despite shorter terms, than his counterparts in redbrick universities, and the Oxbridge professor, despite restricted lecturing and less administration, probably spends more time supervising graduate students than many of those in other universities. There is little idleness, and the results are good; but the induced uncertainty persists.

Despite the recent growth of graduate studies (none of it planned and some of it—like management studies at Oxford—specifically not planned), Oxford and Cambridge remain dominantly undergraduate universities. The legitimate demands of the public service and of an informed public will reinforce college dispositions to persist as such. Even the strongest advocates of graduate studies usually pay at least lip-service to the primacy of undergraduate studies at Oxbridge.

It is through their undergraduates, and not nearly so much through their graduates, that Oxford and Cambridge have made their immense contribution to the nation's life and to its public service. Whereas their graduates have largely gone into university research and teaching—and a considerable proportion of them come from, and return, abroad—their undergraduates have been spread through the professions, the civil service and other departments of public life. Graduates, in their period of graduate study, are less fully affected by the general ethos of their university, by its many-sidedness, by its non-specialist facilities, whilst specialist facilities are qualitatively less different in the various major universities.

The outstanding features of Oxbridge undergraduate education, in marked contrast to redbrick universities, are—apart from the collegiate system itself—the tutorial with one pupil at a time (or at most with two) and the absence of the lecture-examination nexus which dominates redbrick universities.

The tutorial system obviously works unevenly. Anyone who has had to deal with undergraduates from different colleges sees how variously colleges treat their junior members. From that experience in Oxford one comes to suspect that the colleges which have grown fastest and grown big discharge their duties less well than those which have grown slowly or which have remained small. But, however unevenly, the tutorial system does work, and works to meet the need of undergraduates as no other arrangement can. A good tutor can take things up with a man from the point which *he* has reached: what matters is not what the tutor can tell him, but what the pupil can make his own. Obviously, the context encourages the overflow from purely academic and intellectual to social and cultural concerns, where both tutor and pupil are so disposed. The associations sometimes last a lifetime.

Where lecturers are examiners, as they often are in redbrick universities, lecture courses become preparatory discourses for examinations. There is less encouragement for students to read, learn or think for themselves. The situation encourages impersonality and the lack of shared involvement which becomes the style of too-rapidly expanded universities. When examiners feel that they can set questions only on the specific topics on which they have lectured, education suffers a serious short-circuit. Sometimes, students do not even go to the lectures—they rely on being able to copy the notes taken at lectures by their friends. Since not all lecturers are able to make their lectures exciting, and since the lecture becomes the staple stuff of the university experience, redbrick undergraduates not infrequently find much to bore them. Sometimes they are expected to spend twelve to fifteen hours a week in listening to lectures, and sometimes their attendance is obligatory.

In an age of considerable independence on the part of the young, the emphasis on the extra-professional function of academics is sometimes derided by students and neglected by dons. But those who make themselves available to undergraduates —and even also to graduates—find that behind the new student face there are often many old student problems and anxieties.

Pastoral care has, however, not only become rare, it has also been exposed to attack. Even Vice-Chancellors have declared that modern young people do not need the type of concern that traditional universities, such as Oxford, have had for them. Of course, it relieves academics of a burden when they can conveniently discover that young people do not want their attention and advice. But there is no need to accept the students' definition of their situation, much less the definition put forward by a small and strident minority among them. Many academics in redbrick and new universities do, in fact, undertake the extra-curricular duties of the pastoral tradition, but it is doubtful whether they are anywhere taken more seriously than in Oxbridge. The structural arrangements of some institutions of higher education make it difficult for even acutely conscientious teachers to do much along this line.

In Oxbridge the arrangements impose a measure of pastoral concern and sustain it, and as long as the collegiate structure remains intact, does not have too large numbers imposed upon it, and as long as the universities themselves resist the temptation to institute too many narrowly specialized undergraduate degree courses, the benefits of this tradition will persist.

If Oxbridge is attacked for its pastoral concern by academics who reject their responsibility to stimulate and motivate the young people who become their charges, it is also attacked for taking extra-academic qualities into account in the selection of applicants. With these critics intellect alone counts. The 'schoolma'am syndrome'—the idea which teachers sometimes get that the only good end for every bright girl is to become schoolma'ams like themselves—is by no means absent in modern university life. The 'new-image' academics with a narrow professional approach to their 'jobs' sometimes forget that the task of a university is not simply to recruit more academics, but is to educate liberally those whose lives will be lived in other work in the wider society.

Universities have their own ethos and climate, and it is not conditioned by purely intellectual exercises. It participates in a wider, richer range of cultural values. Such an environment may even be necessary to draw out the intellectual best in undergraduates; it is certainly necessary to provide the social and cultural enrichment which a graduate should carry away with him. The cultivation of the intellect is only one of the civilizing processes in which the university is appropriately engaged.

Inevitably where qualities of this kind are prized they must enter into selection as well as into education: the liberal education may be fulfilled at university, but it does not usually begin there. It might begin there for some, but if that 'some' were too many, it would certainly begin for none.

There is one other facet of this matter which Oxbridge critics might bear in mind. More efficient selection methods—more rational, they will no doubt be called—would skim off more effectively the intellectual cream of the schools. Oxbridge gets its full share already, and anything, such as completely centralized selection, which increased the proportion, could only be to the detriment of other universities. Every university should get some people of the highest ability, and having examined in recent years for Oxford, London, three older, and one less old, civic university, and one of the new universities, I am convinced that, as far as my subject is representive, they do.

The alternative would be a hierarchy of universities on the American pattern. However well that arrangement works there, in a system where all universities, even Oxbridge, draw the major part of their revenues from the same public source, it would be something of a national catastrophe, for universities and for undergraduates. The wide diffusion of near-equal educational opportunities at different universities would be impaired, and less favoured universities might be induced like their American counterparts, to become preoccupied with their 'success image' rather than with real academic standards. Against this prospect there is a lot to be said for encouraging Oxford to continue to have regard to qualities other than intellect alone; to take motivation, aspiration, personal interests, talents, qualities of character and even school connection into account in selecting its undergraduates. The unintended consequences of doing otherwise might ramify far beyond the ancient universities.

12

The Age of Majority
(1966)

In the prevailing war of the generations, a truce to refix the age of majority had to come sooner or later. The Latey Committee considering this subject will certainly hear about the concessions which the vociferous and sometimes self-interested spokesmen of one generation demand of the others. They may hear less of the importance of preserving, perhaps of re-entrenching, some of the rights of the old. The issue, ostensibly concerned with the young, is another of those matters which may be viewed piecemeal and narrowly, but which have important consequences for the whole of society. Now that the focus of attention shifts, at the behest of the mass-media, from older people to the young, and as the youth culture increasingly imposes itself on the life of the country, it is the elderly who become the really under-privileged. Affluence, status-striving, and the shift from a production-conscious to a consumption-conscious society put youth at a premium. A narrow legalistic approach to the age of majority, with only the clamour of the youth culture in mind, would be another contribution to our contemporary social malaise.

This said, it must be recognized that our regulation of the age of responsibility has been anomalous, haphazard and incoherent—marriage at twenty-one, or, with parental consent, at sixteen; car-driving at seventeen, motor-cycling at sixteen; buying drinks at eighteen; seeing 'X' films at sixteen, but paying adult prices at fourteen. In a society which long ago lost its ritualized initiation procedures for easing children steadily into adult responsibilities, adolescents, unsure of society's expectations of them, have long experienced acute status-insecurity. Even in the thirties a fifteen-year-old Judy Garland could sing, 'I'm just an in-between too old for toys, too young for boys'. In the fifties and sixties a strident youth culture has made the boys into toys, produced its own deviant life-styles and stimulated the contempt of youngsters for adult society. What were once teenagers' problems have now become society's problems, as the youth culture has mobilized the vast majority of adolescents behind the pop-groups, imposed two or three constantly changing uniforms and disseminated a range of anti-social attitudes.

In the background is the fact that teenage affluence has become a commercial opportunity. The demand for wider opportunities for youth comes largely from businessmen and advertisers who want young people to be spenders and consumers of new lines of fashionable trash. This is the real message behind the steadily developing movement for teenage credit-cards. At one time it was enough to induce teenagers to spend their pocket money or their higher wages on indispensable, but short-lived, novelties and the growing stock of equipment which any youngster who is to win friends and impress people must have. But now adolescents are being induced to pawn their futures by credit-buying of consumer goods with guaranteed in-built obsolescence. The habit is as socially beneficial as smoking marijuana and as addictive as heroin. It is not surprising that the Hire Purchase Trade Association wants eighteen as the age of majority—on the strength, no doubt, of elaborate market research, but with no regard either for the life-long welfare of the adolescents that it hopes to turn into debtors, or for the moral stamina of society.

All healthy societies safeguard their middle-aged and older people—those who, in a period of escalated social change, find adjustment harder than do the young. New productive methods, emphasis on mobility, new consumer goods, all re-allocate social opportunity from the old to the young. A society in which it has long been hard to grow up, has become a society in which it is even harder to grow old.

But old we all must grow: the long-term interest of everyone, and of social order, is in preserving privileges to which people steadily graduate through the life-cycle, and in compensating for the loss of youth's freedom and carelessness by comfort and status in old age. Commitment to the common good diminishes as the 'live now, pay later' philosophy of the youth culture is disseminated—a philosophy which stands in sharpest contrast to the needs of education. The society in which juvenile crime grows, in which the 'rumble' has become a common expression of adolescent disorder, in which drug-addiction increases with great rapidity, is also the society in which youth has 'never had it so good' in a booming youth culture. It is hard to suppose that teenage affluence and teenage delinquency are unassociated phenomena.

The Latey Committee must be aware that youth's acquisition of greater wealth, technical expertise and social influence has not been accompanied by greater social, moral, political or spiritual wisdom. The reverse has occurred. With more power and lower responsibility (to their families, with whom they associate less, and to whom they contribute lower proportions of their income) socialization of the young has become more difficult. If successive generations fail to transmit moral sense, social responsibility, cultural values, standards of taste and good manners, and if education, which once regarded these things as part of its mission, is pressed into a narrow instrumental definition of its aims, then social security will diminish and older people will become the direct or indirect victims of the stimulated demands of the young.

As society has grown more complex, the acquisition of social maturity has grown more difficult. An appropriate personal morality is more difficult to forge when moral confusion prevails within society's institutions. Formal education continues longer, but social control is less effective: the young are indulged, and the postponements and pains which are a necessary part of socialization are shirked as youngsters are allowed to make their own choices at ever-earlier ages. The Latey Committee might address itself to the task of reinforcing arrangements which are in everyone's long-term interests, except perhaps those of the youth culture profiteers.

The specific issues on which the age of majority has some influence have been variously affected by the growth of the modern youth culture. Some items, such as the age of voting, are of largely symbolic significance: others, such as the age at which young people can enter into contracts, have much wider implications for our way of life.

Society would have nothing to gain from a reduction of the age of voting, and much to lose if the age at which contracts could be entered into (including hire-purchase agreements) were reduced. The sensible thing might be to leave both as they are. The tendency for people to marry younger—when not simply a consequence of earlier pregnancy—appears to be more of a short cut to that adult status which adolescents both disdain and yet desire, than to stem from any evidence that marital bliss and marital stability are greater among the young. Although marrage may operate as a useful social control, to reduce the age at which parental consent is necessary would only promote the rift between the generations and legitimate the existing social drift. That physical maturity occurs a little earlier is irrelevant, since it has long been attained well before marriageable age. The crux of that problem is not the age of physical maturity, but the social interpretation which we allow to be put on the physical fact.

The law is ineffective in regard to so personal a habit as smoking, and the obvious benefits of raising the age might have to be foregone unless enforcement could be ensured. Buying drinks presents few problems, but there might be benefits from raising the age for driving, at least to eighteen and perhaps to twenty-one for both motor-bikes and scooters and cars. Juvenile crime and public disorder depend a great deal on easy mobility, whilst a reduction of vehicles on the road could not but improve road safety. Driving would then become one of the first compensations for attaining an age of greater responsibility. If the young are to develop their talents, such deferred gratifications are essential. The Latey Committee need not seek the easy popularity of 'permissiveness'; if they see their task in its wider perspective of the long-run interests of the young and the immediate interests of the community, they will certainly not do so.[1]

[1] Of course, the Latey Committee recommended reduction of the age of majority, and the Government of the day quickly proceeded to introduce legislation to give young people the vote at eighteen. A note of poetic irony was struck soon afterwards when, in early 1969, Mr. Justice Latey resigned his office as Chairman of London University Management Committee, 'immediately after the Union building was occupied by students from the London School of Economics' who were at the time engaged in revolutionary action against the authorities of the School (all of them were, of course,

over the eighteen—Mr. Justice Latey's chosen age for adult responsibilities.
Mr. Justice Latey commented that the situation which had developed was
'wholly beyond the contemplation of anyone when I accepted the invitation
to take on the chairmanship . . .'. The situation provides its own comment on
the knowledge of the youth culture of those who so cheerfully recommended
the reduction of the age of majority. Quotations from the *Daily Telegraph*,
1st February 1969, p. 1.

13

The Hippies: A Sociological Analysis
(1967)

The hippy posters declare San Francisco to be 'the end of western civilization'. The allusion is not merely to geography. It is the only unifying goal of the carefree young people who populate the *hippy scene*. They want to be left alone to 'do their thing'—to do what they like for as long as they like, without the constraints of the mores and laws of the civilization in which they have grown up. The hippies constitute a spectacular but bloodless revolution of young urbanites, who, although they protest against much in society, are non-violent protesters, and who symbolize their attempt to overthrow western values by their home-made clothes, their rejection of the distinction between 'decent' and 'obscene', their disbelief in political solutions, and their desperate attempt to be 'folk'. What sort of society they themselves want, and how it would work, is—as with most rebellions—much less well-articulated than are their ideas about what they are against. Their slogans focus on the Vietnam war; they object to restrictions on personal (and especially sexual) freedom; they dislike the hard-faced, calculating, 'uptight' attitudes of ordinary citizens.

They are unified in their rejection of the social order, without, however, knowing how man is to live when there is no social order. In this sense, they are parasitic rebels, opposed to the every-day, middle-aged values of affluent America—its commercialism, mechanization and bureaucracy; its car-culture, hygiene, and the routinized system of the work-ethic and the quick buck. But, of course, they are the captives of the culture against which they rebel, and their own life-styles are shot through with the assumptions, and are dependent on the facilities, and the prosperity, of the very affluent society that they are so concerned, ideologically, to reject. It is only in the affluent society that such a revolution could occur among the young: it is only where there is a high degree of institutionalized self-awareness (which is the unique inheritance of America as a 'self-made' society, and which has now been so widely disseminated by the mass-media) that men could sufficiently distanciate themselves from their social system, to assume the poses of rejection and 'drop-out' that characterize the hippies.

Like other movements among young people in advanced societies, the attitudes of the hippies are a mixture of sophistication and *naïvete*. There is an acceptance, and an extension of the type of social criticism found among some academics, particularly among social scientists, and most especially among the culturally, *déraciné* elements among them. Academic critics live in a protected sub-culture, heavily subsidized by public money and traditionally protected by strong ideologies of freedom of thought and work conditions. The hippies lack the institutional context, but they claim the same sort of privileges; to the social criticism (more implicit and less articulated in their case—more acted out than spoken out) they add youthful fantasies of Utopia, of absolute freedom, and of the life of the noble savage. They define the institutional context as itself a 'bad scene', and although they have undoubtedly been informed by some of the free-thinking academics of the 1960s, they have implicitly rejected these precursors, and their institutions, with the rest of western civilization.

The hippy movement is completely committed to hedonism. The fun-ethic is dominant. Fun is to be had here and now, for those who just break out and abandon all the inhibiting social training, and the restricting institutional contexts, of modern society. So they fly kites, blow bubbles, distribute flowers and smoke 'grass' (marijuana) both to demonstrate, and to symbolize, their transcendence above social conventions of what it is appropriate for young adults and adolescents to do. If fun, 'doing your thing', is the dominant goal, *now* is the dominant time. Neither past nor future matters to the hippy. He disavows the past, because it represents the social training given by parents, schools, and by straight society generally. He rejects the impress of the future as the imprisoning perspective that teaches men to postpone present pleasure for some remote future achievement, to be gained by conformity to prevailing values, procedures and conventions, in the performance of work.

This deliberately timeless attitude of the hippies, is the paramount rejection of the routines of everyday society, of which time is a principal arbiter. Eat when you are hungry; make love when you feel like it; enjoy whatever is your 'bag' (personal preference); wear what you like—these are characteristic hippy attitudes. The conscientiousness of everyday life; the stable commitments, to persons and enterprises, over time, are rejected for an essentially *laissez-faire* approach to the world. When hippies concentrate on a sidewalk, or sit in the street and cause traffic diversions, they do not—so they would assert—do this aggressively, or to disrupt, but only to show how routines and mechanical agencies, such as clocks and traffic lights, have destroyed human spontaneity. It is in the same spirit that they reject social conventions, which they see as entirely negative in their operation, as curbs on human freedom.

Spontaneous joy is the dominant hippy concern. They reject not only the dehumanizing apparatus of modern living, the bureacratic structures and the impersonal rôle relationships of modern society, but all the values of advanced society. They have abandoned the idea of 'getting ahead'—the dominant American goal—for 'being' now. In their emphasis on sharing what they have (in asking the passer-by for his spare change) they are refusing to develop those inculcated mental attitudes of capitalist society (and perhaps of most advanced society) by which a man bolsters his ego by his possessions. Meanness, lack of generosity, calculation, a disposition to judge others, the search for social status, are all, to the hippies, attitudes of mind that interfere with the individual's sense of himself as 'beautiful', and with his capacity to create beautiful relationships and engage in beautiful, non-productive activities. There is a strong undercurrent demanding that the individual realize himself as an artist, by doing whatever he finds immediately and naturally enjoyable. Implicitly there is a rejection of organized pleasures, of entertainment that is institutionalized, commercial or professional. There is a strong emphasis on life at the local level. 'Where it's at', is always somewhere not too far away, and certainly it is not somewhere that is visible only through a television screen. Doing it oneself for oneself, realizing through activity of one's own (or inactivity of one's own in the use of hallucinatory drugs) is set over against the centralized, technical, impersonal styles of modern entertainment.

To have said all this of the hippies, is to approach their situation and their responses more articulately than they do for themselves. If this is their philosophy, it is not generally known at a level of a set of interrelated propositions. Hippies are casual people. Their relationships are casual, and their conception of the world is equally casual. Their attitudes to American values have a resonance of eastern philosophy, but their positions are not thought out, and the true hippy has no more long-term commitment to a philosophical position than to anything, or anyone, else. He might dabble with Gurdjieff, I. Chang, Maharishi or Bob Dylan—but it is only useful as long as he feels it to be so, as long as it can 'blow his mind'.

But at its best, the hippy refuses to let the competitive, aggressive, possessive and spiteful attitudes inculcated within —and sometimes institutionalized within—modern society, to spoil his nature. At this level it is almost a religious quest, but a quest that demands not the struggle against adverse conditions and mind-sullying experience, so much as the refusal to engage in such experience. At its worst, it becomes the excuse for abandonment of any sort of concern, except in the transient gesture, for fellow-men, and particularly an excuse to ignore longer-term obligations to others, or the framework that makes life endurable for them. If the hippy refuses to be saddled with the emotional responses necessary in all advanced societies, it is because he denies himself a whole range of emotional experience in the undiluted search for instant pleasure. His flight from the boredom of routinized everyday life in the modern metropolis, implies a naïve faith that, once rid of routine, happiness is automatic. As some hippies have found, even the 'love-in' can become a bit of a bore, and even when men set themselves to be free and spontaneous, enjoyment is not always the consequence.

All revolutionary movements betray important continuities with the culture against which they rebel. The hippies, as we have seen, derived something of their perspective from the least assimilated and most critical among social scientists in universities. More directly they owe much to the earlier beatnik movement, from which their hirsuteness and their contempt for hygiene are most conspicuously derived (although, as Herbert Spencer commented, in 1854, hirsuteness is a common characteristic of revolutionaries, the most manifest symbol of nonconformity—to the point of being itself almost conventional). From the Negro sub-culture came much of their terminology (although, as in the case with a word like 'uptight', with considerable shifts of meaning) and many of their more casual attitudes to sex. From the homosexual sub-culture—itself most thoroughly established in San Francisco and New York, the two cities in which the hippies flourish—it has acquired more conscious demands for freedom from interference, and the superficial accoutrements of dress, 'drag' and the erosion of all the external symbols of sex differences.

But in a more fundamental sense, the hippies are a profoundly American movement, even though their postures are being imitated in other American-influenced cultures, at least among the richer nations of Europe. Their extreme casualness in human relationships, appears, to the European, as merely an extension to the extreme of that shaplessness of social relationships that he perceives generally in the United States, and particularly in California. Their strident *laissez-faire* morality, is an extension of the moral indifference of Americans to sumptuary conventions that have prevailed in more traditional societies. Their very exploitative tendency, as a parasitic sub-culture whose members live on subsidies from their relatives, and the charity of individuals who work and earn in the institutionalized world that hippies reject, concedes more to the confidence trickery of the capitalist social order than hippies would care to acknowledge. Again, without quite realizing it, they have picked up and intensified, that strong subsidiary motif of American values, the ideal of 'having fun'. This could never be the self-conscious ideal of a folk-society, which is how many hippies aspire to see themselves—it is, rather, an elaboration of the old American doctrine of 'liberty and the pursuit of happiness', now taken literally and to excess.

The movement is both a cult and a culture, and at times it is something of a self-conscious spectacle. The rediscovery of the self, with the aid of drugs, a book of Buddhist writings, or even with the gospel of St. John, is seen by some as a type of religious quest, although it is religion shorn of all the solemnity of conventional religion. It is not meant to sanctify social arrangements, but rather to legitimize individual behaviour of almost any kind. The central quest is the pleasurable search for the expanded mind, not the anguished search for objective religious truths. Truth, having by modern criticism lost its external referents, has become a subjective condition of awareness, to be gained not by dogmas, liturgies or moralities, but by inner experience—usually with the aid of drugs.

In so far as the hippies have a collective vision, it is symbolized by primitive cultures. The feathers that they wear in their hair are a token of the affinity that they believe they have with the Red Indians, and their persisting failure to fit into white American society. The rejection of acculturation by the Indians is the hippy ideal. They, too, are a tribe, and they, too, might live in a golden age like the noble savage. The rapidly spreading Peyote religion among the Indians, the principal rite of which is consumption of the purportedly hallucinatory peyote cactus button, gives the hippies, with their own commitment to drug-taking, a special sense of kinship with Indians. But the Indians have not reciprocated their enthusiasm, and hippy attempts to settle down among them have left the Indians bewildered at these 'crazy whitemen', and have led to disharmony profoundly disconcerting to the more idealistic hippies.

Politically, in San Francisco and Berkeley, hippies merge with the new radicals, and radicalism has old roots in the student co-operatives in the University of California at Berkeley. The new radicals, however, have abandoned the old self-denying ordinances and the puritanism of radicals of the past, and have accepted something of the new self-indulgence of hippy philosophy. Real hippies, however, are not prepared to accept long-term commitments to campaign for the millennium of socialist society, any more than they are prepared to study and work to get ahead in existing American society. In the psychedelic age, pleasure may be had now—drugs, sex and *the scene* are all available. The left-wing democrats and radicals have to concede that drugs and nude parties are great; they promise to support demands to legalize marijuana; they condemn the 'fuzz' (police)—in their attempt to mobilize the hippy vote, and, more particularly, hippy manpower in their political campaigning. Hippies are broadly sympathetic, but they are not *politicos*: life is for living, now. They joined, in the spring of 1967, in the great San Francisco protest parade against the Vietnam war, but it was the procession, and not the speeches at the end, that they enjoyed. When radicals accused them of having wrecked the solemn occasion with their levity and loose behaviour, the hippy retort was, 'Well, why let Vietnam give you a bum day?'—Nothing is so serious that it should interfere with human happiness.

The central focus of the hippy sub-culture is drugs, and next to drugs, beat-groups and 'instant sex'. In respect of music, the hippies are a market somewhat exploited by the entertainment industry, but many of the groups did, at least begin in a different spirit, until after a taste of success they were willy-nilly, sucked into the commercial system. After that the music, and the psychedelic posters that combine op-art and art-nouveau styles with eye-twisting typography, so devious that only those used to the effect of drugs easily read the message, are merely fed into the hippy *scene* by promoters who are not quite so committed to sharing what they have as are the hippies.

Drugs are even more significant than music. They symbolize the rejection of American values—of parents, the middle-aged, the middle-class, the masculinity cult, the athleticism, and the clean and decent all-American boy. They are a direct way of 'dropping out' of society, and of the world. Simultaneously they provide a new dimension of experience. They are the accepted avenue to happiness, and, indisputably, under their influence what a man experiences is absolutely his own. All hippies are drug-users, whether they use marijuana or L.S.D., or more recently, 'speed' (methedrine). They may, when becoming immersed in a meditation cult go off drugs, as they learn to 'blow the mind' in a new way, but drugs are the *sine qua non* of hippy society, although their use extends, of course, beyond the hippies proper to many other American teenagers and young people who have not dropped out of society. For them drugs are the way to relaxation, and a way, too, as the 'joint' (marijuana) is passed from mouth to mouth, of identifying with a separate, distinctive generational sub-culture.

Just as most hippies believe that involvement in politics would

'bring them down', so they emphatically reject involvement in
the work order. The real hippy neither votes nor works within
American society: he tries neither to buy nor sell, produce nor
consume. They are escapists from the affluent society that sustains them. They have attempted to abandon the pursuit of
gain. They live off each other with their handicraft and publish-
ing enterprises, and they scrounge waste goods that cannot be
sold, and sometimes organize their free distribution among
themselves and to the poor. But in so many respects their sub-
culture is heavily subsidized from outside. Financially, it is subsidized by parental allowances, by odd jobs that hungry hippies
occasionally accept in the capitalist work order, by unemployment pay, and by sale of drugs at high profits to those who are
not part of *the scene*. It is subsidized culturally by the entertainment industry and the mass-media, which sell hippy values in
musical form to a wider public, that does not, by any means,
always know the inner meanings of the latest 'folk-rock' lyrics,
which are often eulogies of drugs and drug-taking. The hippy
economy is a curious pattern of indulgence and penury in a
fringe-world that clings to the styles of student sub-cultures. The
hippy culture both rejects the mass-media, and enjoys a new
covert relationship with them—particularly with the disc-
jockeys. The relationship may be observed in Britain and in
European countries where hippy styles have been imitated, and
where the use of drugs persists as an almost conspicuous display
of notoriety among the pop-cultural heroes who make fortunes
out of relaying, to a wider adolescent audience, the values of
the hippy *scene*, which neither they nor their audiences can
really properly indulge. This structured ambivalence of the
relationship of the hippies to pop-culture and the mass-media,
symbolizes *the scene's* relationship with the wider society. Hippy
culture is viable only as a dependent growth. Even in San
Francisco, effective flight from stark American reality is an
hallucination—and the hallucinatory effect is as much as a
result of the hippy philosophy as of the drugs, and may be, in
its own curious way, very much more addictive. No less than
any other adolescent movement of the past decade, the hippies
are a product of the society in which they live, and there is for
them no alternative context in which to live. But their reaction
to that society poses a very much more radical, and, in many

ways, much more sharply focused discontent than the earlier more aggressive outbursts of young deviants. They have a different social class background, and even if they are not quite articulate about the evils of modern society, and even if they have no effective alternatives to its routine, impersonality and bureaucracy, none the less the hippy phenomenon, if not the hippies themselves, deserves to be taken seriously.

14

Technology and the Socialization
of the Young
(1968)

The environment in which modern youth lives is one that is increasingly influenced by technical equipment. It is not only in the modern factory that this influence is felt: increasingly it dominates offices and even shops. From cash registers to computers, the technical transformation of the world proceeds at an ever accelerating pace. Nor should the word 'environment' cause us to think of this development as merely the backcloth against which our social lives are independently enacted. The technical is much more pervasive in its effects than that. It would be an understatement to say that the technical intrudes into our social relationships—they are, rather, permeated by its influence. Nowhere has the technical transformation of life been more profound than in office work, where the effects of computers and data processing have led to a complete reconception of clerical tasks.

For a very long time, we have been used to the idea that office workers, in the very nature of their work, enjoyed both a different market situation and a different work situation from those of other workers. The work itself could be regarded as something inherently different from that of the work in primary or secondary industry. In the lower middle-class suburbs of Britain, office workers did not 'go to work', they 'went out to business'. And since the tasks in which they were engaged were relatively individuated, and allowed them, in comparison with other workers, some discretion in their performance, there was some justification for the distinction that they made, even though others saw it as mere snobbery. Their work connoted higher prestige; they stood nearer to the sources of authority; they were, as individuals, often known to the management by name; and their personal loyalties were more readily engaged in the interests of the concern than were those of the workers on the shop-floor. Because they were in a position to identify their interests with those of the company, and because their work circumstances were highly divergent, and their sentiments so much in favour of such individualisation, the attempts to unionize office-workers were always faced with peculiar difficulty.[1]

The early office inventions did not appear to lessen these conditions. The fact that office workers were, with the arrival of the typewriter and the telephone, more likely to be women than men, increased the force of many of these factors. Undoubtedly, it made the humanizing of office work all the easier; it probably promoted personal allegiances to the firm, and diminished any sense of solidarity among workers. Nor was identity of office workers with factory workers strengthened by the invasion of the factory floor by women, and the growing proportion of women at work, that occurred in Britain during, and after, the second world war. Concern for distinctions of status, rather than the solidarity of classes, appears to be generally more usual among women, and the increasingly common phenomenon of women working may have enhanced, rather than diminished, this disposition.

What has occurred in office work in the last two decades has been a remarkable development of techniques. What mechanization, in the strict sense, appeared unlikely to do, electronics has succeeded in doing. The many rather individual niches in the office work order are being, where they have not already been, rolled flat by the impact of the new pattern of office equipment. The increasing ratio of capital to labour calls forth demands that are both economically and technologically determined, for a new rationalization of the labour force. The particularism of the office disappears increasingly, except in essentially small concerns, branch banks, and the offices of lawyers, doctors, accountants and architects, and other professional men, and in the institutions—such as hospitals and law-courts —in which professionals still dominate functional operations.

---

[1] See, for an account of these issues, David Lockwood, *The Black-Coated Worker* (London, Allen and Unwin, 1958).

Even in some of these institutions—universities provide an increasingly cogent example, since here, to a degree much greater than in the hospital or the court, the 'processing' of the individual client can, alas, be routinized—the administrative staff grows in size, often disproportionately. And as this occurs, the opportunity for the use of data-processing equipment expands.

The nature of the office, and the skills which office work requires, both change, and in consequence so do, not only the structure of the office, and the human relationships within it, but, also, its relation to the substantive enterprise which it services. It acquires, partly by virtue of the cost and prestige of new equipment, new importance. Nowhere has this been more apparent than in those organizations where, previously, the office was merely a necessary co-ordinating agency—a necessary evil in the eyes of many professionals and factory workers. With the weight of technology behind it, the administration is increasingly able to exert its influence in the policy of organizations and institutions. When the administrative machine is itself dependent on machines, administrative inconvenience becomes an important consideration in what can, and cannot, be undertaken. It would, however, be a mistake to suppose that this might indicate an enhancement of the significance of the office worker as such: it is the technological complex, not the influence of the workers, which grows in significance.

Some aspects of the rationalization which Max Weber long ago saw as characteristic of bureaucracy—the deployment of human beings in co-ordinated hierarchies of authority; the articulation of well-defined spheres of competence; the distinction of private abilities and contracted skills; the impersonality of the rules governing work—now become re-located in the system. They cease to be specific to intrinsic human relationships, and are increasingly embodied in the equipment of the office. Whereas, in the past, men adopted the model of the machine in making an organization, now, the machine replaces the human components of the system. Machines themselves become the bearers of the rationality that is implicit in their operation. Thus, the office revolution lifts the burden of rational organization from the rôle-players; it becomes a consequence of the use of the equipment, to which the workers now need only to adjust. Obviously, office workers continue to behave rationally at work; perhaps, indeed, since the equipment is more relentless than were the human agencies of bureaucracy in the offices of the first half of the twentieth century, they are constrained to behave more rationally. But the rationality is not now necessarily a manifestation of their personalities, nor a consequence of the socialization, or (more especially) of the secondary socialization to the job, that they have undergone. Rather it is built into the external order within which they operate. The consequences of these developments, not only for the styles of social relationship in office work, but also for the manifestation of personal integrity, the exactitude, mutual reliability and the sense of work-commitment, all of which were demanded of, and frequently were evident in, clerical workers in the past, are not yet apparent. The formal requirements for the employment of office workers, which have, in any case, become perhaps less stringent in regard to total personality dispositions, and certainly more stringent in respect of strictly technical competences, during the course of the present century, will probably undergo further change. There is, in the new situation, less need to control the whole person in all his attributes and activities, since control is now, in effect, passed to machinery. The older virtues, which were virtues relating to the totality of a man's personality—his 'character', as such a written statement of recommendation was appropriately called in Britain before the second world war—become increasingly irrelevant to competent office performance. Work activity becomes more closely defined, and the guarantee of the worker's performance relies less on his personality, and more on the maintenance and the precision of the machines which regulate him. The employer need no longer demand that his staff should be sober, frugal, industrious, clean-living, decent and conscientious, since these general attributes of character are decreasingly significant for the segmental involvement of the new style of office work, in which the range of work discretion is so much narrower that the effect of such general dispositions is very much reduced.

The inclusive morality of the past, in which integrity of character was the best guarantee of work performance, is less necessary as an agency of social control at work, and a segmentary morality replaces it. Thus, the need for the employer to show more general concern for workers declines as effectively for office staff today, as the need to care for productive workers outside the terms of the contract, and in periods when men were 'laid off', in the industrial revolution. The personal and human elements of the situation give place to the rationale of routinization. The idea of the job in which human relationships matter—perhaps for some time more of a myth than a reality in many offices—becomes even more tenuous, and this despite the concern of companies to emphasize their welfare schemes, benefits and personnel departments. The company which proclaims that it 'cares', perhaps does nothing more than to stimulate new cynicism. Segmentary participation has long been the basic work reality for most office workers, but until recently the situation was at least one in which men still dominated, rather than adjusted to, the machines. The idea of the importance of human relationships existed, and offered ideological support for a type of morality of involvement that made office work in many ways different from work in productive industry.

In the past, office workers were probably of more importance than their numbers alone might suggest, in setting a certain moral tone, not only in the work order of society, but also in some areas of public life. They were, it may be said, often people with pretensions, and pretensions can often be important in feeding aspirations, in inducing men to live up to a higher standards than those which they have inherited. The informal socialization which went on in the office, appears to have promoted this process. In periods of scarcity of work, the office worker's reputation was important to him in keeping his employment, and it was a reputation that had to be sustained in a wide variety of life-circumstances outside the immediate activity of the office. It manifested itself in diverse social and civic concerns, in voluntary associations and religious movements. Standing where they did, associated with, but not participants in, higher styles of life than their own, there is every reason to suppose that office workers might be people with particular self-awareness of their social rôles, and disseminators of particular types of social values. As their work condition changes, these particular associations of the life-styles of an important social stratum, will undoubtedly disappear.

Because their work situations are less effectively under the control of the workers themselves, they are likely to be more rationally organized, and the elements of job individuality will certainly be reduced. With heightened dependence on equipment that is itself dependent on complete rationality of operation, the work situation of office staff will be more effectively subject to external constraint. All this suggests that, in time, a process of education will evolve that pays less attention to the inculcation of what, in the past, we have regarded as important virtues, and less attention to the promotion in individuals of the spirit of rationality. Education for leisure is a slogan already with us: man, less stongly socialized to consistency, rationality and commitment in his extra-work situations, might be more disposed to play, recreation and artistic creativity than the common man has been in the past. But the *contexts* in which he works, and, perhaps increasingly, those in which he is educated, votes, encounters the law, prays and plays, will be highly rationalized and increasingly impersonal in their impact. The rationality that they espouse will rest less on the internalized values of individuals, and more on values implicit in the equipment (and machines embrace a culture, in the anthropological sense of the word—and project it). The moral attributes that were once important to the work order, and that had so much importance in creating a way of life in western society, may become less significant in each of the various segmentary participations of men in the plural society. New patterns of socialization will lead to the internalization by individuals of values increasingly divergent from those embraced within the increasingly technologized external order. The demand that rational behaviour should stem from inner promptings and moral dispositions, carefully nurtured by that style of 'exacting affection' in childhood, so well exemplified in the late Victorian lower middle and respectable working classes, will slacken. Instead, required responses will be exacted by the constraints of the technically-ordered external world. Man will act in accord with the rationality embedded in the machine, rather than that issuing forth from their own educated dispositions. This disjunction between internalized values and those embraced in the external order, may be the source of new tensions and new discontents in society, as men identify rational restraints with the bureaucratic enemy. The new Ludditism may arise because men have, paradoxically, become free individually from the exacting rationality that a bureaucratic society will externally impose upon them. Permissive morality, following free expression in early childhood, as the styles of education for the future, may reflect the reduced demand for complete moral control in the work order of modern society, consequent on machine control. The work order has long been the most consistently co-ordinated part of the social system, and its demands, in the past, for the internalization of moral values that guaranteed performance, have forged western man, and shaped the civic, political and legal order—the total social context—in which he has lived. As work relies more on the values implicit in machines, and less on the internalized consensus of values among men, the old conflict of the individual versus society may acquire, and perhaps is already acquiring, new vigour.

As rational systems grow, and the automation of the office is such a system, they eliminate the need for shared mores, norms and values. These qualities need no longer be cultivated in man —so it appears—since the functions they performed have become embedded in institutional arrangements. Industrialization, the division of labour and the remoteness of the production-consumption nexus that it created, made work a highly objectified and highly visible activity, and an area of life in which men had to be socially controlled. But social control of highly differentiated activities is difficult, and industrial societies came increasingly to rely on the internalization of a set of value-orientations, instilled in the primary and secondary socialization processes, as the best guarantors of work performance. The professions apart, this was nowhere more evident than in office workers. But, in industry, machines have steadily replaced the need for both external social control and the internalization of moral dispositions useful to the work order. With mechanization, and more especially with automation, the productive work order had less need to demand a range of moral attributes from its participants: the conveyor-belt could more precisely elicit controlled responses than the process of internalization of valuable moral attributes could ensure. A similar process of change now begins to affect the office worker.

One side-effect of the intensive process of internalization of moral virtues that occurred in western society, was a particular development of commitment to civic values. The quality of interpersonal relations, and of the public order, seems to me to have acquired a distinctive texture in those societies that underwent an early and prolonged industrialization process. But this quality appears to have few, if any, specialized agencies to sustain it. There is much ineffective grumbling about growing public squalor, and about the much lowered commitment to their jobs of, say, postmen, shop assistants, civil servants and office workers generally. There are sustained complaints from the courts and from law-enforcing agents, about the decline in public and civic virtues. But it appears that when a high level of internalization of particular moral dispositions ceases to be so necessary for the work of society, other social institutions, and other social concerns, are inadequate to sustain the sense of moral obligation at this high level. Moral consensus appears to be no longer a prerequisite for the functioning of the social system, which now relies on the automation of a wide range of instrumental skills and facilities. And yet the social system under such conditions—unmediated by deeply laid and widely shared value orientations—is likely to operate more impersonally and bureaucratically than hitherto, and to be less moderated by sympathy, fellow-feeling and humane discretion. The social context, the state, the work-place, the arenas in which social institutions function, are all likely to appear as more coercive. On objective assessment, of course, coercion may have been sometimes greater, exploitation and petty tyranny more abundant, in a more personalized system; but the objective assessment may be less important than the sense of comprehension of, and involvement in, the working of things. Office workers have, until very recently, been relatively immune from experience of this kind, and as a group they may have played an important part in mediating and reducing the impersonality of institutions.

In the future, office workers are likely to be less differentiated from other workers in life-style, social commitment and willingness to take responsibilities in civic and social affairs, than they have been in the past. The consequences for the texture of social relations, and for the tenor of public life, may be serious, since office workers have been those whose aspirations and pretensions have helped to diffuse to wider groups of the working classes a sense of social responsibility, a readiness for voluntary effort, and a willingness to be educated. The nature of their work demanded that they should acquire a detached commitment and a disinterested goodwill. They acted for others, mediating command and authority, transmitting orders and information. As intermediaries, they needed to acquire a more acute awareness of the rôle-obligations of others than was ever the case with workers whose principal interaction was with materials or machinery rather than with people. As long as the office remained a human environment, it was a veritable school for the acquisition of knowledge and sensitivity about the interaction of personality and rôle. Unreflectingly, sociological theory paid tribute to the office and office workers, in taking it as the model circumstance in which rôles became articulated and where work became most completely organized by the specification of interrelated rôle-performances. It was in the office that men learned how to disengage private emotions from public performances, and to accept the distinction of rôle and person: for whilst *élites* may have acquired this faculty in other institutions, it was the office which demanded it on a wide scale from workers. In being inducted into office work, the young person underwent a process of socialization for his rôle. He learned the importance of disinterested goodwill in working with other people, and a civil responsibility that transcended particular loyalties or partialities—to sex, kinsmen, neighbours or generations. (Anyone who has visited underdeveloped countries knows how difficult is such a training in disinterested goodwill, and that office workers in such societies are still highly partial to kinsmen and tribesmen, and susceptible to bribery from others.) The attitudes and responses learned by the office worker inevitably carried over into his everyday life. The process by which the office became a vital part of the work order, was also a process by which whole generations of workers were heavily re-socialized.

Office workers were recruited largely from the more able, self-conscious and educable among the working classes. For many, office work was a rise in social status: those who took it up were recognized as being upwardly socially mobile. Moving up the social scale to better work, entailed the acquisition of a different culture, gentler and more polite styles of conduct, as well as more acute perception of social rôles. The other side of the matter, was that office workers were often not regarded as

workers at all by labourers and factory hands. His social pretensions were objectionable to them, just as his unwillingness to
acknowledge the similarity of his economic circumstances to
theirs was an affront to the socialists among them.

The technological transformation of office work manifestly
reduces the objective distinctions between that sort of work and
work in industry. The peculiarities that encouraged highly
refined distinctions of status in the office have been eroded, and
the similarities of the office worker's condition with that of
other workers, as non-owning classes, has become more evident.
But it is not only here the consequence of technological development is felt. Perhaps more important than this political consequence, is the consequence for the styles of morals and manners
that men acquired through the finely articulated relationships
of people in office rôles. If these relations were sometimes
heavily preoccupied with status differences, they were also
often not less humane for that. Men were located and identified
in respect of other men, not by their relation to machines. As
surely as technology de-moralizes work rôles, it must lead to
some degree of de-moralization of social relationships and social
involvements. The boredom of working with machines will be
reinforced by the loss of those subtle distinctions and refine-
ments that formerly characterized inter-personal relationships.

The effect of technology on office work has been taken in this
essay as not *merely* an illustration of a wider social process of
technical innovation. The socialization of workers for office
rôles has been regarded as having been especially important in
the general dissemination of civilized values. The loss inflicted
by technological transformation is not confined to changing
work relations in the office itself. It entails the loss of that disinterested goodwill in the extra-work involvements of office-
workers, and in their example to others. But what is going on
in the office may *also* stand as a representative of the technological transformation of contemporary society.

Because of the reduced significance of inter-personal trust and
of the need for a stable reputation, and the loss of those incre-
ments of status that were the reward for acquiring and maintaining good character, older persons in our society have very
much less 'purchase' in their activity as socializing agents,
whether in the process of primary socialization of children, or

in the secondary socialization of adolescents to adult rôles. Their loss of standing because they know less of new industrial and administrative processes is one factor, but more important is the waning significance of moral dispositions in work relations. The old balance of acquired moral restraint on the one hand, and social reputation on the other, has broken down. The effort to acquire civilized attitudes is no longer so worthwhile: the machines don't care.

Neither do the employers. The nexus that provided the economic underpinning for civic virtue has gone. Technological development has not been alone in promoting the changes in socialization, of course. Socialization necessitates the constraint of uncivilized beings who are induced, cajoled, coerced, into more civilized responses. Emulation and distinctions of status were, as manifested in the office work structure, one of the less coercive agencies of the process, and it may be that they were, for that reason, more effective than the grosser threat of economic sanctions. But undoubtedly, the change in work relations has been reinforced by the conditions of full employment since the second world war, which has acted as a powerful dissolvent of the moral attitudes of middle management. As the demand for workers with well-attested characters has diminished, as work relations have become increasingly relations with machines, rather than with other people, so, too—and perhaps autonomously—patterns of child-rearing and early schooling have changed. Much less restraint of baby, and 'free expression' for toddlers, are the order of the day. The union of these two shifts in the demands made—on adults at work, and on children in general —has been consummated, with the aid of the mass-media of communication, in the 'permissive morality' for adolescents.

All these processes must qualify the views of any who might be inclined to a theory of technological determinism. Yet, in respect of secondary socialization, the influence of technological change cannot be lightly gainsaid. Its importance is only enhanced when it is recalled that secondary socialization (to which, especially in its wider implications beyond work activities, far less attention has been paid than to the socialization of the infant child) may, much more than early life experiences, determine the styles of *social* interaction and the expression of *civic* (as distinct from *private*) virtue. Whatever may be the personality dispositions laid down in the earliest years of life, the way in which response is summoned in rôle relations, and the way in which restraint is imposed by civic standards, largely condition the quality of our everyday life. Young people in the 1920s may have been no less possessed of strong aggressive drives than are those of the 1960s, but then they were socially constrained to manifest those impulses in very different combative enterprises (whether in sport or in gang-fights) from those that have now become commonplace (whether football hooliganism or student demonstrations). These changes in the social manifestation of aggressive drives, and the much less effective communication of civic standards, owe a great deal to technological changes.

What has been happening in the office—a sphere of which, even two decades ago, few realized the scope for technical innovation—has been happening in schools, universities, hospitals, and in the organization of recreation, quite apart from the production plants where the process began earliest and has gone furthest. The entire social context in which men live, and in which the young are brought up, has been steadily dehumanized as equipment has become more extensively employed, and as it has imposed its own rhythms, its own imperatives of scale, on human activities. Men themselves are organized increasingly into machine-like structures. We acknowledge this when we refer to the operations of communication and decision-making in any large concern as 'the machinery'. Men do not simply adjust to the new technology and its routine, but they find themselves participating with each other as if they, too, were parts of the machine. Their mutual reliance is increasingly reliance on technical competence in machine-like operations, without intrinsic consequence for other facets of their lives.

What diminishes, and what sometimes even disappears, in such relationships is personal trust. Primary relationships, between parents and children, spouses, lovers and friends, are relationships of total personal trust. Trust is given by, and reposed in, the whole person: it is manifested in character and in its consistency. But in relationships modelled on machine-like activities, trust is not diffuse and general, but highly specific. At work, we rely less on persons and more on technical rôle performances. Even leisure, dominated by cars, television and other equipment, demands that men's behaviour towards each other should be governed by the requirements of the equipment. The diminution of personal trust presents a paradox: we first learn trust in total relationships as children, but later we must confine it to narrowly-defined performances in specified places and at designated times. To socialize the young, relationships of trust are essential. But, increasingly, adults participate in a world where trust is limited and technical. Into these segmentary relationships, adolescents have to receive their secondary socialization. Although diffuse human interaction is essential to the process of civilizing babies, for secondary socialization in the technological society, *human* experience is intrinsically less relevant. Adolescents must, thus, unlearn their total trust, and re-learn—learn to behave more like machine parts, without the discrimination, discernment and subtlety that, in the early phases of the development of administrative and office work, were stimulated in the worker. This whittling down of trust in social relationships is not unassociated with the development of cynicism: it leads to the mistrust that adolescents now so widely express of our technologized social system.

Young people are sometimes well aware of the impress of technology on their lives, and manifest their awareness in their boredom with their circumstances and with the localities in which they live, and in their flight from these things, and in riot and rebellion. In a rich but routinized society there is a frantic search for excitement—for irregular, unprogrammed, spontaneous action. There is a demand for a 'happening', *here, now* —not *there* in the television studio. Drugs, wanderlust (so different from the institutionalized *Wandern* of continental apprentices of the past), extremes of noise, dress, dirt, hirsuteness, physical contact and sensual experience—all indicate the search to break out of the routines of the rational, affectionless technological order of the modern world. The rejection of science by so many Sixth Formers, the disruption of universities by students are part of the same response. At other social levels, among those less capable of rationalizing their needs in intellectual terms, and less capable of choosing for themselves what to do about their lives, there are the outbursts of hooliganism and vandalism. At both levels there is often a curious incapacity to see those people whom they are against as even being human beings—such has been the effect of technology in destroying the subtle comprehension of persons and rôle-players.

A significant element in youthful unrest in the technological society is their gregariousness and the restless search for community and fellowship. The 'be-in' and the 'love-in', and the mindless slogans ('Make love not war') reveal the extent to which there is protest against the affectionlessness of the world. Yet the transience, shiftlessness and haphazard gregariousness of young people do not provide a context in which the security and assurance of sustained relationships is realized. The crudity of the youthful response does not restore the human relationships, the shared values, mores and conventions that the technological transformation of society has displaced. The machines have incorporated and encapsulated man's rational procedures. They have not incorporated the discretion and discernment of which human beings are capable when they implement rational precepts, in moderating the logic of a situation with human care and concern. Worse—they have even impaired the capacity of men to regulate their affairs with discerning affection and disinterested goodwill. And of this, youthful dissidence is itself adequate evidence.

It would be facile to assume, as some have done, that the encapsulation of rationality into machines, frees men from the constraining necessity to moderate their desires. Even the complete automation of all industrial and administrative processes would not eliminate the need for man's acquisition of self-discipline, and hence, would not make obsolete the maintenance of a stable structure of social mores. Even if men need merely respond to the stimulus of equipment in their work activities, none the less their leisure, their political arrangements and all their social involvements demand a high measure of conformity to receive social values. Civic proprieties and many specific commitments to other people (not general slogans about universal brotherhood) continue to be as necessary as—perhaps more necessary than—ever before. Yet, as we have seen in the specific example of office work, if the work order does not impose upon us such socialization, in that sphere where it could be most readily imposed, what agencies will summon those attitudes and restraints by which, voluntarily and without the abrasive operation of law unmediated by internalized values, men maintain the pattern of stable social order?

15

The Youth Culture, the Universities and Student Unrest
(1968)

Student disturbances in Britain in the last three years have been the local, and as yet somewhat muted, manifestation of widespread student unrest in the western world. In part, the British events have been no more than superficial imitations of behaviour that has become fashionable elsewhere. That imitation should occur, and that students in Colchester and Leicester should be inspired by (or even interested in) what students do in Berkeley, at Columbia or at the Sorbonne, is itself a new phenomenon. With ideological promptings, students have come to identify themselves as a 'class'. The concept of students as a class would not have arisen, however, without the growth of a somewhat different idea; that of youth as a separate stratum of modern society, with values and a way of life of its own. And this idea is an important element in the intermittent, desultory but deepening conflict between the generations that has been steadily developing in industrial societies in the last decade.

A sociological analysis of the student riots might appropriately begin with discussion of generational conflict, and of the emergence of the youth culture, which has been fostered by agencies very different from those now active in promoting dissent among students.

The youth culture which reflects the uncertainty about values and status in contemporary society, finds its fullest expression in organized recreational activity—in the entertainment industry. Student unrest is merely the most recent, but, because of the readiness of student leaders to seek ideological legitimation, and to stimulate more direct action, and because of the concentration of the young in educational institutions, in some ways the most dangerous, manifestation of the generational struggle.

The conflict between the generations, symbolized in the hippy motto, 'Don't trust anyone over thirty', is, today, more pronounced than conflict between races, and, as a cause of dramatic popular disturbances, it has eclipsed the class struggle, which is now institutionalized in the arbitration process, orderly 'go-slows', and, not much less orderly, strikes. Teddy-boys, Yobos, Mods and Rockers, Hippies, and the continuing aggressive youth pop-culture have been diverse, but vigorous, manifestations of one unconscious movement. It has had no ideology, no special organization (although in the entertainment industry it has approached that in a somewhat oblique way), and no means of recruiting. But now that the struggle has reached the universities and young would-be intellectuals have been drawn in, a Marx may yet come forth to provide it with ideological coherence.[1]

Although war between generations characterizes many animal species, all human societies have hitherto regulated or neutralized the wish of the young to acquire the power, status and prestige of the old. This has been the more necessary because of the complexity of human culture, and the fact that transmitting it from one generation to another is a slow, protracted and delicate process. The seniority principle is universal, but industrial society, with its premium on innovation, has modified it increasingly in order to recognize, and reward, individual achievement. Hitherto, an individual might anticipate old age with pleasure, as a time when declining physical energy would be compensated by social esteem for experience: in industrial society, old age is but a time when physical decline is compounded by negative prestige, parsimonious charity and, often, by social neglect. The emphasis on social mobility implies that

---

[1] That Marx should be invoked by the student revolutionaries indicates the failure of ideology to catch up with social processes. Student discontents do not spring full-grown from Marxist or Maoist premises: these are merely the convenient terms in which they can be expressed and justified. The theories that are employed are, of course, somewhat inappropriate, since the goals of the generational struggle are—inherently—confused and contradictory.

the old, because they can no longer move up, begin to lose the status they already have, to the young whose potential is not yet spent.

The means of 'getting ahead' ('achievement-orientation' as American sociologists define this characterizing value of industrial societies) has itself become highly routinized. If the old can be much more readily displaced than in the past, that occurs, in general, only as the young submit themselves to the rigours of a complex educational selection system. It is partly against this system that the young are rebelling—most consciously within the institutions of higher education, and less consciously in other ways. Chief among these other ways has been the use of that department of modern society where achievement is least routinized—the entertainment industry in which social mobility (adequately acknowledged in money and acclaim, if not in complete social esteem) may take place swiftly, and without society's elaborate selection procedures. Youngsters, sometimes as a 'group', may move from being back-street nobodies to being 'stars' overnight. Such is the myth, and sufficiently such is the possibility. In the course of the last fifteen years, entertainers have become predominantly adolescents (or slightly older people who pass themselves off as such). This has not simply been some mysterious 'change in style'. Despite the insignificance of the numbers involved, entertainment has been conspicuous as an avenue of mobility where youngsters are unhampered by the need for qualifications. Young people in general go through a phase when they absorb all the publicity of show business, and they derive vicarious pleasure from identifying the show business symbols of upwardly mobile youth. The increased involvement of adolescents in entertainment has been a response—in many ways a calculated response—by promoters of mass entertainment to the shift in the distribution of income that has occurred in Britain since the last war. It is not that the executives in the entertainment industry realized that men have a desire for status congruence—that the young would want more social esteem (and eventually more power) to match their higher incomes. It was rather that they saw that profit must be made from those consumers with most surplus, and they are now the young. The youth culture has thus been largely created by the entertainment industry, and the gap between the generations has been made increasingly manifest. Entertainment values have more and more depicted that youthful dissidence that other, more conservative societies have always deflected and contained. Mass entertainment has captured the principal agencies of expression in contemporary society, and is now the 'normal' way in which men expect their leisure time to be filled.

One form of social dissidence is delinquency—incidence of which is always highest among the young, and modern entertainment has disseminated a number of delinquescent styles. 'Mods', 'rockers', and 'hippies' all owe their names to types of pop music, or attitudes towards it; pop culture heroes parade their deviance in respect of drug-taking and sundry other offences; young music groups have adopted bizarre, deviant-sounding names, to promote the idea of being 'with it'—and to remind older, conventional people that they are quite clearly 'without it'. Governments have been prepared to tolerate, and even to endorse with passing honorific notice, these styles, disregarding the alarm with which each new departure has been greeted by many of the public. That these developments portended a more dangerous development of youthful dissidence and revolt, was scarcely foreseen, but since the assault on public convention and morality was so little resisted, the insatiable demand for sensations, stimulated in their audiences by the mass-media, has led to more conscious challenge of the institutions of society.

Entertainers who have won acclaim as symbols of dissident youth, by getting away with well-publicized deviant (and sometimes criminal) behaviour, have created a sentiment among the young that 'we do whatever we like'—an attitude recently reiterated by people as different as Mick Jagger and Daniel Cohn-Bendit. The demand to 'do what we like' is a demand for power, and one which in its *naïveté* and its anti-social (and anti-human) implications is more radical than the weapons of the old class struggle—the strike and industrial sabotage. Until the generational struggle affected the places where youth was concentrated in large numbers—the educational establishments—'doing what we like' was no more than a posture of bravado, possible only for youth culture leaders with enough money to cock a snoot at conventions and sometimes at the Law. But once the universities became involved in the generational struggle, the idea of 'doing what we like' ceased to be a gesture of individual deviance, and became inextricably mixed with mass action. Before that occurred, however, demands for freedom from conventional, customary, moral and—eventually—legal restraints were disseminated and endorsed by pop entertainers and pop journalists (who are by no means confined to pop newspapers or pop television programmes) as part of that sensationalism on which mass appeal and mass circulation now depends. Their endorsement has been self-perpetuating and self-enhancing, since each novelty must be more vivid than the last, not as a contingent necessity of genuine processes of technical change, but solely because change of style has become vital to success and to profit-making in very competitive industries.

That the young have been most affected by the new entertainment values arises because it is always the least socialized members of a society (those with least informed taste, and least understanding of social values) who are most vulnerable to sensationalism and the appeal to primitive appetites. In our society they are also those with the largest uncommitted incomes, and this fact has stongly influenced styles of entertainment. Demand for freedom from restraint in dress, sex and drugs was prompted by the profit-motive in that part of society where least talent and highest reward are often so erratically combined. The mass-media have increasingly taken on entertainment values, and as the old regional and class sub-cultures of the past have, in face of the increased social mixing in modern society, broken down so the locus of sub-cultures becomes the generational group. The most prominent of these is the youth culture, and its style is determined by the less cultured elements in society who now dominate the media of communications, and who make their livings from sensationalism.

In no previous age have the enemies of a received cultural tradition—which relies on inculcated restraints, internalized discipline and the steady acquisition of taste and knowledge— been not only so little impeded, but so positively abetted by such massive resources of accumulated capital. Legislators have rushed forward to endorse the transfer of rights and status to the young, mistaking those social changes that have been induced by publicity for change that is necessary to maintain harmony with economic and technical developments. The report of the Latey Committee is an indication of the extent to which officials have been 'conned' into believing that 'the wind of change' is some sort of autonomous, real force. But the *potential* enemies of culture are recruited from those who are also its *potential* inheritors—the young. The effect is to make it more likely that they will destroy, rather than receive, the fruits of civilization.

The growth of dissident entertainment values and of the youth culture is part of the context of contemporary student troubles. Spock-ism in child-rearing; 'free expression' in early education; the permissive morality advocated by self-styled 'liberals'—are other elements. Students today have been much more exposed to these influences than could have been the case in the past. Just as they are no longer predominantly the children of a social *élite*, so, too—such is the complexity of the bureaucratic structure of our society—despite the call to be the 'leaders of tomorrow', they no longer necessarily expect to become an *élite* themselves. Students are no longer a class apart from youth in general: the universities have lost their distinctiveness of culture and commitment. Students are now more completely identified with the younger generation, even if they are a particularly articulate, privileged and readily mobilizable part of it. Until recently, the values of the entertainment industry, and the demand for purely 'privatized' standards of morality gave the young little to act collectively about. Imitation of behaviour abroad (where university problems are, in many respects, quite different); some political exploitation; the diffusion of a few slogans from revolutionaries and sociologists —these things have been enough to give the dissidence of youth a collective focus. As universities have become less distinctive places, and have lost their style as ivory towers in which people might read and think, and as students have been less specifically prepared for an ivory tower experience, so their identification with the youth culture has been strengthened. It could not become complete until issues for collective action were found, until the essentially negative and somewhat mindless values of the pop culture could be made into formulae for group responses. But even then, it might not have come about if universities had not themselves abandoned so much of their former mission.

(*1968*) *Youth Culture, Universities and Student Unrest*

The distinctive values of the university were, in the past, the basis for the social control, and the self-control, of students, but these values have been rapidly eroded since the war. Apart from the general factors already considered, there have been causes of this process of erosion quite specific to the universities themselves. The espousal of the new disciplines—from the technologies and business management to subjects such as 'how to teach English to foreigners'—has brought uncertainty to the values, and amorphousness to the structure, of universities. The university tradition itself has been further diluted by using the name 'university' for many education institutions with quite different purposes and functions. Most central of all the causes of decay has been expansion. More *has* meant worse. This has not been so much a matter of admitting people with less intellectual capacity, but of admitting people who were less committed, had less self-control, and who were less adequately socialized for the university experience. The increased influx of people less prepared to take on university values, has come just at the time when universities themselves—troubled by amorphousness, uncertainty and loss of their specific character—were less capable of communicating the spirit and values of academic study. The contemporary explosiveness of students is the best commentary on the expansionist policy of the recent past.

Rapid growth in some disciplines has led to the recruitment of junior staff who have themselves suffered all the inadequacies of the expanding universities: they cannot transmit university values because they never really received them. So the deficiencies in communication and socialization have grown. Many of those who have been prominent in recent disturbances in Britain, as elsewhere, have been junior lecturers and students in sociology, a subject that has grown at a rate unprecedented for any discipline in British academic history. Some of these young men, appointed before they had completed their apprenticeship either to their subject or to academic life, felt that the promised land of opportunity had become a desert, as the inevitable competition with too many colleagues of equal status began to make its demands. High aspirations, sufficient achievement to give taste of success, and competition that made further success difficult—were enough to cause some to displace their anger on to the system. The universities were rotten. Sociology, in particular, had a fund of theories that could be used as 'scientific' explanations of the corruptness of the system. That disenchantment with their personal status was a cogent factor is strongly indicated by the particular slogans they extracted from the corpus of sociological literature—slogans about power.

Societies that encourage high aspirations to stimulate men to achievement create intense frustration for the many who aspire to more than they can attain. In the youth culture at large, frustration finds vent in sundry wanton aggression and vandalism, in deviant behaviour and the thwarting of authority, and in vicarious pleasure of identification with pop culture heroes who have 'made it'. Frustration has been slower to mount among students, who have been used to seeing themselves as relatively privileged, and for many of whom, until recently, access to the human cultural heritage was in itself a special kind of intrinsically satisfying achievement. As the mass-media has diffused money values and the fun ethic, schoolboys and students have acquired an awareness that, even for the relatively advantaged, achievement rarely matches aspiration, and that in a more and more rationally organized society tight bureaucratic rôles are all that most will achieve. The work ethic has gone, and in the face of the novelties of entertainment, that these rôles are dull is disputed by none. As university disciplines and the goals of education have changed, the compensations of having an informed mind and cultural appreciation are not now much emphasized. Politicians have unwittingly furthered the cynicism by justifying expanded educational expenditure as a contribution to national productivity. But students have come to resent the idea that, in accepting a ministry grant, they have pawned their souls to become deployable computer-fodder. The promise of governments that universities were a national investment has been quickly falsified by the disruption of universities by student protest.[1] Yet in public pronouncements about uni-

[1] This particular case of disruption might, because of the dramatic character of its incidence, have an important consequence if it impresses economists, planners and technologists who are wedded to a theory of progress by the development of more efficient machines (including bureaucratic machines) that progress in fact depends on the frailty of human

versities, these ideas have seriously weakened those traditional academic values that were far more effective in eliciting student commitment—that education is for the enrichment of the individual, and that from such individuals an important, but latent, social benefit accrues.

Students were not the vanguard of the struggle between the generations. They came in to it late, and long after the values of contemporary entertainment had been disseminated to the young. The aimless, incidental vandalism of down-town adolescents and football hooligans only slowly became a style—legitimized by revolutionary slogans—for students, or for the minority among them who are the hard-core rebels. Even when students joined the struggle, they did not start from the ideological position that later became their justification. In Berkeley, trouble began with trivial issues, sanctified as the right of free speech (so trivial that it subsequently became the right of 'filthy speech'). Dissent proliferated through a series of minor causes, from the summoning of police on to the campus (seen almost as a medieval place of sanctuary, were the normal legal writ should not run, but which, oddly, had no particular moral code of its own) to the right to use loud-speakers at rallies; disputes about the places were rallies might be held; and the inappropriateness of the American Navy having a recruiting table on university premises. Gradually, the issues became increasingly political, as ideologues made the natural and normal tensions of institutional life into causes of dissension. But the politically-minded were not alert at the outset. They did not start the troubles, and only slowly realized just how vulnerable were universities to disruption once minor matters of regulation could be elevated into keen conflict over values. Only slowly were Marx, Marcuse and Guevara called in to legitimize the struggle. But once this could be done, dissent could be communicated. Local, minor, administrative issues—about personnel (as at L.S.E.[1]) or facili-

---

beings. Neurosis, deviance, crime, addictions, desultory rioting and suicide —most of them increasing steadily in their incidence in recent western history—are danger signals about the speed, and perhaps about the extent, of social and technical change.

[1] The case referred to here is the appointment of Dr. Adams as Director, which brought about the first spasm of demonstrations at the London School of Economics in 1966–7.

ties (as at Hornsey School of Art), or rules that no one was interested to enforce (or perhaps even to break—as at Oxford)
could not be made focal points for the expression of conflicting
values, and the promotion of the struggle. For most students, of
course, the grand theorists and the revolutionaries are as
irrelevant as ever they were, but for a vigorous minority (who
can, over specific grievances, or in response to official action,
win the sympathy of others) they have become the names for
the banners, the faces for the posters and the coiners of slogans.

The process of student unrest has, thus, been from local discontents, inherent in the student condition, to international
ideologies. Yet, an agitator bent on destroying contemporary
society must by now see that modern universities are institutions almost inviting disruption. They have depended, more
than most institutions, on a fiduciary relationship, and for all
kinds of reasons, and particularly because of the dissemination
of alien values to the moden young, the basis of trust has now
been seriously threatened. Without trust, the effectiveness of
such sanctions as those that universities have evolved, is impaired, since they, so much more than factories, ministries,
political parties or even trade unions have exercised discipline
in a context of shared values and close personal relationships.
For a long time British universities were small enough, and
problems local enough to prevent dons and students from regarding themselves as self-conscious 'classes'. Discipline in universities was less exacting than that expected of citizens in city
streets. And yet, these were large institutions, bringing together large numbers of energetic, young people who experienced a relatively common circumstance that might, by a Marxist, readily be defined as 'dependent' and 'under-privileged',
imposed by an identifiable 'opposing' class of dons. Had not
younger members been socialized to academic values and university allegiance, universities would, long ago, have been
places almost ready-made for a class struggle—especially the
more impersonal French, German and American universities.
In the 1950s, some British dons spoke despairingly of the growth
of attitudes of 'us' and 'them' among students, but no one, at that
time, sought to make political capital out of a distinction already
growing in the minds of students in the expanding universities, in
which direct contact between staff and students was diminishing.

Why, then, did modern western universities not become centres of conflict before now? Principally because the values that they so much more clearly embraced in the past, were communicated to, understood by, and subscribed to, by their clientele.[1] As repositories of the cherished ideals of civilization, the universities had, until recently, been effective in transmitting and disseminating these values: their mission was approved widely in society. The coming of the youth culture has challenged these values, although that challenge has been recognized as such only since it acquired distinct political expression.

As British universities have expanded, some students have come to accept a radical interpretation of their 'class' position. Social circumstances have changed so much that it is surprising that only so small a part of the students have actively embraced the new teachings. For when men can, in imagination, no longer encompass their world; when they can no longer be wholly acquainted with its social contours through interpersonal relationships, then, they need to make sense of it in grosser, more abstract, terms. 'Class' is just such a category— unneeded as long as relationships are human, but a ready formula by which to perceive entities bigger than one can adequately know by direct experience. In a situation being transformed from personal to impersonal relationships, new concepts are especially appealing, not only to help people to comprehend the world they live in, but also to provide them with a sense of identity, and values to judge by and live by. Human beings, in this impersonal context, may now be regarded as representatives of a class—one's own, or one which one's own is set over against. In a complex structure this exercise is enhanced by the concept of rôles. Men become rôle performers, and their relations with others are dictated by their rôles. The larger the agglomeration, the more persuasive become the concepts. The large university lends itself still (in a way in which many departments of industrial society no longer do) to the cruder analysis in terms of 'class', but—although the student ideologues are hostile to a rôle-ordered society they have, by living in it, learned impersonal rôle responses, and they are quick to portray administra-

---

[1] These values varied in different national traditions, being more specifically 'intellectual' in France, 'scholarly' in Germany, 'social' in Britain and 'pragmatic' in America: but this is irrelevant to the present argument.

tors and dons as ciphers (not real people) who merely represent that other class. The mass university, like the mass factory of the nineteenth century, is an amorphous and bewildering world, and one which, to many of those involved, has lost coherent meaning and stable values. It is a place where personal and local difficulties can now be readily given almost cosmic significance when a few abstract categories are applied. The bulk of students are not, of course, taken in. But there are real tensions inherent in the student experience, and these have been exacerbated by recent university expansion. Again, students are susceptible to the plausible interpretations that confer a sense of self-importance and class destiny—the significance of which is confirmed by press publicity. Yet the class division in universities is largely derived from the impress of the youth culture and its values. It is not really a class division at all, because it is based on a distinction between generations, which change in the course of time; and it is peculiar to institutions in which the young are only temporarily involved. These are the central contradictions in the ideological position of the student militants.

The problems of modern universities are not caused by either the students or the ideologues. They arise principally from the errors of governments and university authorities themselves. Expansion, amorphous subjects and bureaucracy have occasioned the dilution of, and deflection from, the universities' traditional mission. Student unrest is less a cause of trouble, so much as a symptom of the latent malaise, which, now that the goodwill of students is being lost, could lead to the breakdown of universities as national institutions. Specific problems differ from one country to another. Thus, the fourteen points of Nanterre, issued by French students, include demands for facilities and arrangements (increased staff contact with students; increased recognition of teaching in relation to research) which are taken for granted in Britain. The persistent note in the recrudescent troubles at Berkeley was for 'face to face' seminars, more contact with staff: there was even an organization which gave itself the (to British ears) strange title of 'the committee to establish community'; and one of the voluntary remedial groups that sprang up to promote new personal contacts, called itself 'Touch'. Whatever the local variations, however, the response of students has shown similarities greater than those conferred on their unrest by the common jargon of the agitators who carry the message of rebellion from one 'campus' to another. The common note has been rebellion against impersonal bureaucracy and the loss of human relations.[1] Even small universities have now acquired the ethos of large ones (some of them deliberately in earnest of their intention to become large) and the impersonality of their style has been symbolized by the pre-stressed concrete. Against both, men find it hard to make evident their individuality, and, in the shadow of each, 'human' meanings are eclipsed. Nowhere is the inhumanity of modern architecture more evident than in the new university buildings; nowhere is bureaucratic administration more of a travesty of an institution's traditional values.

Declining consensus about values in Britain has been reflected in universities. Intellect, untempered by taste, character, disposition or even commitment to academic work, has been elevated as the sole criterion on which candidates for university places are admitted, even though we know that universities do not live by brain alone. Reliance on intellect for admission has accompanied reliance on business-management procedures in the running of universities. Lecturers so disposed, could, thus, abandon moral obligation to care about students, since this should now be the concern of specialist welfare officers: academics came increasingly to see themselves as being there on account of intellect, not on account of character, moral disposition or goodwill to others.

Curiously associated with this development has been the impress of pop values on official attitudes, in the competitive effort to sell the new universities by appeals to the young that emphasized enlarged freedom and the abandonment of moral concern.[2] Such abandonment is, of course, an implicit rejection of

---

[1] The degree to which faculty members have lost direct contact with students in the large departments of many universities in Britain would make an interesting study. During the period of the closure of the London School of Economics, two agitated parents, concerned about their daughter's education, mentioned disarmingly that she, after months at the School, knew the head of her department only as a face on television.

[2] Reporting to a commission of inquiry into Oxford University in 1964, Lord Fulton, then Vice-Chancellor of the University of Sussex, said that unless Oxford relinquished its measures of pastoral care it would, in the

the task of cultivating in the young the values and perspectives of the university. Some dons have been so eager to dissociate themselves from the moral values of schools that have made a virtue of disbelieving what headmasters write. Some have spurned letters of recommendation from headmasters in which applicants for university places were described as 'reliable', 'of good character' or 'loyal', mistakenly assuming that those of whom less positive things were said were likely to be more intelligently critical. They failed to recognize that without certain basic dispositions, or the prospect of fostering them, education itself could not proceed.

Recent university failings; militant agitators; the inherent tensions of the student condition have coalesced with the sense of generational division promoted in the youth culture to prompt student disturbances. The fun ethic of the entertainment industry is also evident: the 'demo' is, to pick up a phrase from the entertainment world, 'where the action is'—perhaps in a more literal way than the entertainers ever intended. Demos have become a fun thing to do. Entertainers, bent on destroying traditional culture (from which there was for them no living to be made) have perhaps overplayed their hand. Sensationalism, as they have encouraged it, has come to a point where no new sensations that they can provide can be other than routinized and boring. The dissident values developed in entertainment have promoted a general climate of dissidence in which new forms of social action can occur. The 'protest songs' which were, to the entertainers, merely profit-making, have become, to the clientele, political programmes. Youth has learned that 'do it yourself' excitements have the genuine pleasure of the unexpected and the improvised. Life has again become more exciting than commercial entertainment, but now it is society—not nature—that is available for conquest. The demonstration—not yet so serious that many heads get broken, and directed against only the straw authorities that universities and colleges provide—is a perfect form for such excitement. The permissive context of the university makes it the perfect place.

---

future, compete unfavourably with new universities which had already abandoned such concern. Making an even more vigorous bid for popularity with the youth-cultured young, the Vice-Chancellor of Essex University said that his would be a university without rules.

The freedom that students enjoy so that they may pursue their studies much as they choose, rests on the assumption of self-discipline. That, in turn, presupposes easy association of young undergraduates with older members who know and sustain university values. With the breakdown of relationships the equation has now collapsed. Proper cultivation of the young rarely takes place. Yet the tradition of freedom is still invoked, even though the discipline has largely gone. Universities would be reluctant to call in the police to restore discipline, and even if they did, and gentler as police are in Britain than in Paris and Columbia (where their brutality did so much to intensify student solidarity) their presence would scarcely re-establish the circumstances in which student self-discipline could be re-elicited.

Perhaps because of the resistance of many intellectuals to purely commercial values, the ethos of the youth culture and the mass-media has only belatedly had its consequences among students. Only long after the street brawls of the Teddy-boys and the *Halbstarken* of the mid-1950s, and the beach-fights of the Mods and Rockers, and the football hooliganism, have the universities experienced the same generational discontent. Specific causes may differ and, it has, in this context, taken on an ideological interpretation, but many of the general causes lie in the process of cultural change promoted by the mass-media.

The ideology, fed on the writings of C. Wright Mills and Herbert Marcuse, makes power the central issue for the more self-conscious protesting students. The ideologues have learned the paradox of legitimacy—that authority depends, short of physical coercion, on the acquiescence of subservient groups. Yet power has rarely been a subject of concern for academics, and its locus is not easily discovered in universities. Behind the slogans about power is the discontent of young people in a world where stability of prospects and the security of old horizons have been lost. Aspirations have been encouraged to grow, but achievement is uncertain. The struggle for status has become more intense, while it has become less certain just what status consists in; in what ways it might be achieved; while the rewards attached to it are themselves continually amended by egalitarian govenments. Piece by piece, the legislation of the last decade or two has rent the fabric of the known social order, and has unwittingly destroyed the premises on which social decencies rested. The students' prospects of graduating into a social *élite*, inheriting the values of a culture, and exercising power, have receded as universities have become mass-institutions, and because power *élites* have themselves become less identifiable in the bureaucratic structure of modern society. These dimmed prospects may be a special part of the unconscious stimulus of student protest. Despite the relative privilege they enjoy in comparison with other young people, students are aware of being relatively deprived in regard to the certainties that were enjoyed by students in the past. 'Relative deprivation' is a widely invoked sociological theory to explain deviant and 'compensatory' behaviour. Perhaps it applies to student movements: perhaps behind the nebulous, self-contradictory idealism, there lurks self-interest and wounded hopes for personal advantage as well as confusion and the search for meaning and identity.

16

Social Values and Higher Education
(1968)

I. A SOCIOLOGICAL APPROACH TO VALUES

'Values' is a key concept for sociologists, and yet, in contemporary sociology, it is often simply assumed that everyone knows just what is meant by the term. Social values may be regarded as institutionalized preferences in social action and thought. As such they may be discussed as categories at different levels of generality, and as the attributes of groups of varying degrees of size and persistence. Values specify both the ends, and the appropriate means by which ends are to be attained. They may be the subject of conscious pronouncement within a social system, or they may be much less explicit. The sociologist sees them as attributes of all social systems from long-persisting civilizations, national or regional societies, to local communities, particular social strata, formal organizations or self-selected voluntary bodies. The values of the smaller and incorporated group may often be more specific than those of its encompassing society, the values of which it may accept as the framework within which its own ends are to be achieved, although this need not always be the case. Regional societies may dissent from specific values espoused by the wider nation-state of which they are apart; divergent social strata may have markedly different preferences about the desirable ends of life, and, in some cases, have very different conceptions of what means are appropriate to their realization; self-selected voluntary bodies may explicitly reject the most fundamental and general of the values embodied in the nation state or in the continuing civilization of which that state is a part. Quite small, value-conscious voluntary bodies may come into being to challenge, if not to change, the fundamental value-assumptions of the wider society, or to take sides in the struggle between conflicting values for social realization. Whilst religious bodies are the most obvious examples of such a position, educational agencies have also been committed to particular values, and whilst they have often been involved in the communication of traditional values from one social stratum to others, they have often also seen their mission as transformative of the values espoused in society at large.

Sociologists—perhaps to emphasize the ethical-neutrality that they so much prize—describe as 'value-orientations' the governing criteria by which social behaviour and the operation of social institutions may be characterized. The preferred ends and means of a given culture may be designated in particular ways, usually as one of each of four or five sets of dichotomous characterizations. Thus a society may prefer, and reward, instrumental activities rather than affective activities, and whilst all cultures strike some balance between them, the point of that balance varies widely, moving towards more complete dominance of the instrumental in advanced social systems, where there has been a long process of capital accumulation, of more-round-about methods of production, and the imposition of long-deferment of gratifications of an affective kind. A society may distribute social honour according to ascriptive criteria, such as birth, or according to ability. It may prefer work activities to be organized into highly specific rôles, or it may prescribe arrangements that entail for everyone highly diffuse social obligations. Social prescriptions may be applied according to objective criteria with the universality that that implies; or they may be of more particular application according to arbitrary qualities of subjective importance.[1] These orientations of value have an obvious evolutionary implication, although this has not been the primary concern of the sociologists who have employed these concepts. Evidently they

[1] The formulation of value-orientations that has now become widely accepted in sociology is owed to the work of Talcott Parsons: see especially, *The Social System* (London: Tavistock, 1952). Some of his categories echo the less elegantly formulated evolutionary continua introduced by L. T. Hobhouse, *Social Development* (London, 1924).

describe a shift from subjective, local and concrete applications of judgments, to objective, universal, pragmatic and abstract applications. The social systems that manifest this change grow larger, more elaborate and—in the sense of their capitalization and their division of labour—more efficient. The ultimate ends —and perhaps the absolute values—grow more remote. These changing orientations conceal, however, the shifts that occur in substantive values, which is the level at which value change is directly experienced by men in society (even if a matter of less interest to theoretical sociologists). It is with changes in substantive values that this essay is primarily concerned.

A direct statement of the values of a society may sometimes be obtained from any of its intelligent members. The values mentioned are attributed to the whole society. Thus: 'In this country, we believe . . .'; 'The British have never . . .'; 'Our people hold . . .'. Such statements present the ideal values of the society. Eighteenth- and nineteenth-century travellers, the Tocquevilles, the Schaffs, the Brices, even at their most sociological, dealt in generalities of this kind, describing the commitments embodied in institutions, and what was often referred to as the 'national character' of a people. The discerning traveller also knew that there were discrepancies between 'ideal' values and 'actual' values; he recognized social norms and the extent to which they were regularly evaded privately, and even publicly ignored. Men have some considerable consensus in their evaluations. It may be summarized in proverbs, folk-lore, exhortatory advice, or even in a code. But men also acknowledge a distinction between formal codes and actual practice. Society constrains, but men resist, evade, withdraw. More than this, men recognize that not only individuals, but sometimes groups and even departments of state, evade or ignore their obligations according to the ideal values of the society.

All societies necessarily permit a margin of defection from ideal values, although that margin varies between societies, and also within the same society at different times. When the margin is wide, men talk of 'moral decline'; when very narrow, of 'puritanism'. The margin is an area of tension and uncertainty, particularly when there are pressure groups within society seeking to widen it or diminish it. (Since, in the past, values were largely embedded in religion, such pressure groups were mainly of puritans or 'revitalizers' who sought to reduce discrepancies by making practice conform to the ideal: today, in secular society, the pressures are exerted in the opposite direction.) Since values are not always stated with precision, uncertainty, incoherence and contradiction characterize the margin. These uncertainties have their own function for social cohesion, and perhaps no society could maintain order without the flexibility that they permit.

Societies that steadily relax moral prescriptions and become 'permissive' tend either to be those that have become heterogeneous by incorporating former enemies, or by the intrusion of aliens, or at least of alien culture, or to be societies that have undergone radical change of circumstance—such as defeat in war or loss of empire. Societies become puritanical in periods when internal differentiation brings forth new classes that crystallize out, seek social hegemony, and attempt to articulate, and impose, their world-view by cultural reappraisal and revitalization. In seeking dominance, such classes often terminate the creativity of the past, which had been facilitated by the 'permissiveness', and even the corruption, of the older code of ideal values.

In all societies, particular agencies have existed to express ideal standards of value. Although religion and morality have not been intimately associated in all societies, in major civilizations, those functionaries concerned with placating the supernatural have often become agents of social control. The old clearly exert this claim over the young, and in societies in which seniority and authority converged, and where control over the supernatural was regarded as more important than control of the natural order, ideal values attained cogent expression. Reiteration of social ideals by these agents prevented the margin of defection from becoming 'too' wide. It is the particular problem of advanced, complex and pluralistic societies, that such agencies have disappeared as specific substantive values have lost credibility through cultural relativism and social diversity. In these societies instrumental and pragmatic value orientations remain, but men's ultimate ends become more diversified, uncertain and vague than ever before. This throws a particular strain on the process of socialization—the upbringing and the

education of children, and on those agencies responsible for it
—schools and universities.

II. HYPOCRISY AND CYNICISM

All societies, as part of the condition for men living together,
embrace some measure of hypocrisy. Given the constants in
human nature, the selfishness of men, the competitive search
for the scarce commodities of wealth, power, prestige and sexual
gratification (for the regulation of all of which the institutions
of society exist) hypocrisy becomes indispensable to society's
continuance. Hypocrisy is necessary to induce men to strive
towards ideal values in their own conduct, and to exact these
standards from others. It encourages men to meet in the pretence that each is honest, moral and all that an ideal member of
the society should be, even though experience frequently con-
tradicts this expectation. Pretence civilizes relationships, facilitates social intercourse and reduces fear. It is the real *social
contract* in which men are engaged.

Although this social contract has usually been unconscious,
intellectuals have periodically sought to 'enlighten' other men
about it, and sometimes some members of those classes least
socialized and least admitted to 'civil society' have, albeit
crudely, seen through the pretences of their 'betters'. But until
the mass-media of communication developed, and until there
came into being a body of publicists who were prepared to exploit simple democratic assumptions, the discrepancies between ideal values and actual practice were of no general interest. But in the modern world, and largely through the
efforts of publicists seeking scandals to expose, the hypocrisy
by which ideal values were supported has been destroyed. The
latent functions of pretence have been lost, and an important
lever by which men were induced to behave better than otherwise they would, has been thrown away. The emperor—society
—has lost his clothes, or is steadily being stripped of them: it is
not clear that he can function naked.

Sociologists have—in a way that is perhaps now becoming
old-fashioned—seen the source of men's values as society.
Obviously, values do not inhere in individuals: they are not
innate. They are acquired by social participation. They are,

as Durkheim expressed it, part of the external constraint that men living in society experience.[1] In western society, social values were attributed to the will of God: Durkheim saw God as the objectification of society, and the reference point for social cohesion.[2] Values were a social property, and although men were rarely directly conscious of it, this was implied when they sought criteria by which to judge the behaviour of others, and justification for their own. Much as a man might defect himself, he wanted others to maintain ideal values. Once general belief in God waned, values lost something of their apparent objectivity. When the rôle of privileged strata, members of which had strong interest in the maintenance of social order, became the burden of political attack, that loss increased.

When the objective status of values is doubted, and when the fact of widespread hypocrisy is brought forcibly and frequently to public notice, not only is the validity of particular values doubted, but the belief grows up that society needs no common substantial values. That sense of reassurance that many men derive from common values is spurned. The quality of social order that value-consensus produces is held to be 'false consciousness'. Those who seek to promote moral causes are subject to scrutiny, and their ulterior motives are suspect. The hypocrisy that acted as a social lubricant before is now exposed, and society experiences widespread cynicism. Increasingly, men are thought to be no better than they need be, and there is more direct reliance on direct legal sanctions to prevent what is conceded to be universal self-interest from passing into frankly criminal behaviour.

Both hypocrisy and cynicism coexist in many given social situations, of course, each using one side of the margin as a base line by which to manipulate the other. Hypocrisy is evident when ideal values are accorded formal subscription, and this subscription is employed to enforce a measure of day-to-day conformity with them: cynicism is evident when everyday standards are involved to debunk ideal values. Both are an attack

[1] This concept is introduced in Emile Durkheim, *The Rules of Sociological Method* (Glencoe, Illinois: Free Press, 1938), and is invoked implicitly or explicitly in much of his subsequent work.

[2] Emile Durkheim, *The Elementary Forms of the Religious Life* (Glencoe, Illinois: Free Press, 1954 (originally published 1912)).

on the margin, but cynicism appears—perhaps because this is the phenomenon most evident in the present age—much the more radical form of assault.

Large societies have always manifested variations in the extent of the margin, and in the opportunities for defection given to different sub-groups within them. In societies encouraging creativity and enterprise, the margin had to be wide enough to permit innovatory experiment, whilst not being so wide that moral defections destroyed the assumptions of social intercourse.[1] A frequent device in societies has been to exempt particular individuals or classes from the normal obligations of the ideal moral code—institutionalized, for example, in the case of the *berdache* of some Siberian and North American tribes, who, acknowledged as a man-woman, was both teacher and counsellor; or in the tolerance of Bohemianism in nineteenth-century Europe.[2] Such individuals or classes have usually been ambivalently viewed: the tensions of ordinary men in regard to them, seeing them as creators and benefactors but also as parasites and immoral wastrels, is as old as Socrates. The modern university evokes something of the same response.

In the recent past, the margin of difference between ideal and practical values has been sustained differently within different social strata. Among upper classes defection from normal obligation was tolerated because such classes were beyond social regulation: status might compensate for inadequate morality. On the other hand, the upper-class man might seek social acclaim by becoming an exemplar of the moral code—by being a gentleman besides an aristocrat.[3] In Britain, the middle

[1] The fear of deviation was evident in much of Catholic history in medieval times, hence the very slow relinquishing of prohibitions on various types of scientific experimentation.

[2] That such areas of licensed deviation grow only slowly is evident from the long absence of such sub-cultures in the United States in the later nineteenth and early twentieth centuries, and the migration of American writers to Europe. Henry James once declared that he felt that he was the only man in America who was not in business.

[3] A somewhat different case occurs in societies that are strongly Puritan: here the social values are most strongly espoused by the *élite* religious stratum, and where this religious *élite* also becomes a social *élite* (as it did most effectively in non-aristocratic contexts, especially America) the process of communicating values to lower strata necessarily takes different shape—in that

classes were the custodians of ideal values, and, in Victorian times and in the early twentieth century, moral worth was their primary claim to status. Veblen's attribution to the American middle class of conspicuous consumption, was merely the commercialization of a more profound middle-class trait—conspicuous hypocrisy.[1] The lower classes stood in need of the moral code by common consent of their social superiors, but were not expected to show spontaneous dedication to social values. Communication of values to them, the process of gentling the people, was an important enterprise for some members of higher classes; their acquisition was a principal agency of self-help and mobility for the workers themselves, particularly evident in the development of strong working-class religious movements, such as Methodism, Salvationism and Pentecostalism. Typically, for the classes among which they grew, they overstated, in crude black-and-white terms, the moral message—so much so that the many middle-class people at first mistrusted their enthusiasm, until they saw that this type of sect socialized men 'to the dominant values' of the society (and perhaps oversocialized them, although that was no harm).[2] Increasingly, in the nineteenth century, educational agencies were added to religious agencies as the communicators of values, but with one important difference. Whilst in embarking on educational enterprises, from the late eighteenth century onwards, the churches became increasingly concerned with moral injunctions and exhortation, education, as it later slipped out of the control of the church, was progressively infused with more procedural and instrumental perspectives, and steadily lost its substantive moral content.

The location of particular values in particular social groups has come to be of less interest to sociologists, than the change in value-orientations evident in advanced societies when com-

---

case the communication was from the churched to the unchurched. The consequence was one in which puritanical views persisted longer.

[1] The concept of 'conspicuous consumption' is extensively employed by Thorstein Veblen, *Theory of the Leisure Class* (New York: Macmillan, 1899).

[2] The importance of sects of this type in communicating to outsider and deprived classes the dominant values of the society, was made evident by Benton Johnson, 'Do Holiness Sects Socialize in Dominant Values?', *Social Forces*, 39, 4 (May 1961), pp. 309–16.

pared with less-developed societies. The shift is from the high evaluation of expressive and affective acts as ends-in-themselves, to the high evaluation of instrumental, purposively-rational activities, that in a process of 'infinite progress' have always further ends in view. Successful performance replaces inherent quality: the clever man is prized more than the man of integrity; intellect is more useful than morality. But these shifts may also be looked at in relation to changes in social structure. They represent the shifts from a world organized in small communities to a world in which, increasingly, there is the prospect of one open-ended society (open-ended in the sense that, by migration and mobility, there is no evident foreclosure on what the individual might achieve or where he might go).

The shift from community to global society creates marked tensions however, and not least in the loss of a sense of identity and the loss of inter-personal trust which were so fully evident in face-to-face communities. Such communities were marked by a high degree of affectivity: what bound men and what they shared was emotional involvement. In the global society what binds men and what they share is a set of bureaucratically sustained relationships. Whereas identity was confirmed by a web of kinship, and individuals were located in terms of fixed relationships with others, in the new society men are identified in terms of occupational achievement. Success becomes a principal way in which individuals are taught to identify others and themselves. Whereas relationships were marked by reliance on personal dispositions, in the global society relationships are reliant on technical capabilities and rôle performances. Whereas, in the community men knew so much about each other that there had to be tolerance of pretence and hypocrisy, in the global society men are manipulated, and trust (gullibility, as it would now be called) becomes a positive liability, since public relations is conducted on the basis of persuading men of what they would not otherwise believe: cynicism becomes a necessary defence mechanism.

Since men do not, however, come to abandon community life all at once, tensions persist in the transition. Men still discriminate in personal relationships, even though they espouse universalistic criteria as the ideal of the modern world. They still display allegiances to kin, locality, linguistic group and nation, and perhaps also to race.[1] Occasionally, in the uncertainty of the open-ended society, they reassert these particularities with additional vehemence, as they search for the security of the past from the impersonality of the future—so might be seen Scottish and Welsh nationalism in the mid-twentieth century. But the broad trend is evident—society operates on values of greater universality, expressed in language of a high level of abstract generality. The shared substantive values, and shared social experience of stable community, in which they were embedded, have gone. Only at levels of very high abstraction, in propositions about freedom and equality before the law, are values shared. The expansion of life activities in a highly mobile society gives people wide ranges of choice of behaviour and of life-styles, and wide diversity of values prevails. It is about techniques of evaluation that consensus occurs in modern society, rather than about substantive values as such. Not the ends, but only the means are subjects of assent. So that values have less to do with morality and more to do with technique.

---

[1] Allegiance to race is an especially interesting case: a race as such has no concrete community attributes of its own. It is like 'class' an abstract way of conceiving social divisions (even though the grosser criteria of race are more objective, and more conspicuous than those of class). Communities have often been composed of people from one race, but this was not in itself important, since values arose from the fact of community, not from the fact of race. When men perceive humanity—and much more cogently now when they perceive the nation-state society—as 'races' they engage in the same sort of exercise as when they perceive society as 'classes'. They use abstract concepts to which they seek to fix specific attributes of identification. This way of comprehending society could arise only when communities were in decay, and when men sought other entities from which to extract the virtues, reassurances and certainties that belonged to communities. Like classes, races are not concretely known phenomena: the contours of such a category pass far beyond the individual's actual acquaintance with the world, and because of this they cannot possess the attributes of communities, much as men try to engraft them. Identity with these categories is forced, and in many respects learned, conscious and mediated. It would be sterile to inquire to what extent race consciousness and class consciousness are 'false'—they are self-evident facts of the modern world—but because primary identification with these abstract categories is achieved only through strident propaganda, indoctrination and casuistic ideologies, when compared with the unreflective quality of community commitment, one sees how remote they are from immediate apprehension and direct experience of the real world. See also above, pp. 227–8.

The changes in law reflect this process. There is permissiveness about wide areas of interpersonal relations at the level of personal dispositions (birth-control, sex, abortion) and increasing regulation of technical arrangements (traffic control, zoning, industrial operation).

III. VALUES AND HIGHER EDUCATION

In our recent history, higher education has espoused a variety of moral, civic, academic and cultural concerns. The individual being educated was expected to manifest certain virtues as defined by the social mores, particularly in his public relations, with the representatives of the social order (political, religious and stratificational) and to show appropriate respect for the institutions of society. Beyond the more learning of facts, he was also expected to have acquired, or to be acquiring, an education of emotions—the control of impulse; the restraint of feeling and its expression; the acquisition of detachment and objectivity; a distanciation and a charity in dealing with delicate and difficult moral matters; a spirit of inquiry, and the rules of critical appraisal. With all he was exposed to an environment where high regard was given to the cumulative achievements of human creativity which embodied cultivated taste and emotional control.

The commitment of educational agencies to values of this kind was dependent on similar evaluations prevailing within the wider society. Schools and colleges were socializing agencies concerned with more elevated aspects of the process than those found in the family. Teachers of particular branches of learning were necessary to provide the young individual with an all-round experience of knowledge and culture, which, even though his own parents may have had the same experience, could not, in its many-sidedness, have been transmitted by them. Schools and colleges were dominated by particular social classes and their values, but they regarded these values as *the* values of civilization, and they regarded themselves as their custodians. Since schools were religious foundations they, like the church itself, gave overt and explicit expression to ideal values, which they presented, as nearly as possible, as real values, and for this their concern with the socialization of the young was the justification. In the neutral sense in which the word is here employed, schools were institutions that legitimized hypocrisy. In part, this was often evident to schoolmasters and sometimes also to pupils, but the exhortatory function of education was fully accepted.[1]

The value commitment of educational institutions was present in both formal and informal ways. In residential schools informal socialization was most extensive, but in some measure it took place in all schools. The disciplines—classics, history, religion—were heavily suffused with conceptions of virtue, and part of their function was to communicate these. The self-image of educators, and the charters of educational institutions, were based on the concept of mission. Pastoral care was as central as academic disciplines, and each expounded the themes of the balance of freedom and discipline, community loyalty and self-expression. Society itself was informed by the idea that men were 'in care'. God cared and so did his agents, and this idea was even more emphasized in schools.

Educational institutions have changed as society has changed. The concept of the college as a moral community has disappeared with the disappearance of the concept of society as a moral community. Regulations, like laws, have become the technical definition of freedom, and are much less mediated by shared mores, conventions and subtle, internalized restraints. The change has been evident within disciplines; in the way in which they are studied; and in the socializing aspects of educational institutions. Disciplines have changed both in relative distribution, and in intrinsic character. In large part, value-free sciences and pragmatic technologies have replaced morally-committed humanities. The new subjects have a very different orientation to values. Nowhere is this so apparent as in the social sciences, and particularly sociology, which, in the years 1960–8, has expanded more rapidly than any other discipline

[1] Particular constellations of values in educational institutions have differed between western societies. American schools, responsive to the national need to absorb immigrants and to americanize them, emphasized adjustment as a primary value: English schools, existing in a society that had experienced more continuity than either continental European countries or the United States, transmitted the values of upper classes and were concerned with personal integrity, deference and reserve, and community loyalty—which may be summarized by saying that they were 'character-oriented'.

has ever expanded in British educational history. Sociology is methodologically agnostic: values are treated as *phenomena*. Ethical-neutrality has been the slogan of this subject (even though today there is a reaction against this 'scientific' position among many social scientists). Cultural relativism, and the analysis of values in relation to the social circumstances in which they have arisen and been cultivated, became the weapon by which all values might be debunked, and more especially, by which the received ideal values stemming from classes often so different from those from which the social scientists had themselves come, could be 'de-objectified'. Special pleading for intellectuals, and their values, was the way out of dilemma about the loss of all objective points of reference.[1]

The new disciplines steadily acquired larger proportions of resources, and larger proportions of students. But the stance of the new disciplines also affected the old. Even English Literature and Theology came increasingly to espouse the new scientific approaches, to doubt the values—of piety or aesthetics—that they had for so long taken for granted. The instrumentalism of science has come to be accepted, not only in the procedures of all, or almost all, disciplines, but also in their conception of their goals. The point of studying has largely ceased to be the end of becoming the cultivated, educated man: it has become the acquisition of a good job (or the experience of a good time in the free environment of the university—although this is a less than licit end as far as the institutions themselves are concerned). If students embrace educational experience for essentially extrinsic ends, educators, and more especially politicians, have come to regard education as a mere means to economic national well-being. The justification for increasing state finance of education has been that students are 'national resources' from the 'pool of ability', that might be processed to become better-qualified brains for work of 'national importance' to ensure 'increased output' and the improvement of the 'balance of payments'. Education as an enrichment of the individual, through which *he* might cultivate inner resources by

---

[1] Both Auguste Comte and Karl Marx contributed to this development in their different ways, and were guilty of this sort of special pleading, but the best example of this line of argument is found in Karl Mannheim, *Ideology and Utopia* (London: Routledge, 1952).

learning to temper his dispositions, and acquire civilized interests, the competence for civic participation, standards of virtue
and a sense of humanity—has been largely lost sight of. The
good life, the better self, the liberal spirit, are not now the terms
in which education is discussed. The change may not be unrelated to contemporary student unrest.

The shift in educational ends has been accompanied by the
abandonment of pastoral concern in many educational institutions. 'Free expression' as a theory in the nursery has its consequences in the academy. The disappearance of unifying substantive moral values in society, and the impress of scientific
and value-free procedures in academic subjects, has made the
educator's task of communicating values in informal ways virtually impossible. The academic stance of value freedom has extended from issues to persons. There is an unwillingness to
judge men morally, and faith that, given the opportunity to go
their way, individual adolescents will find—and it is sometimes
even supposed that they have already found—the values by
which to organize their lives. In any case, it is argued, values
are private matters, and individuals are not justified in inter-
fering with others in these things, no matter what the disparity
of age, experience and knowledge. That common values have
any bearing on the *quality* of social life goes unnoticed. This
'privatization' of values is increasingly accepted in educational
institutions: the only values about which consensus is sustained
are those that govern procedures, not those that define ends.
In the past, academics were frequently aware of the ambivalence of the two sorts of rôle that they performed in relation to
the young—as mentors *and* judges, as teachers *and* examiners.
Today both types of rôle are challenged. Some among the
young find repugnant both the paternalism and the authority,
and indeed the very process by which any assessment of competence is made. Even the objective criteria of intellectual performance—shorn of all judgment of moral fitness—are challenged by the more radical protesters, since assessment conflicts with the very abstract principles of equality and non-
discrimination that they associate with the projected global
society of mankind.

The impatience of these students arises, at least in part, from
disbelief in the procedural values of modern society—cost-

efficiency criteria are the obvious example. In part, it stems from the disillusionment occasioned by cultural relativism, and the celebration of the loss of distinctions between communities and nations. Yet there is a curious half-concealed hankering for precisely that reassurance and security that small communities with strong substantive values have enjoyed in the past. Most of all, there is the impatience with the self-evident hypocrisy of institutions that evoke ideal values and connive in their evasion: the necessity of hypocrisy in social life is the aspect of sociological learning that the protesting students have failed as yet to learn. One example of the exaggerated hypocrisy into which institutions have now—with their abandonment of substantive values—sometimes fallen, and which reveals the fragility of the social process, may at this point be in order.

Many educational establishments defend their regulations (hours of visiting by members of the opposite sex, for example) by emphasizing the importance of maintaining the public image of the institution, and the danger of loss of reputation should liberal policies lead to moral misdemeanours becoming publicly known. Instead of espousing certain substantive values, they appeal to the fact that significant others are believed to espouse them. Instead of sustaining a manageable hypocrisy by proclaiming ideal-values, knowing that such values are not always, and perhaps not often, fully realized, they make self-evident the hypocrisy of their position, by appealing to expedient publicity values. As long as publicists demanded that 'advanced' institutions should socialize young people to traditional values, educators could cover their divergent 'privatized' value positions by an appeal to the expediency of enforcing ideal morality. But what publicists have been doing is only incidentally to reinforce traditional values: essentially they have been exploiting the tensions of the margin between ideal values and social practice. As social structure changes, and as instrumental values become more widely adopted, so educational institutions may find that their defence for socialization is weak. Instead of educators appealing to public values in defence of the restraints they seek to impose (restraints that might be better defended in other ways) students, as yet uneducated, might appeal to the new permissiveness against the civilizing values of educational institutions. Instead of universities proclaiming a civilizing mission, they will, because of their own failure of nerve, find their values being dictated by a less educated society, and by the less civilized sections of it, the journalists and the young.

IV. SOCIAL CHANGE AND MORAL CHANGE

The particular values that educational institutions espoused in the nineteenth century were largely those of a community-organized society. The new settled industrial areas did not, as yet, destroy the sense of community of the rural past. The neighbourhood was often highly solidary, and so was town and region. The particularistic values of a local allegiances of the mass of the people persisted, even if to their bases of kinship and locality had been added an element of social class, and even though the abstraction, 'class', was beginning to challenge the more concretely experienced collectivities of men. Schools were well placed to adopt community values, being themselves communal in shape and, sometimes, in spirit.

Because the individual is well known over his whole lifetime, and because all his daily doings are easily observed, the small community controls its members simply and, as it appears to them, 'naturally'. In the early development of industrial society, the new division of labour made such spontaneous community control increasingly difficult: men no longer knew so certainly just what were the legitimate time-dispositions and work-activities of other men. Social control grew difficult as individuals moved from one social context to another—home, school, work, pub—each with its different mores, and each in different company. As towns grew, the impersonality of the environment and the diversity of the mores of those dwelling within them increased, particularly in metropolitan centres. Social control steadily came to be exercised by the impersonal agency of watchmen, policemen, probation officers, welfare-workers, traffic wardens, town planners. And the controllers themselves had also to be controlled by those in higher echelons.

No society relies solely on agencies of external control to ensure social order: all demand internalization of norms. But industrial society could probably not have evolved without more extensive and more intensive internalization. Although perhaps less important than the changes in patterns of child-rearing, local elementary schools were an important new agency of socialization, and before them, the Sunday schools. Schools exercise social control, but primarily their concern was not to *control*, but to *socialize*, children. Although schools have always had custodial functions, custody was not their primary concern. They derived their specific substantive values from the model of earlier schools of the more privileged classes. In some respects, schools also socialized parents, by making their parentage more public: many parents who might not otherwise have been concerned about the child's development, took the teacher as an important referent in seeking to avoid social shame. Children did so more directly, and learned the values of more cultivated, more socially respected, and certainly more publicly-conscious persons than otherwise most of them might have encountered in so close and important a relationship.

In the developing industrial order, the conscientious worker became an important factor. Since work rôles were increasingly complex, it was necessary to rely on a man's conscience to augment whatever supervision (social control) was possible. Since the nexus between working and eating had, by the division of labour, become tenuous, the character of a man became the insurance of his willingness to work. As the work order grew in complexity and technicality in the twentieth century, and especially after the second world war, character became increasingly irrelevant to a man's work. It became a less significant assessment of a man's competence. The control of men, having, in early industrialization, come to rely on other men, specialists in control, and on heightened internalization, came now to be a matter more of man's compliance with the machine. The conveyor-belt is supremely uninterested in a man's character. It dictates his work-rhythms, and, in very large part, makes him a 'good enough' worker, given certain minimal conditions. The employer need not now rely on a man's dispositions: a man may be drunken, lazy, addicted to beating his wife and still be all right as a worker. The worker who was described morally, becomes the worker defined by time-and-motion study. Moral change becomes possible because moral behaviour is no longer underwritten by economic need. The intense socialization of the Victorian era, ceases to be demanded in the work sphere and thus ceases to be undertaken, despite the consequences for public order.[1]

These changing social processes condition the way in which value orientations change. From the substantive values of the past are substituted the instrumental regulations of the present. From the concern for the quality of whole persons, society passes to concern with narrow specialized competenences, and ignores the fact that rôle-players are also men who might have social significance (as well as a private life) outside his work rôle. Oddly, the instrumental regulation appears—from the rebelliousness of contemporary youth—to be even more oppressive than the moral restraints of the past: no doubt, this is so because the old morality was mediated by mindful men, the instrumental regulation by mindless machines.

The morality that the schools were engaged in inculcating was rooted in communities where most of life was lived with whole persons: schools were themselves such places, and, as long as they were dominantly residential, so were universities. As the work order changed, however, the values espoused in educational institutions were exposed to assault. For the new work order they were 'out of date'; education of that kind was a waste of time and money; old disciplines were useless; new subjects defining ever narrower and more technical skills (business management; hotel management; brewing; food science; and the many refined divisions of the sciences and technologies) were what business demanded of the universities. Yet if, because the economic sector of society rejected them, these old substantive values were no longer disseminated in educational institutions what was to become of men's enjoyment of their non-work activities, and what was to ensure the maintenance of public order and public decencies?

Other social changes facilitated moral change. The new society was more impersonal, and the moral ideas and social values learned in the context of community life were less easily applied in the new contexts. Value judgments became more difficult to make, because so many activities now seemed autonomous of individual decision, and, against the machines, emo-

---

[1] This argument is extended in somewhat different context in Chapter 14.

tional preferences were meaningless. Property became less personally owned, so attitudes to property changed: many things appeared to belong to nobody, and men who had learned about personal loyalties and decencies from the community-influenced process of socialization, saw no harm in taking what was nobody's. Mobility and profitability were prized, and sustained commitments and established loyalties became old-fashioned and quaint. Men were absolved from the need to give expression to social values in many departments of their lives, and even lack of fellow-feeling was to be justified if they were 'only doing their jobs'.

Men could divest themselves from moral responsibility in the new society, and new rationalizations came to their aid. Psychological theories, which penetrated education deeply, removed from the sphere of blame and praise many aspects of action, and introduced, by concepts of 'the unconscious', 'defence menchanism', 'displacement' and wide extensions of the category of mental sickness, new excuses for what was once morally condemnable, and unconscious motivations for what once was seen as morally laudable. Sociological explanations took the process further: individual deliction was subsumed in a deviancy potential that was related to broad social conditions, and hence again somehow 'excusable' because, in these terms, explicable. The new phenomenological style of discussion—itself so morally neutral—communicates, perhaps without conscious realization on the part of those concerned, a new moral indifference. This indifference presents itself as 'tolerance' and as a value with special application to private life (although it appears to have less cogency in public life than it had in the past).

Social control has not been, and cannot be, abandoned in society, but of necessity it now operates more mechanically, without the mediation of widely held and shared values. Since socialization to substantive values appears to have become less intense, when social control operates it does so more firmly and more abrasively, precisely because it no longer has the support of internalized mores. The law imitates the mechanical operation of the new types of control found in the factory. Offences become increasingly technical, and they arouse less guilt and less shame than did the moral offences of the past. Since the individual's responsibility to the rest of society is concealed by the complexity of regulation, and since he is excused by modern theories of human behaviour, his offences appear more as technical and impersonal infringements than as a moral misdemeanour.

This development is often represented as the extension of individual liberty, although this extension is jeopardized because the individual's own choices are less protected from the wayward expression of their liberty by others. What this extension costs, is the loss of a deeper sense of shared involvement in society, from which individuals in the past acquired their sense of personal worth and of social order. The change is manifested at all levels of social life, but, should illustration be necessary, dress, which is both personal and yet so public, provides an indication of the moral change that has occurred. Dress was once controlled formally, and in more recent times was decreed by shared standards of propriety: ridicule was the lot of those who too far deviated from acceptable styles. In communally strong societies, such as Spain, modern styles are still subject to social disapproval: beatniks are still objects of open derision in central Spain. But in northern Europe, in fifteen years we have come to abandon our moral concern about dress. Dress was once *public* behaviour: now it is increasingly purely personal expression. The individual has acquired an enlarged arena of freedom: his complexes and compulsions may be manifested without much social disapproval. Society has lost one thread in the web of social control that defines relationships among men. This is a trivial, but conspicuous, example of the fact that men no longer quite so much care about other people, as they become increasingly islands, entire of themselves.

V. OLD VALUES AND NEW GENERATIONS

The values inherited by contemporary society were those that defined and secured a measure of social order for the life of communities in the past. The contours of such communities were fixed, visible and comprehensible, but in a mobile world the contours shift, the local unit ceases to reflect the wider order which men formerly believed existed, and the part men play in the wider society loses recognizable shape and meaning. The way in which a man is known, elicits responses, performs his obligations, have all become more impersonal, mere symbolic expressions of social involvement. His status is accorded by the manipulation of symbols, but these are no guarantee of intrinsic worthiness. Worthiness itself has become an obscure criterion.

As groups are drawn into the mass society, men reach out for moral certainties, for values by which the world might be defined, the individual located, related to it, and provided with a sense of meaning. Their desperate need has sometimes led them to embrace bizarre caricatures of what they want, for traditional moralities, once destroyed are hard to resurrect. Sometimes a charismatic leader is trusted to restore order and balance, and the revitalization movement he leads may—as in Germany in the inter-war years—become a grotesque perversion of the rural, atavistic values in the name of which it marshals some of its support. Or the need leads to the formation of new patterns of group life as men build new communities to establish moral certainties, as immigrants have often done—a recent example being the espousal of Pentecostalism by formerly Roman Catholic Italian and Puerto Rican immigrants to the United States, and country people in the new urbanizing conditions of Latin America.[1] These are attempts at adaptation, and they are also the search to rediscover the moral certainties of a world that has been lost. What such groups provide is often of only immediate value for the members themselves, but they may also present the idealized values of the traditional communities of the wider society, even though, as that society becomes mobile, impersonal, corporate and massive, these values cease to inform wide areas of public action.

Modern societies do not maintain a consensus of values, so much as increasingly common instrumental value-orientations. These are the accepted ways of proceeding towards the attainment of goals which are non-terminal and vague—such as self-interested achievement. The procedures that are enjoined on men are not sacred, substantive values, and once the distinction is established it becomes impossible to agree with those

[1] For an interesting account of Puerto Rican sects, see R. Poblete and T. D. O'Dea, 'Anomie and the "Quest of Community": the Formation of Sects among Puerto Ricans of New York', *American Catholic Sociological Review*, 21, 1, 1960, pp. 18–36.

sociologists who write, 'A society is held together by its internal agreement about the sacredness of certain fundamental moral standards.'[1] This may have been true of the past, but there is nothing of the sacred about co-ordinated rôle performances, and much less that is moral (as distinct from technical or legal) in the way in which men are rôle-related in contemporary society. The rules, by which rôles are performed and related, do, *in a sense*, hold together a modern society by sustaining its highly complex economic, political, juridical, educational structures. But it is the institutional framework and its demands, not the consensus of moral concern of men for each other, and for their social order that undergirds the society. It is not the substantive values that men have in common, but their willy-nilly involvement in the widely embracing demands of the rationally constructed system that men share. There is nothing sacred about this: it summons no affection, and arouses little emotional commitment except hostility.

The decline of the substantive morality of the past needs no documentation. The changes in the law, the increasingly diverse values presented by mass-media, the rejection of what were, even fifteen years ago, 'common decencies', are evidence of it. This is not merely the change of moral rules, it is the rejection of substantive morality as such, made possible because men are mechanically rather than morally controlled. The restraint needed for men to live together peaceably is asserted less in moral terms about the sacredness of the community, than by operation of the law. Society's demands on individuals were ever irksome, and individuals—particularly the young, who rarely understand to what extent they depend upon society—often welcome the new freedom. The balance of freedom and discipline so much emphasized in the past (and nowhere better illustrated than in academic discipline and academic freedom) has broken down. In a curious, back-handed way what is realized is not the vision of Karl Marx, backward-looking and communitarian, but that of Herbert Spencer, of a time when men would not exist for society, but society for the individual. In large part, the relationships have changed from those characteristic of a village fiesta, in which all generations were

[1] Edward Shils and Michael Young, 'The Meaning of the Coronation', *Sociological Review*, 1, 1953, pp. 63–81 (p. 81).

involved, to those of a modern dance-hall, where each individual (and it has become individuals rather than couples in modern dance styles) requires the other people *only* to provide the atmosphere in which he can act out 'his thing' in what may, without travesty, be called isolation. There needs to be no real concern for the others, only a set of regulations for motor operations. Civility prevails perhaps, even friendliness, but the friendliness is often only the prostitution of genuine affection (still known of course in the family and in courtship relations, and, sometimes, though perhaps decreasingly, in adolescence) expressed in anodyne questions and comments, not meant in themselves, so much as used to lubricate otherwise abrasive rôle-relationships.

The decline of stable communities promotes the establishment of much less mediated relationships between the individual and the agencies that operate for the whole society—the state in its various departments, the big industrial companies, and, above all, television. In the mass society, individuals are isolated, the society atomized. Ideas are transmitted less through social groups—kinsmen, neighbours, associates—and more directly to the individual. Information and values are no longer sifted, censored, mediated by the stable community, but come direct from a complex and bureaucratic agency which operates for profit, prestige or power, and offers gratifications to individuals in return. The appeal to primitive appetitites can be more direct because of the absence of the mediation of those who know one personally. Indeed, social groups may appear increasingly to be nuisances in the individual's way—as the agencies trade on man's hedonism and on their ability to circumvent normal social controls in their presentation of information and values. Thus they can offer, more daringly than ever before, the prospects of vicarious sexual stimulation, hallucinatory experience, profit, power, or other gratifications without any of the restraints that occurred in the past. The individual would, in the past, have forfeited reputation had he sought enjoyment in any other than conventionally acceptable ways, but in the anonymous society such control is no longer effective. The climate changes then, and demands grow, largely from those who make profits, for the abandonment of the irksome human relationships that prevailed in the past. Hence there is demand for elimination of censorship; for the rejection of all legislation that might be regarded as paternalistic (licensing laws, Sunday observance, gambling restrictions); for new sexual permissiveness; for changes in the law in regard to at least 'soft' drugs. Things that once were largely controlled by families and neighbours, are left to the state, as the community diminishes, and the powerful agencies that profit from exploiting man's more primitive appetites put pressure on the state to change its laws.

As the agencies that communicate values change, so the values themselves change. The mass-media and the advertising agencies compete for attention, less and less restrained by the decencies of the past, and increasingly impatient of whatever restraints remain. As restraints are removed so the quality of public order changes. But the competition of the media leads men to new cynicism in regard to their claims: from a society that operated on extensive trust among men, we move to a society in which distrust becomes a necessary feature of self-protection.

The changes in society have been so rapid that the differences in value-commitment may, at the present time, be almost generationally observed. The conflict of the generations is now something very much more than the old biologically-modelled struggle of new bucks and old bulls, that older people refer to when the wish to find solace for themselves about contemporary trends. The conflict is not a struggle by the young to occupy positions of seniority, but is the attempt to eliminate seniority. The young have been exposed to new values—the emphasis on youth; on the moment, on activity, and on enjoyment, and most of all on change, which is the central value of the system. Not all the younger generation espouses these values equally, of course, and those who do, often do so with contradictions, obscurities and in consistencies. They are not values with the intrinsic substance to command consensus in society, since they are highly individualistic, and they are embedded in particular sections of society: most of all they lack any commitment to social continuity. They are values in sharp contrast with the old morality, and they have fullest expression in that section of society, the entertainment industry, that has replaced religion as the principal expressive agency for social values.

The emphasis on 'fun' is, of course, in sharp contrast to the instrumental value-orientations of advanced industrial society. It represents in itself a rejection of instrumentalism, and the somewhat frenetic insistence on 'having fun' in our society is no doubt itself an exaggerated reaction to the way in which so much of everyday life is becoming routinized and desiccated. Such a reaction is also evident in another ill-accommodated element—the search for some of the values realized in the community-based society of the past, which may be called affectivity values. The strong modern emphasis on sexual experience, and the romanticization of it, whilst often accepting the casualness of sex in mobile society, also very strongly suggests the search for a relationship that will be, in the words of the pop songs, 'for ever'. The particularism of local communities is rejected by the highly mobile young people of today, whose impressions are no longer acquired from life in a fixed locality, and who frequently declare their own localities to offer them nothing but boredom. And yet, these same youths also manifest highly exaggerated local loyalties in their behaviour before, at and after football matches: this, too, may be regarded as a distorted pathological symptom of a deeply-felt need. The discrimination made between 'us' and 'them' among football crowds is in sharp contrast with the demand—also made largely by the young—that all racial, national and sex discrimination should be eliminated.

The principal form of discrimination accepted by the young is based on age differences: older people are not to be trusted. But mobility, casualness and superficial acquaintance under the banner of age-group solidarity all militate against the emergence of any enduring orientation even for those people who are (temporarily) young. In the modern, technological world, human beings are highly expendable. They are overtaken and consumed by rôle-commitments. It is only the young, and especially those who, as students, have ill-defined rôles, who can ride such a cause, and youth's a stuff that won't endure. But youth-inspired social disruption—probably now something that we must learn to live with for the rest of all our lives—is what happens when one generation has abdicated (partly voluntary and partly by force of circumstances) responsibility for socializing the next.

VI. THE DILEMMA FOR HIGHER EDUCATION

Contemporary continuing processes of social change place institutions of higher education in an especially delicate position, because they are agencies of advanced socialization; because they, perhaps more fully than any other institutions in society, feel the impact of the young as a collectivity; and because they experience, in the changing character of disciplines, and the changing social rôle of knowledge, the fundamental shifts in the orientations of society. It is not without significance that the disturbances about values, and the principal upsurges of young people have occurred not in factories, but in universities. When workers strike it is almost always for pay or improved conditions: it is evident, even without a Freudian interpretation of a displacement of tensions, that students at present protest on any of a variety of excuses. Protest is itself the posture of the young who have any pretensions to awareness of the world. Part of the stimulus arises, however, from precisely the cause of football hooliganism—action is demanded in a society that has become routinized and tedious, in which life has become so unhazardous that hazard has to be manufactured. The remoteness of decisions, and the impersonality of the system, the scale and the complexity (even of universities in the way that they are now organized) makes life hard to understand, hard to make sense of, intellectually and, even more, emotionally.

In the process of rapid change, universities have operated on a wide variety of divergent assumptions. Just as shared values do not hold societies together, so they do not hold universities together. Universities are maintained by a highly institutionalized pattern of operation. Within this framework many divergent demands and expectations struggle persistently for realization. Today, the struggle has become much more overt, and much more stratified—largely along generational lines (there is some considerable degree of convergence, but no absolute coincidence, of particular generations and particular strata in these divisions). The operation of universities has been largely informed by their embodiment and enactment of moral and cultural ideas that can be said to have arisen largely in the last century. Commitment to academic work; self-discipline; the importance of educating the emotions as well as the mind;

259

the benefit of easy association of older and more experienced minds (and men) with younger and less experienced ones—these were some of the assumptions and values. But the values of the universities have been shifting, sometimes by deliberate choice, and sometimes less consciously. When one recalls the Report on Halls of Residence prepared for the University Grants Committee only a decade ago, one is presented with values that quite a number of people in universities would today regard as 'old-fashioned' to the point of quaintness. Change has been rapid, but would be defended by some as appropriate to the need to 'keep up with the times'. There appears to be no other criterion of value to be invoked but this contentless concept of change.

We have noted how the humanistic orientation of universities has diminished, and universities have increasingly abandoned older substantive values for new operational values. The ends of the universities mission in the world have been pushed from view: they have now receded beyond a point where it is decent to inquire about them. Those who do are regarded as being wishy-washy, unpragmatic, impractical idealists. The means have become the primary focus—how to push more people through for the sake of national productivity. The quality of the experience and even the quality of the product become irrelevant considerations, as long as the institutional structure remains and *appears* to be doing something of the same job. The ideals of educating people *better*, and giving them a more meaningful experience, are surrendered in order to go through the motions of educating more people. More students go through without any of the transformative experience that a university should offer—unless the acquisition, by some, of generalized hostility to society be taken as the purpose of the exercise.

This development, too, may be seen as a perverted and pathological symptom, analogous to the exaggerated and perverted local loyalties manifested in football hooliganism. Universities did, in the past, sustain values that promoted criticism of the wider society as a useful end. Whilst universities supported in some measure the idealized values of the social system, they also maintained, in the nature of intellectual inquiry, a critical and questioning approach to the world. The apparent contradiction was resolved in the high-mindedness, emotional control and detachment that, at its best, characterized these exercises. Healthy scepticism about social arrangements was part of the best in the university tradition, but that scepticism did not lead men to become anti-social. Aware of a measure of hypocrisy in society, members of the university community did not then engage in the type of exposé now so much presented by the Sunday newspapers and the B.B.C., and imitated by student newspapers. The onslaught on received substantive values, in the interests of the new instrumentalism, and the permissiveness it encourages in the private sectors of society, has led to the souring of healthy scepticism. Cynical hostility to society has followed for at least a sizeable section of those in universities, and the universities, increasingly committed to the new instrumentalism, find it hard to maintain themselves as communities.

Among many dissident students, the new value-orientations are, of course, as much a focus of attack as the old. Whilst they reject the paternalism—at least in name—they also attack the universities for serving the technical-military-industrial complex. They are—perhaps not unreasonably—affronted when Vice-Chancellors discuss 'university productivity' and when they are referred to as 'output'.[1] Their demands for association in the running of universities are perhaps to be seen as a demand not so much to be consulted about the technical decisions that inevitably have to be taken in the organization and administration of complex institutions, but as a demand for more contact with dons, for treatment as human beings rather than as potential adjuncts to the bureaucratic machine of the state and industry. It is, perhaps, the demand for some sort of affiliation to a meaningful community. That it is dressed up in political terms merely reflects the current ideologies of discontent which are the means by which students are mobilized.

In this, the protesters are themselves the victims of the highly instrumental values against which they protest. They believe that representation in university decisions will give them the sense of identification that they lack. This in itself illustrates their unawareness of the complex and technical character of the decisions undertaken in modern organizations. But it also indi-

[1] See, for example, *Universities and Productivity*, papers collected for a Conference convened through the Vice-Chancellors' Committee and the Association of University Teachers, 21st March 1968.

cates the extent to which they have come to assume that the modern, formal, instrumental relationships are significant. It reflects the breakdown of good personal relationships in universities, and of the sense of the university as a community engaged in a shared enterprise. That representation would do nothing to satisfy their complaints, nor to affect the operation of universities is unseen by them—and sometimes unseen by the university authorities themselves. Formal student representation is not a solution of the problem of the universities, so much as a device that might help to prevent the problem of universities being solved. Universities are, even today, agencies of socialization. It is not surprising that young people should be bewildered by them, for their first encounter with mass institutionalized life is in universities. Appropriately, the universities continue to present demands on their unsocialized entrants, but increasingly they do it without the mediation of sustained human involvement and concern that socialization itself requires. Universities once shared the diffuse, affective concerns for students that characterize educational institutions for younger people, but now that that character has so largely gone, it is not surprising, that there is protest at the growing impersonal character of higher education. The growth of size of the universities has itself both occasioned the new protests and facilitated their expression. Universities command little, perhaps no loyalty, from many of their students, although this was a marked feature of their character in the past. Hence students can now turn with hostility on what only a few years ago would have been referred to as their *alma mater*. It is no longer that for many of them, and its affective leverage has gone. Instead of commanding affection and loyalty in its students, it awakens, at least in a significant minority, hostility and aggression, ludicrously conjoined with demands for closer association.

Education is a part of socialization, and commitment is best elicited where individuals can be engaged emotionally, in a controlled, detached spirit, as well as intellectually. As reliance for education has shifted to more technical processes; as the numbers involved have grown to the point where the individual is frequently anonymous; as specialization has widened the intellectual gulf between teachers and students, the possibilities of such emotional engagement have been lost. Personal contact of an educative kind between teacher and taught has diminished, and increasingly the young socialize each other. In the uncertainty of a world with highly divergent expressions of value, and in universities that retain many of the forms, but less of the substance of personal concern, it is hardly surprising that this socialization leads to attitudes and actions of radical discontent.

Educators and sociologists generally point to the environment in the explanation of particular social problems. This has been largely the perspective of this essay. But the environment is not merely a matter of better material facilities, particularly in contexts in which socialization is taking place. If, as the evidence from infant socialization strongly indicates, personal regard is a vital element in adequate socialization, the routinization of procedures in universities will not of itself improve either the process or the product. It may, indeed, as has been suggested here, help to eliminate that human concern by which a distinctive culture is transmitted. The commitment to human culture —to the things that man has wrought, and to the refinement of his sensibilities, intellect and critical faculty—is surely a part of education. It is not a part that can be sustained by the mere training of men to adapt themselves to increasingly technical rôles. It requires the cultivation of what might—without any religious overtones—be called the human spirit. In its perverse way, student discontent may be regarded as the demand for the servicing and the feeding of that spirit.

The 'fun ethic' itself is part of a protest, itself no less perverse, against the way in which instrumental values squeeze joy out of life.[1] It is a reassertion that men should enjoy themselves. It is itself expressed through commercial agencies that give expression to a demand that is profitable, and which they at-

---

[1] Of happiness we have, of course, no measure. One cannot but be impressed by the frequency with which young people profess boredom. It is a factor recognized by criminologists in explaining juvenile delinquency. On a wider canvas, it is also clear that surfeit of entertainment dulls response, and our society is one that devotes immense resources to continuous entertainment. Another indicator is the way in which adult pleasures of yesterday are no longer pleasurable, and are thought fit only for children: yesterday's political ditties are today's nursery rhymes; yesterday's great novels are today's schoolboy's stories; yesterday's great poetry ends up in today's 'O' level syllabus, where any suggestion that it once gave pleasure to people is an incredible idea to many of those who have to learn it.

tempt to satisfy after their fashion. We cannot here discuss the
extent to which expanding entertainment, and its impersonal
provision themselves preclude spontaneity and joy, and result
in the boredom to which so many of our young people give
voice. But we can recognize the extent to which the fun ethic
and the professional entertainers offer *immediate* gratifications.
Inevitably, that sort of pleasure must be superficial and primitive, uncultivated and sensational. Protesting students also
demand the instant. They seek 'action' and want to be 'where
it's at'. They will not wait until their demands are discussed or
considered. But the educational process cannot be instantane-
ous. The acquisition of faculties by which to enjoy the world,
and particularly to enjoy man's cultural products, can be only
slowly acquired. There is in this time-perspective a vital difference in the values that universities espouse and the values of the
contemporary youth culture. The 'free universities' that have
been proclaimed—particularly in America—are, of course, an
attempt to realize the impossible goal of instant education—the
chance to talk out the tensions, to put the world to rights. They
are anti-universities, since they reject the inevitable slowness of
the process of accumulation of knowledge, artistic insight and
critical discernment. What they do offer, however, is the appearance of community—albeit sect-like, dissident and unstable—
but still a group of which the contours can be known, and in
which some sort of identity might be established.

The community-ordered world has gone. And it may be that
only in that world could values be enunciated that appeared
to men to be intergrative of societies, because they were integra-
tive of communities (which may be a gross sociological error).[1]
It may be that only in a world of that kind, full of little traditions that were periodically transformed by priesthoods and

[1] Emile Durkheim, who first propounded this thesis in *Elementary Forms
of the Religious Life*, op. cit., did so with reference to Australian aborigines,
in whose tribal life the community and the society were scarcely distinguishable, since the society took cognizance of itself only as it assembled as a
community. The relevance of the thesis to vast and complex industrial
societies may well be questioned, although it may have had cogent application to the traditional society of the past which was a summation of many
communities, and which saw itself as a community, as far as it saw itself at
all.

aristocracies into great traditions, could art be created, and its appreciation be cultivated. If all this is so, nothing that universities can do will much affect things. The struggle between instrumental values in the work-order, and increasingly throughout the social system, and of the fun ethic in leisure hours, may continue, and between them squeeze out of existence the cultivated values of the past. Rapid social change may impress people, as they seek to compress more into their lives, that 'life is too short' for the slow acquisition of sensitivity, human concern, a sense of history and an appreciation of humanity's past achievements and products. Because so much will be realized so much more quickly in the technical sphere, men may come to believe that 'having it now' is imperative, even though human relationships and human values are not capable of instant realization.

The new symbols may increasingly be those that are simply instrumental in communicating objective and accurate quantities—the old symbols of value systems, religious beliefs and artistic creation (the meanings of which are, paradoxically given their supposed function, already often known only to specialists) may lose that lingering resonance that even now they retain, and by which they evoke man's aesthetic appreciation. Art, as the reflection of man's communion with the world and with his fellow-men, as the product of both objects and the emotion that the artist intertwines with external reality in representing it, may become a backward thing, despised because it lacks objectivity and perhaps because it lacks the immediacy of the extended external world that will become more widely visible and apprehendable. If all this occurs, then the university as it has been known thus far, will have no place in the world. Its successor will be concerned only with 'findings', rather than with knowing by appreciation.

But the technological society of the future will come into being only if men are prepared to assume the rôles necessary for its operation. In a paradoxical way, the hippies and the student protesters of the present time, may be an indication that many men will not be so prepared to accept the uneasy balance between instrumental values and the fun ethic. Certainly, their protest is ill-informed, fogged by irrelevant slogans and misplaced aspirations, and underwritten by naïve ideas of Utopia.

But protest as such may not be misplaced. The modern university is in danger of forgetting its mission, even though the student protesters do not adequately comprehend what that mission was and might be. That mission already has its powerful enemies in the universities, men who have pawned themselves to the future with no clear idea of what the purpose of their enterprise is, and without realizing that human frailty may yet be the issue on which the technological dream founders.

The university might yet seek to reorientate itself to the task of slowly inducing appreciation of human achievements, of restoring as a central concern the communication of cultural values, and recognizing as a worthy mission the attempt to induce young people to cultivate their inner resources. It would mean considerable reallocation of funds between disciplines, it would mean a reappraisal of the functions of contemporary education, and it would mean a critical assessment of those teaching methods that have become technological. But if it meant that students acquired a wider and deeper sense of involvement, not only with the university, but with the development of the best in human culture, and recognized again the university as a repository of real values, not merely an arena of power-struggles, the change might save even the technical developments of our civilization. It would not matter if the frontiers of knowledge were pushed back more slowly, if we recognized that the cost of making them move more quickly might be man's inability to cope with knowledge, and his increasing misery at knowing neither his social world nor his inner self.

Index

Figures in bold type indicate the central reference to a particular subject

Abortions, 175, 244
Abrams, M., 43*n*.
Academics, 107, 111, 114, 128, 196, 232, 247
  contact with students, 75, 76, 102, 114–15, 120–2, 132, 134, 138, 142–3, 187, 229, 232, 262
  expansion and, 74, 136
  values of, 78–80
Achievement-orientation, 60, 70, 71–2, 95, 98, 164, 178–9, 220, 225; *see also* 197, 254
Advertising, 23, 24, 29, 45
Affectivity, 65–6, 235
Affluence, 14, 163, 169, 190, 191, 195
Alienation, 24, 26, 38
America, 15, 47, 175, 228*n*., 240*n*., 264
Anonymity, 48, 89, 166, 169, 171, 176; *see also* 256
A.U.T., 85, 114
Authority, 22, 36, 37, 204, 232, 237, 247

B.B.C., 28, 46, 167, 261
Bendix, R., 59*n*.
Berkeley, 200, 218, 226, 229
Birmingham, University of, 74, 118*n*.
Blackett, P. M. S., 135*n*.
Blumer, H., 41*n*.
Bowlby, J., 176*n*.
Bradbury, M., 17, 140*n*.
Britain, 15, 16, 19, 21, 30–1, 53, 73*ff*., 142, 192, 202, 204, 207, 228*n*., 240*n*.

Bureaucracy, 24, 195, 197, 203, 207
  in universities, 134, 229, 230; *see also* 209, 256, 261

California, University of, 18, 200
Cambridge, University of, 73, 135*n*.
Capitalist economy, 15, 30; *see also* 166, 191
Censorship, 175, 257
Child-oriented society, 168–9
Child-rearing, 214, 223, 250
Cinema, 21, 41, 42, 45, 49, 50
Clark, B., 68*n*., 143*n*.
Class(es), 30, 86, 94, 127, 160, 162, 178, 203, 205, 240, 244, 246
  as a conceptual category, 38, 218, 227, 228–9, 249
  crime and, 179, 182
  mass-media and, 86–7
  middle, 54, 59, 90, 161, 171, 201, 209, 240
  struggle of, 38, 219, 221, 227
  upper, 38, 54, 56, 240
  values of, 175, 237
  see also Working Class
C.N.D., 17, **33–40**, 170
  as millennial movement, 34–5, 37
Communities, 91, 234, 242, 243*n*., 253, 254, 258, 264
Community, 90, 193, 249, 264
  breakdown of, 88, 99, 162, 170, 175, 177, 180, 242, 245, 252
  in universities, 80, 144, 146, 261, 262
  search for, 217, 248
  values of, 48, 249, 251, 254

Competition, 24, 54
  in universities, 76, 103, 109–10, 230
  of mass-media, 92–3, 257
Comte, A., 246n.
Credit cards, 191
Crime, 42, 173, 175, 182–3, 192
  mass-media influence on, **41–50**, 183
Criminality, 17, 23, 97, 173
Culture, 25, 32, 35, 54, 244, 265
  cultural diffusion, 44, 52
  cultural goals, 21, 70
  cultural heroes, 27, 44, 127, 202
  cultural relativism, 237, 246, 248
  of machines, 209
  opposition to, 77, 79, 82, 223
  universities and, 77–8, 82–3, 85, 107, 110
  see also Youth Culture
Cynicism, 24, 35, 208, 216, 238–9, 240, 261
  in universities, 80, 81, 85, 225
  mass-media and, 45, 257

Delinquency, 36, 41, 86, 156, 159, **173–84**, 221, 263n.
Delinquents, 42, 183
Democracy, 38, 39, 170, 176
  and education, 142
Demonstrations, 33, 34, 38, 83, 215, 231
Demoralization, 14, 213
Deviance, 13, 36, 181, 203
  and mass-media, 44–50
Discipline, 53, 54, 70, 168, 169, 255
  in universities, 81, 84, 128, 227, 259; *see also* Social control
  self-discipline, 90, 176, 217
Dress, 29–30, 31, 88, 199, 222, 253
Drugs, 171, 198, 200, 201, 202, 216, 221
  addiction to, 175, 179, 192
Durkheim, E., 239, 264n.

Education, 23, 53–5, 56, 74, 131, 192, 226, 241, **244–66**
  and democracy, 142–3

and entertainment, 182–3, 231
  university, 76, 81, 128–9, 145, 185, 188, 231
Élite(s), 13, 51, 80, 111, 212, 223, 233, 240n.
Employers, 207, 214
Entertainment, 16, 89, 91–2, 94–5, 111, 182, 197, 202, 220, 264
  education and, 182–3, 231
  idols, 87
  public control of, 100
  values of, 92, 131, 167, 180, 183, 221, 222, 223
Essex, University of, 231n.

Family, 13, 25, 29, 48, 56, 88, 94, 96, 174, 256, 257
  and crime, 173, 184
  decline of, 65–6
  -life, 26, 31
Fashion, 29–30
Films, 27, 152, 190
Fitzpatrick, J. P., 175n
Floud, J., 58n.
Flugel, J. C., 175n.
France, 15, 228n.
Fun-ethic, 112, 167, 196, 231, 263, 264; *see also* 258, 265

Generations, War of, 13, 66, **86–100,** 190, 218, 219, 221, 226, 257; *see also* 22, 35, 126
Germany, 15, 49, 54, 56, 159, 254
Giddens, A., 146n.
Gray, B., 43n.
Guevara, C., 226

Halsey, A. H., 58n.
Hedonism, 169, 196, 256
Himmelweit, H., 42n.
Hippies, **195–203,** 219, 221, 265
Hire purchase, 98, 191, 193
Homosexuality, 175
Hooliganism, 49, 97, 98, 159, 165, 171, 177, 215, 216, 259, 260
Hughes, E. C., 61n.
Hypocrisy, 238–9, 241, 242, 248, 261

Identity, Social, 65, 96, 225, 233, 242; *see also* 223
Ideology, 15, 18, 28, 59, 127, 219, 227, 243*n*., 261
Income, redistribution of, 13, 22, 23, 30, 94, 98, 163
Inflation, 14, 22–3, 113–14
Intellectuals, 37, 77, 219, 238, 246

Johnson, B., 241*n*.

Keele, University of, 133*n*.
Knowledge, 55, 57, 61, 106, 107, 244, 247, 259, 264, 266
diffusion of, 51–2
growth of, 103

Labour Party, 39
Latey Committee, 98*ff*., 190–2, 193, 223
Report of, 18
Leeds, University of, 19, 112*n*., 115*n*.
Legislation, 97–8, 99, 174, 232, 257; *see also* 192–3, 222
Leisure, 24–6, 37, 96, 156, 209, 217, 265
Lipset, S. M., 59*n*.
Lockwood, D., 205*n*.
London School of Economics, 193*n*., 226*n*., 230*n*.
London, University of, 189, 193*n*.
Loyalty (Loyalties), 166, 170, 212, 231, 245, 252, 258
in universities, 80, 262; *see also* 83

Manchester, University of, 73, 140*n*.
Mann, P. H., 115*n*.
Mannheim, K., 246*n*.
Marcuse, H., 226, 232
Marijuana, 196, 200, 201
Marris, P., 115*n*.
Marshall, T. H., 61*n*.
Martin, F. M., 58*n*.
Martin, J. M., 175*n*.
Marx, K., 214, 219, 226, 246*n*., 255
Marxist analysis, 38, 219

Mass-Media, 16, 26–8, 131, 171, 181, 185, 196, 202, 225, 227
and crime, **41–50**
and the young, 91–2, 95, 124, 190
and values, 27, 72, 93, 94, 132, 182–3, 222, 255
Merton, R. K., 68, 173*n*., 179
Methodism, 176, 241
Mills, C. W., 232
Mobility, 88, 89, 178, 179, 191, 241
geographic, 31, 252, 258
social, 38, 58–9, 60, 71–2, 127, 176, 212, 220
Mods and Rockers, 86–9, 93, 96, 97–8, 219, 221, 232
Money, 23, 24, 28, 31, 156
values, 48, 225
Morality, 35, 99, 161, 171, 172, 207, 221, 237, 251, 255, 257
permissive, 210, 214
standards of, 151, 152, 211, 237
More Means Worse Argument, 75, 101, 224
Morrison, Fines, 153

Naegele, K., 72*n*.
Nanterre, 229

O'Dea, T., 254*n*.
Oxford, University of, 19, 73, 135*n*., **185–9**, 227, 230*n*.

Parents, 25, 57, 58, 85, 90, 93, 99, 126, 174, 176, 196, 215–16, 250
and universities, 82, 119, 125
relation to teachers, 59, 250
Peers, R., 115*n*.
Peyote religion, 200
Poblete, R., 254*n*.
Police, 26, 34, 49, 87, 88, 100, 154, 155, 160, 172, 232, 249
Power, 37–8, 117, 127, 164, 219, 220, 225, 232, 238, 256
Press, 112
and crime, 41, 49
and universities, 77, 113, 125
Pretence, 238, 242
Pretensions, 208, 213

Professional ethic, 61–2, 63
Professions, 63, 69, 77, 205–6, 210
Protest, 34, 38, 40, 170–1, 217, 225, 259, 261, 263–5
  hippy, 195, 265
  movements of, 38, 198
Punishment, 97

Race, 29, 243*n.*
Racism, 39, 243
Radio Luxembourg, 45
Rationality, 181–2, 206–7, 209, 210, 217
Rebellion, 157, 230
  of students, 83
  of youth, 22, 27, 87, 125, 126, 170, 195, 251
Rebelliousness, student, **218–33**
Redfield, R., 52*n.*
Religion, 14, 200, 237, 257
Research institutes, 143
Residence, University halls of, 82–3, 106, 115–16*n.*, 132, 138, 144, 145–9, 260
Rewards, 23, 62–3, 64
Riots, 21, 40, 86, 87, 157, 218
Robbins, Committee Report, 17, 105, 123, 133, 135*n.*, 144, 185, 186
Roles, 48, 64, 98, 176, 206, 208, 213, 214, 215, 217, 228, 235, 251, 255, 258, 263
  commitment to, 70–1
  conflicts defined, 66*ff.*
  diffuse and specific, 60*ff.*
  obligations of, 65, 212
  performance of, 67, 69, 212, 242, 255
  relationships, 65, 68, 197, 215, 256
Russell, C. B., 151, 153–6, 158, 160, 163, 171
Russia, 56, 59, 64

Salvation Army, 176, 141
San Francisco, 195, 199, 200, 201, 202
School(s), 28, 43, 47, 48, 53, 54, 66, 70, 88, 120, 180, 196, 230, 244–5
  as institutions, 68–70, 249–50
  meals in, 25, 58
  size of, 69–70, 90, 98–9, 162, 180
  transmission of values in, 55–6, 245
Science(s), 56–7, 105, 245, 246
  rejection of, 216
Scuttlers, 155, 156, 158
Selznik, P., 68*n.*
Sex, 96, 164, 171, 222, 244, 256
  -ethics, 58
Sheffield, University of, 112*n.*, 115*n.*, 141*n.*
Sherif, M. & C. W., 178*n.*
Shils, E., 255*n.*
Singer, M., 52*n.*
Social change, 13, 22*ff.*, 150, 159, 191, 258, 265
  and universities, 74*ff.*
Social control, 31, 42, 88, 97, 99, 160, 192, 224, 237, 249, 256
  at work, 207, 210
  breakdown of, 36, 89, 90, 159, 161, 177, 253
  in relation to socialization, 174–5, 176, 252
Social Enquiry, techniques of, 19, 42–4, 50, 93, 116; *see also* 115–16
Social selection, 57*ff.*, 165, 220
Social structure, 97, 157, 242, 248
Socialists, 35, 200, 213
Socialization, 13, 93, 94, 168–9, 173, 177, 192, 209, 213, 216, 244, 250, 252, 258, 263
  by teachers, 57, 60, 62
  in universities, 76, 84, 120, 124–5, 224, 258, 262–3
  related to social control, 174–5, 176, 252
  secondary, 13, 176, 208, 210, 212, 213–14, 241
Sociology, 19, 224, 225, 234, 245, 246
Spain, 253
Spencer, H., 199, 255

Index

Spock-ism, 223
Status, 26, 29, 165, 190–1, 197, 205, 213–14, 219, 225, 232
  generational, 97, 193
  symbols of, 98, 254
  uncertainties of, 152, 163, 171, 218
Students, 17, 33, **106–49**, 186, **218–33**, 246, 248
  as a class, 218, 223
  commitment of, 76, 77, 102, 123–4
  consultation with, 114, 261, 262
  disillusionment of, 117–22
  experience of, 82, 260
  motivation of, 75, 101, 103–4, 123, 246
  protest of, 83, 159, 263–4, 265
  relations with academics, 75, 76, 78–80, 102, 114–15, 121–2, 134, 187, 227, 229, 232, 261
Success goals, 28, 29, 94–5, 126–7, 164–5, 178, 242
Sussex, University of, 133n., 230n.
Swastika daubing, 49

Teachers, 25, 76, 93, 102–3, 169, 247
  as socializers, 57–9, 65, 67, 126, 167
  mobility of, 70–1, 99, 162, 180–1
  role of, **51–72**
Technological determinism, 214
Technology, 105, **204–17**, 245
  development of, 13, 22–3, 73, 265–6
  in universities, 104, 110–11, 141, 144
Teddy boys, 21, 82, 86, 158, 219, 232
Teenagers, 21ff., 44, 168, 201
Television, 41, 92–3, 100, 215
  and crime, 46–50
  values of, 72, 92, 183
Them and *Us*, 24, 80, 119–20, 227, 258
Trust, 213, 215–16, 227, 242, 257; *see also* 254

Tumin, M., 72n.
Tussman, J., 18
Tutorial system, 75, 101, 108, 124, 140–2, 144, 186–7

Undergraduates, 81, 102, 123, 132, 137, 186–7, 232
  and youth culture, 125–6
  courses for, 18, 187
Universities, 13, 17, 18, 132, 185, 198, 215, 216, **218–33**, 251, 259
  academic staff of, 74, 75, 77, 111, 229
  administration of, 76, 77, 80, 137–8, 143, 145, 148–9, 206, 230, 261
  American, 74, 189
  competition within, 76, 103, 109–10, 230
  departmentalism in, 132–3
  examinations in, 81, 85, 139–40, 145, 187
  expansion of, 73–5, 101, 106–7, 109–17, 132–4, 224, 229
  lectures, 122, 138–40, 187
  permissiveness of, 79, 81, 125, 128, 231, 248–9
  redbrick, **73–85**, 106, 186
  size of, 134–40
  see also Residence, University halls of, *and* Tutorial system
University unions, 82, 119n., 133n., 132
U.S.A., 30, 31, 59, 199

Values, 22, 24, 27, 32, 51, 53, 85, 89, 100, 151, 173, 175, 176, 180, 210, 213, 229, 230, **234–66**
  American, 198, 199
  and education, 55ff., 60, 64, 71, 234ff.
  conflicts of, 71–2, 96, 129, 131, 227
  mass-media and, 44–8, 183
  middle-aged, 195, 201
  of office workers, 208
  of young people, 92, 97, 131, 179

271

Values, *contd.*

  substantive and instrumental, 235–6, 241, 243, 248, 251, 252, 254–5, 261, 265
  transmission of, 91, 163, 228
  university, 73–4, 77, 81, 83, 84, 106–8, 116, 119, 123, 188
Vandalism, 179, 181, 216, 225
Veblen, T., 241
Violence, 13, 21, 37, 165, 171, 177
  and mass-media, 43–4, 87
Voting age, 192–3

Walker, N., 175*n.*
Wallas, G., 90
Weber, Max, 206
Work, 24, 88, 154, 197, 213
  office-, 204*ff.*, 214, 217
Work ethic, 26, 195, 225

Work-order, 166, 202, 209, 210, 217, 250, 265
Work-role, 22, 250
Workers, 22, 23, 24, 166, 204–9, 211
Working Class, 30, 38, 90, 129, 209, 211, 212
  cultures of, 90, 212
  ghettoes, 160
  ideals of, 59

York, University of, 123*n.*
Young, M., 255*n.*
Youth Culture, 18, 29–32, 44, 86–7, 97, 120, 150, 157–8, 159, 163, 165, 167, 180, 182, 191–2, 212, 263
  and universities, 77, 111–12, 117, 123, 125–8, **218–33**

Zweig, F., 148*n.*